AF567131

THE KLEINMAN EDITION

*A Torah theme for every day of every week,
blending profound perspectives
from all areas of Torah literature –
Scripture, Mishnah, Jewish Law, Mussar/Ethics,
Tefillah/Prayer, and Hashkafah/Jewish Thought –
collected for daily study.*

ArtScroll Series®

THE KLEINMAN EDITION

A TORAH THEME FOR EVERY DAY OF EVERY WEEK FROM ALL AREAS OF TORAH LITERATURE — COLLECTED FOR DAILY STUDY.

Rabbi Yosaif Asher Weiss
General Editor

OF TORAH

VOLUME 3

DAILY STUDY FOR THE WEEKS OF

וישב-ויחי

VAYEISHEV–VAYECHI

Published by

ArtScroll • Mesorah Publications, ltd

FIRST EDITION
First Impression ... November 2006

Published and Distributed by
MESORAH PUBLICATIONS, LTD.
4401 Second Avenue / Brooklyn, N.Y 11232

Distributed in Europe by
LEHMANNS
Unit E, Viking Business Park
Rolling Mill Road
Jarow, Tyne & Wear, NE32 3DP
England

Distributed in Australia and New Zealand by
GOLDS WORLDS OF JUDAICA
3-13 William Street
Balaclava, Melbourne 3183
Victoria, Australia

Distributed in Israel by
SIFRIATI / A. GITLER — BOOKS
6 Hayarkon Street
Bnei Brak 51127

Distributed in South Africa by
KOLLEL BOOKSHOP
Ivy Common
105 William Road
Norwood 2192, Johannesburg, South Africa

ARTSCROLL SERIES®
THE KLEINMAN EDITION — LIMUD YOMI / A DAILY DOSE OF TORAH
VOL. 3: VAYEISHEV–VAYECHI

ISBN:
ISBN 10: 1-4226-0141-2 (hard cover)
ISBN 13: 978-1-4226-0141-9 (hard cover)

Typography by CompuScribe at ArtScroll Studios, Ltd.

Printed in the United States of America by Noble Book Press Corp.
Bound by Sefercraft, Quality Bookbinders, Ltd., Brooklyn N.Y. 11232

DEDICATION OF THIS VOLUME

It is our privilege to dedicate this volume
in tribute to the memories of our fathers and uncle

R' Avrohom Abba Goldenberg ז״ל
ר' אברהם אבא ב״ר צבי ז״ל

He taught us to live with love of Torah, yiras Shamayim, and deep dedication to chessed. Like Avraham Avinu, his was a life of constant chessed, combined with great dignity, righteousness and humility.

His family's sole survivor of the Holocaust, he built a living, flourishing memorial to the kedoshim.

R' Yosef Eliezer Brieger ז״ל
ר' יוסף אליעזר ב״ר יעקב יצחק ז״ל

He embodied the love of Torah of his forebears: *Rashi, Maharal, Shach, Bach,* and R' Mordechai Banet and, as the sole survivor of his family, he maintained their heritage. Though torn from the Galanta Yeshiva in 1941 as a 16-year old, he retained his lifeblood, his passion for Torah study, and, in America, rebuilt a family in the image of the one that was destroyed.

All his life, he learned every free minute, and became a repository of vast Torah knowledge.

R' Yaakov Shlomeh Lebovits ז״ל
ר' יעקב שלמה ב״ר משה הלוי ז״ל

Orphaned at 11, in Chust, he went to work so that his younger siblings could receive a Torah education. He married Faiga Sicherman and, *b'chasdei Hashem,* both survived and replanted a home of Torah and *hachnasas orchim* in America.

Their home was open to all, especially those who were spurned by others. By providing love and support, they nurtured many people back to lives of Torah.

We pay tribute to the matriarchs of our family

Mrs. Chaya (Sicherman) Goldenberg שתחי'
Mrs. Malka (Karfunkel) Brieger שתחי'
Mrs. Faiga (Sicherman) Lebovits שתחי'

With personal sacrifice for our Torah *chinuch* and the constant osmosis of being in *chessed*-filled homes, they imbued us with their values. Words cannot convey our gratitude to Hashem for the blessing of having such beacons of goodness.

May they all be blessed with many healthy years to enjoy *nachas* from all of their children, grandchildren, and great-grandchildren until the coming of Mashiach.

Leon & Agi Goldenberg and their children:

Mendy, Estie, Efraim, Rivka, and Chava Blau,
Shiffie, Chanie, and Rikki Grossman,
Abi, Shoshana, and Yehudis Goldenberg,
Tzvi and Leilie Fertig,
and Yitzy Goldenberg

The Kleinman Edition

To our fathers and grandfathers, daily Torah study was the first priority. It is fitting, therefore, that we dedicate this Limud Yomi Series in their memory

Avrohom Kleinman ז״ל

ר׳ אברהם אייזיק ב״ר אלכסנדר ז״ל

נפ׳ י״ב שבט תשנ״ט

After years of slave labor and concentration camps — years when he risked his life to put on *tefillin* every day! — he courageously rebuilt. Wherever he was — in)P camps, Poughkeepsie, Borough Park, or Forest Hills — he was a one man *hiruv* novement, before "*kiruv rechokim*" was a familiar phrase. Everyone was drawn to his enthusiasm for Yiddishkeit.

His home was open to anyone in need, even when there was barely enough for family.

All his life he felt close to his Rebbe, the Nitra Rav, and to the father-in-law he never knew; their *sefarim*, *Naos Desheh* and *Lechem Abirim*, were part of our Shabbos table. He was a caring and gentle man whose life was defined by his love of learning Torah, *gemillas chasadim*, *kiruv* work, *hachnasas orchim*, *askanus*, and love for his family. He left a noble legacy that we are honored to perpetuate.

Mendel Indig ז״ל

ר׳ מנחם דוד ב״ר מרדכי שמואל ז״ל

נפ׳ ט׳ אדר ב׳ תשס״

"It was as if a *maloch* protected us," he used to say about the dark years of Churban Europa. He lost almost everything — even the *tefillin* that he put on every day until the very end — but he kept his spirit, his *emunah*, his dedication to Torah, and his resolve to rebuild.

He became a living legend of Torah, *chesed*, and service to his Bensonhurst community. His home was open to anyone in need, and there was always enough room for guests. His *succah* was the largest in the neighborhood, and he always found a way to bring endangered relatives to America and help them become established.

After he retired, he devoted himself to learning and bringing others close to Yiddishkeit, especially immigrants from the former Soviet Union, teaching them to put on *tefillin* and reuniting them with the Judaism of their ancestors. It is our privilege to carry on his glorious legacy.

We pay tribute to our mothers

Ethel Kleinman תחי׳

Rose Indig תחי׳

To us and our children and grandchildren — and to all who know them — they are role models of *emunah*, *chesed*, love and wisdom.

Our mothers שיחיו and our fathers ז״ל planted seeds of Torah in America and produced magnificent *doros* of children, grandchildren, and great-grandchildren following their example. May Hashem continue to bless our mothers with good health and many nachas-filled years.

Elly and Brochie Kleinman and their children

Deenie and Yitzy Schuss Yossie Kleinman Aliza and Lavey Freedman

and families

With dedication to the principle that Torah study should always be available,
the following generous and visionary patrons
have dedicated volumes of this series:

VOL. 1: BEREISHIS-VAYEIRA / בראשית־וירא

Elly and Brochie Kleinman and family

In memory of their fathers

ר' אברהם אייזיק ב"ר אלכסנדר ז"ל – Avrohom Kleinman ז"ל

ר' מנחם דוד ב"ר מרדכי שמואל ז"ל – Mendel Indig ז"ל

and in tribute to their mothers שתחי' לאוי"ט יבלח"ט

Ethel Kleinman

Rose Indig

VOL. 2: CHAYEI SARAH-VAYISHLACH / חיי שרה־וישלח

Motty and Malka Klein

for the merit of their children שיחי'

Esther and Chaim Baruch Fogel Dovid and Chavie Binyomin Zvi

Elana Leah and Natan Goldstein Moshe Yosef Yaakov Eliyahu

In honor of his mother שתחי'

Mrs. Suri Klein לאוי"ט

In memory of his father

ר' יהודה ב"ר דוד הלוי ז"ל נפ' כ"ז אדר ב' תשס"ג – Yidel Klein

In memory of her parents

ר' אשר אנשיל ב"ר משה יוסף ז"ל נפ' ג' שבט תשנ"ט – Anchel Gross

שרה בת ר' חיים אליהו ע"ה נפ' כ"ד סיון תשס"א – Suri Gross

And in memory of their grandparents who perished על קידוש השם in the Holocaust

ר' דוד ב"ר יעקב הלוי ע"ה ופערל בת ר' צבי ע"ה הי"ד – Klein

ר' מרדכי ב"ר דוד הלוי ע"ה ולאה בת ר' יעקב הלוי ע"ה הי"ד – Klein

ר' משה יוסף ב"ר בנימין צבי ע"ה ומלכה בת ר' יחיאל מיכל ע"ה הי"ד – Gross

ר' חיים אליהו ב"ר מרדכי ע"ה וויטא בת ר' שלמה אליעזר ע"ה הי"ד – Gartenberg

VOL. 3: VAYEISHEV-VAYECHI / וישב־ויחי

Leon and Agi Goldenberg

Mendy and Estie Blau — Efraim, Rivka, and Chava

Shiffie Grossman — Chanie, and Rikki

Abi and Shoshana Goldenberg — Yehudis

Tzvi and Leilie Fertig

and Yitzy Goldenberg

In memory of their fathers and uncle

ר' אברהם אבא ב"ר צבי ז"ל – Abba Goldenberg ז"ל

ר' יוסף אליעזר ב"ר יעקב יצחק ז"ל – Joseph Brieger ז"ל

ר' יעקב שלמה ב"ר משה הלוי ז"ל – Yaakov Shlomeh Lebovits ז"ל

and in tribute to their mothers שתחי' לאוי"ט יבלח"ט

Chaya (Sicherman) Goldenberg Malka (Karfunkel) Brieger

and their aunt — Faiga (Sicherman) Lebovits

VOL. 14: THE FESTIVALS / מועדי השנה

The Teichman Family (Los Angeles)

In memory of their parents and grandparents

שמואל ב״ר יששכר דוב ז״ל – Sam Teichman ז״ל

ליבה בריינדל בת ר׳ יהושע הלוי ע״ה – Lujza Teichman ע״ה

רחל בת ר׳ אלכסנר סנדר ע״ה – Rose Teichman ע״ה

יצחק אייזיק ב״ר אברהם חיים ז״ל – Isaac Nae ז״ל

◈ Publisher's Preface

King David said: גַּל עֵינַי וְאַבִּיטָה נִפְלָאוֹת מִתּוֹרָתֶךָ, *Unveil my eyes that I may perceive wonders from your Torah* (*Psalms* 119:18).

Shammai said: עֲשֵׂה תוֹרָתְךָ קֶבַע, *Make your Torah study a fixed practice* (*Avos* 1:15).

Rav Saadiah Gaon said: The Jewish people is a nation only by virtue of the Torah.

The Torah is the essence of the Jewish people, and not a day should go by without Torah study. How much learning should there be? Just as the Torah itself is infinite, there is no limit to the effort to master its contents. The task does not end when one bids farewell to the academy and enters the world of work and business. All over the world, study halls are filled before dawn and after dark with men plumbing the depths of the Talmud and other works. Before and after their workdays, they overcome fatigue with a relentless desire to absorb more and more of God's word.

To such people, **The Kleinman Edition: Limud Yomi / A Daily Dose of Torah** will be a welcome supplement, an enrichment that offers glimpses of additional topics and a means of filling the day's spare minutes with nourishment for the mind and spirit.

To those who as yet have not been able to savor the beauty of immersion in the sea of study, this new series will be a vehicle to enrich their every day with an assortment of stimulating Torah content.

We are gratified that Volume 1 of this new series has been phenomenally well received. Many people have told us how they are filling once-empty gaps in their day with these "daily doses," and how this work has stimulated them to do further research in these subjects. As King Solomon said, תֵּן לְחָכָם וְיֶחְכַּם־עוֹד הוֹדַע לְצַדִּיק וְיוֹסֶף לֶקַח, *Give the wise man and he will become wiser; make known to the righteous and he will add [to his] learning* (*Proverbs* 9:9).

Each "Daily Dose of Torah" includes selections from a broad spectrum of Torah sources (see below); in combination they provide a multi-dimensional study program. Each selection can stand on its own, or, ideally, serve as a vehicle for further research and enrichment. These components are as follows:

- ❑ ***A Torah Thought for the Day***, focusing on a verse in the weekly *parashah*. The discussion may revolve around various classic interpretations, or it may offer a selection of insights and lessons that are derived from the verse. This section will draw from a wide gamut of early and later commentators, and will enhance the reader's appreciation for the wealth of Torah interpretation and its lessons for life.

- ❑ ***The Mishnah of the Day,*** presenting a Mishnah selection every day, with text, translation, and concise commentary, adapted from the classic ArtScroll Mishnah Series and the Schottenstein Edition of the Talmud. This daily dose will begin with Tractate Shabbos, and continue through Seder Moed.

- ❑ ***Gems from the Gemara,*** presenting some of the Talmud's discussion of the daily Mishnah. Thus the reader will "join the academy" of the Talmud's question-and-answer clarification of the laws and underlying principles of the Mishnah.

- ❑ ***A Mussar Thought for the Day,*** building upon the theme of the *Torah Thought for the Day*, by presenting an ethical or moral lesson drawn from the masters of Mussar, Hashkafah, and Chassidus. This selection will stimulate thought and growth — and be a welcome source of uplifting ideas for times when the reader is called upon to speak at a *simchah.*

- ❑ ***The Halachah of the Day,*** presenting a practical, relevant halachic discussion, beginning with the thirty-nine forbidden categories of Shabbos labor. The selections are adapted from Rabbi Simcha Bunim Cohen's popular and authoritative works, which are part of the ArtScroll Series. [These brief discussions are not intended to be definitive. Questions should be directed to a qualified rav.]

- ❑ ***A Closer Look at the Siddur,*** broadening the reader's understanding of the rich tapestry of *tefillah*/prayer. The Shabbos Daily Dose will focus on the Shabbos prayers. And once a week, this section will discuss such universal themes as the Thirteen Principles of Faith or the Six Constant Commandments.

❑ ***A Taste of Lomdus,*** a special weekly feature that will present a brief but in-depth discussion of a Talmudic subject, in the tradition of the Torah giants whose reasoning and novellae are the basis of research and study in advanced yeshivas. Every day, there will be a challenging "Question of the Day," related to the theme of the day. The answers for the questions will come at the end of each week.

Each volume of the Daily Dose of Torah Series will present a capsule study program for twenty-eight days. The annual cycle will be comprised of thirteen four-week volumes, covering all fifty-two weeks of the year, and a fourteenth volume devoted to Rosh Hashanah, Yom Kippur, and the festivals. We are confident that the complete series will bring the excitement of Torah study to countless people, and that many of them will use it as a springboard to further learning, both independently and by joining *shiurim.*

The Kleinman Edition: Limud Yomi / A Daily Dose of Torah is dedicated by **ELLY AND BROCHIE KLEINMAN,** in memory of their fathers ז"ל and in honor of their mothers שיחיו. The Kleinmans have long distinguished themselves as generous and imaginative supporters of Torah and *chesed* causes. With warmth and kindness, they have opened their home countless times to help institutions and individuals. They have richly earned the respect and affection of all who know them, and we are honored to count them not only as major supporters of our work, but as personal friends. They and their family bring honor to the legacy of their parents.

This volume is dedicated by our good friends **LEON AND AGI GOLDENBERG.** They are justly renowned and admired for their support of a wide array of Torah and chessed causes, much of which they do anonymously. One of their major concerns is to foster Torah study, and we are gratified that they see the Daily Dose as a vehicle to increase learning among students of Torah, and to introduce it to people who have yet to savor its beauty. This dedication is in memory of forebears who survived the Holocaust with their faith and love of Torah intact, and with a strong commitment to plant new seeds in America. We are proud that the Goldenbergs consider this series as a fulfillment of that commitment.

The editor of this new series is **RABBI YOSAIF ASHER WEISS,** Rosh Yeshivas Ohr Hadaas, Staten Island, who is also a distinguished editor of the Schottenstein Editions of the Talmud Bavli and Yerushalmi. Rabbi Weiss' reputation as a noted scholar and educator will be justly embellished by the Daily Dose Series.

We are grateful to **RABBI RAPHAEL BUTLER**, the dynamic and innovative founder and president of the Afikim Foundation, who conceived of this concept and had a significant role in its development. We are proud to enjoy his friendship.

We are grateful to the outstanding *talmidei chachamim* who are contributing to this series: **RABBI YOSEF GAVRIEL BECHHOFER, RABBI REUVEN BUTLER, RABBI ELIYAHU COHEN, RABBI ASHER DICKER, RABBI MAYER GOLDSTEIN, RABBI BERYL SCHIFF, RABBI MORDECHAI SONNENSHEIN, RABBI MOSHE UNGAR, RABBI YISROEL DOV WEISS, AND RABBI ZEV ZIONS.** The quality of their scholarship shines through every page. We thank **RABBI SIMCHA SHAFRAN** for allowing us to use his *sefer Maadanei Simchah* as a source for some of the Questions of the Day.

The beauty and clarity of the book's design is yet another tribute to the graphics genius of our friend and colleague **REB SHEAH BRANDER**. As someone once said in a different context, "I can't put it into words, but I know it when I see it." It is hard to define good taste and graphics beauty in words, but when one sees Reb Sheah's work, one knows it.

ELI KROEN, a master of graphics in his own right, designed the cover with his typical creativity and good taste. **MOSHE DEUTSCH** had an important hand in the typesetting and general design. **MRS. CHUMIE LIPSCHITZ**, a key member of our staff, paginated the book. **TOBY GOLDZWEIG, SURY REINHOLD, AND SARA RIFKA SPIRA** typed and corrected the manuscript. A special thank-you to **GITTEL TOVA WEISS**, for her contributions to this volume.

MRS. MINDY STERN proofread and made many important suggestions. **AVROHOM BIDERMAN** was involved in virtually every aspect of the work from its inception, and **MENDY HERZBERG** assisted in shepherding the project to completion.

As this new series continues to take shape, we express our great appreciation to our long-time friend and colleague **SHMUEL BLITZ**, head of ArtScroll Jerusalem. His dedication and judgment have been indispensable components of virtually every ArtScroll/Mesorah project.

We are grateful to them all. The contributions of ArtScroll/Mesorah to the cause of Jewish life and Torah study are possible because of the skill and dedication of the above staff members and their colleagues.

It is an enormous privilege to have been instrumental in bringing Torah knowledge to the people of Torah. There are no words to express our gratitude to Hashem Yisbarach for permitting us to disseminate His Word to His children.

Rabbi Meir Zlotowitz/Rabbi Nosson Scherman

Cheshvan 5767 / November 2006

פרשת וישב
Parashas Vayeishev

פרשת וישב

SUNDAY

PARASHAS VAYEISHEV

A TORAH THOUGHT FOR THE DAY

וַיֵּשֶׁב יַעֲקֹב בְּאֶרֶץ מְגוּרֵי אָבִיו בְּאֶרֶץ כְּנָעַן

And Yaakov dwelled in the land that was the sojourning place of his father, the Land of Canaan (*Bereishis* 37:1).

Rashi's comment (printed in his commentary to v. 2), citing the Midrash, is well known: "Yaakov desired to dwell in peace — immediately, there leaped upon him the turmoil of Yosef." *Rashi* seems to have inferred that Yaakov's "dwelling" mentioned in the verse is not just a simple statement of his arrival at home after many years; rather, it is indicative of Yaakov's yearning for rest and peace, after his many years of hard labor in Lavan's house, and following the danger posed to his physical safety by his brother Eisav. [Although a wish for some tranquility would seem not to be a great sin, it aroused the ire of Hashem, as *Rashi* continues: "The Holy One, Blessed is He, says: Is it not enough for the righteous that they have the World to Come in all its glory waiting for them, that they wish peace in this world too?"]

Perhaps, an allusion to the mind-set of Yaakov can be noted in the verse itself, which contrasts the "dwelling" of Yaakov with the "sojourning" of his father Yitzchak. Although Yitzchak lived all his life in one country, never leaving Eretz Yisrael, he never "dwelled" there; in his mind, he was merely a sojourner, making his way through the "entranceway" that is this world into the "banquet hall" of the World to Come. Yaakov, however, upon returning to Eretz Yisrael, wished to feel truly at home after his many years of wandering and hardship; he wanted to dwell where his father had only sojourned. This was unacceptable to Hashem.

Rav Reuven Feinstein sees another layer of meaning in the contrast made by the verse between Yitchak's "sojourning" and Yaakov's "dwelling." He notes that the dispute between Yosef and his brothers was the first step in the chain of events that ultimately led to the descent to Egypt. Why did that chain of events have to begin now? Rav Feinstein suggests that Hashem planned to fulfill the prophecy of *your children will be strangers in a land not their own . . . for four hundred years* that had been told to Avraham (*Bereishis* 15:13), by counting those years as beginning from the birth of Yitzchak, so that the Jews would have to remain in Egypt for only 210 years (indeed, that is what transpired). This could only be done, however, if Avraham's children, starting from Yitzchak, saw themselves as being "in a land not their own" (as Eretz Yisrael had not been officially given to them, but to their descendants).

Indeed, Yitzchak felt this way, viewing Eretz Yisrael simply as a land in which he sojourned. But when Yaakov returned and wished to *dwell* in the land as his own, he threatened to make this calculation untenable. Accordingly, Hashem set in motion the chain of events that would cause the Jews to descend to Egypt.

MISHNAH OF THE DAY: SHABBOS 9:3

The following Mishnah seeks sources for several unrelated laws: מִנַּיִן לְפוֹלֶטֶת שִׁכְבַת זֶרַע בַּיּוֹם הַשְּׁלִישִׁי שֶׁהִיא טְמֵאָה — *From where* do we know ***that a woman who discharges semen on the third day*** after having relations with her husband ***is tamei?***[1] שֶׁנֶּאֱמַר ,,הֱיוּ נְכֹנִים לִשְׁלֹשֶׁת יָמִים" — ***For it is stated: "Be prepared for a three-day period."***[2]

The next law:

מִנַּיִן שֶׁמַּרְחִיצִין אֶת הַמִּילָה בַּיּוֹם הַשְּׁלִישִׁי שֶׁחָל לִהְיוֹת בְּשַׁבָּת — *From where* do we know ***that we may bathe the*** infant who has undergone ***circumcision on the third day*** after his circumcision, even ***if it falls on the Sabbath?***[3] שֶׁנֶּאֱמַר ,,וַיְהִי בַיּוֹם הַשְּׁלִישִׁי בִּהְיוֹתָם כֹּאֲבִים" — ***For it is***

NOTES

1. The Mishnah (*Mikvaos* 8:3) teaches that a woman who discharges semen that was introduced to her body through relations with her husband becomes *tamei.* However, this is only the case as long as the semen is still viable, and capable of fertilizing an egg. The Tanna of our Mishnah holds that semen in a woman's body retains that capacity for three days after she has relations with her husband (including the day they had relations). Hence, semen that she discharges during these three days renders her *tamei.* The Tanna seeks to identify the Scriptural source for this law (*Rav; Rashi*).

2. *Shemos* 19:15. This verse is stated in connection with the Giving of the Torah at Mt. Sinai. The verse ends: אַל־תִּגְּשׁוּ אֶל־אִשָּׁה, *do not approach a woman* — i.e., do not engage in marital relations. The purpose of this commandment was to ensure that at the time the Torah was given, no Jew would be in a state of *tumah* due to having had relations, and hence hindered from participating in this momentous event.

Since a man who becomes *tamei* through the emission of semen may purify himself by immersing in a *mikveh* that same day (see *Vayikra* 15:16), a three-day preparatory period would not have been necessary for the men — they could have immersed themselves immediately after relations, and been *tahor* and prepared to receive the Torah. Perforce, the waiting period must have been intended for the women. In specifying a three-day waiting period, the Torah teaches that women are rendered *tamei* by a discharge of semen for three days after they have had relations (*Rav;* see *Rashi* here and to *Exodus* 19:15).

3. I.e., which verse supports the opinion cited in the Mishnah (below, 19:3) that even on the third day after circumcision, the baby is still considered ill enough that we may suspend the laws of the Sabbath for him, as we do for any critically ill Jew? Such a

stated: "And it came to pass on the third day, when they were in pain."[4]

The third law:

מִנַּיִן שֶׁקּוֹשְׁרִין לָשׁוֹן שֶׁל זְהוֹרִית בְּרֹאשׁ שָׂעִיר הַמִּשְׁתַּלֵּחַ — ***From where*** do we know ***that we tie a strip of red*** wool ***on the head of the goat that is sent away*** to Azazel?[5] שֶׁנֶּאֱמַר ,,אִם־יִהְיוּ חֲטָאֵיכֶם כַּשָּׁנִים כַּשֶּׁלֶג יַלְבִּינוּ'' — ***For it is stated: "If your sins will be like crimson, they will become white as snow."***[6]

NOTES

suspension would allow us, for example, to boil water with which to bathe the baby, since bathing him in warm water has a curative effect. Moreover, if the boy's condition on the third day permits suspending the laws of the Sabbath, then certainly his condition on the first and second days warrants the same suspension (*Rav; Rashi;* cf. *Rambam, Hil. Milah* 2:8, who holds that the third day is *worse* than the first two). [This discussion refers to a child who does not exhibit any unusual signs of reaction to his circumcision. One who does exhibit such signs is obviously considered critically ill, and we would be allowed to suspend the Sabbath laws for him even without any special Scriptural derivation (*Rama, Orach Chaim* 331:9).]

4. *Bereishis* 34:25. Scripture teaches that on the third day after the men of the city of Shechem were circumcised, Shimon and Levi seized the opportunity provided by the men's post-operative weakness to attack the city. Thus, it is apparent that even on the third day after circumcision, post-operative danger remains.

5. On Yom Kippur, in the Temple, two identical goats were brought to atone on behalf of the entire nation. One was slaughtered in the Temple as a *chatas,* and its blood was sprinkled in various places in the Temple. The other goat was led out to a wilderness area to be cast off a precipice known as Azazel (see *Vayikra* Ch. 16). The Mishnah (*Yoma* 6:6) teaches that the one who led the goat out to the Azazel area would take a strip of red wool and divide it in two, tying one half to the goat's neck and the other half to the rock at the top of the precipice. He would then push the goat down the mountain. As the goat fell, the wool would miraculously turn white. This was a Divine sign that the sins of the people were forgiven. Our Mishnah inquires as to the Scriptural origin of this practice (*Rav*).

6. *Yeshayah* 1:18. The Mishnah understands the prophet's words as an allusion to the practice of tying the strip of red wool onto the head of the goat, and its turning white as a sign of forgiveness for the nation's sins.

QUESTION OF THE DAY:

How many years elapsed between Yaakov's return to Canaan and the sale of Yosef?

For the answer, see page 54.

GEMS FROM THE GEMARA

פרשת וישב

SUNDAY

PARASHAS VAYEISHEV

Our Mishnah cites a verse that concerns the Giving of the Torah. The Gemara to this Mishnah discusses the Giving of the Torah at great length. One of the teachings cited (88b-89a) is that of R' Yehoshua ben Levi, who said that when Moshe ascended to the Heavenly heights, the ministering angels said before Hashem, "Master of the Universe! Why is someone born of a woman among us?" Hashem answered, "He has come to receive the Torah." The angels then said before Hashem, "The coveted and treasured [Torah]! [The Torah] that You stored as a treasure for 974 generations before the world was created! You intend to give *that* to flesh and blood?! *What is a mortal that You should remember him or the son of man that You should recall him?* (*Tehillim* 8:5). *HASHEM, our Lord, how grand is Your Name in all the earth [already]! Therefore, You [would be better served to only] bestow Your glory upon the Heavens!*" (ibid. v. 2).

Hashem turned to Moshe and said, "Give them an answer."

Moshe responded, "Master of the Universe! I am afraid lest they burn me with the breath of their mouths." Hashem said, "Take hold of the Throne of My Glory [for protection], and then give them an answer." [This itself was a response to the angels — that only man can be part of the lower world and yet reach the Throne of Glory. Only man, then, deserves the Torah (*Rif* to *Ein Yaakov*).]

Moshe argued, "Master of the Universe, the Torah that You are giving me, what is written in it? *I am HASHEM, your God, Who has taken you out of the land of Egypt*" (*Shemos* 20:2). Moshe then addressed the angels, "Did you descend to Egypt? Were you enslaved to Pharaoh? Why should the Torah be yours?" Moshe continued, "What else is written in [the Torah]? *There shall not be unto you gods of others* (ibid. v. 3). Do you live among the nations who worship idols? What else is written in it? *Remember the Sabbath day to sanctify it* (ibid. v. 8). Do you engage in any labor from which you would need to rest? What else is written in it? *You shall not take [the Name of HASHEM, Your Lord, in vain]* (ibid. v. 7). Are there any business transactions among you [that might lead to vain oaths]? What else is written in it? *Honor your father and mother* (ibid. v. 12). Do you have a father or mother? What else is written in it? *You shall not murder; you shall not commit adultery; you shall not steal* (ibid. v. 13). Is there envy among you? Is there an Evil Inclination among you?"

The Gemara relates that the angels conceded the point. Thus, we find at the end of the psalm (*Tehillim* 8:10): *HASHEM, our Master, how grand is Your Name [in all the earth];* here it is not written: *Bestow Your glory upon the Heavens.* Moreover, all the angels became friends of Moshe, and each gave him a gift, as it is said (ibid. 68:19): *You ascended to the heights, you captured a captive, you took gifts because of man;* that is to say, in reward for bearing the insult when the angels called you "a man," you took gifts. Even the Angel of Death gave him something, as it is said (*Bamidbar* 17:11-12): *Moshe said to Aharon, "Take the fire-pan and put on it fire from upon the Altar, and place incense" . . . He [Aharon] placed the incense and atoned for the people . . .* It then says (ibid. v. 13): *He stood between the dead and the living* etc., *and the plague was checked.* The Gemara concludes: If the Angel of Death had not told Moshe this secret [that incense has the power to halt a plague], how else would he have known it? Thus, this knowledge was the gift Moshe received from the Angel of Death.

A MUSSAR THOUGHT FOR THE DAY

Many of the masters of *mussar* grapple with the question: What sin did Yaakov commit in wishing to live in peace, that resulted in the turmoil of Yosef descending upon him? Do we not find that many *tzaddikim* live their lives peacefully?

One approach to this question is found in the words of the *Ksav Sofer.* He suggests that in finally coming to the safe haven of Eretz Yisrael after his years of dealing with Lavan and Eisav, Yaakov desired to reach a level of material comfort and security so that he could concentrate on his *spiritual* future with no distractions. But this level was greater than Hashem desired it to be. Although Yaakov's motives were pure, Hashem created man with the predisposition to always desire more materialism; as the verse states (*Koheles* 5:9): *He who loves silver will never be satisfied with silver,* no matter how much he obtains. Thus, Hashem understood that it would be dangerous for Yaakov to attain the level of comfort he sought; instead of providing him with the ability to pursue his service of Hashem in peace, it would ultimately prove a hindrance. For this reason, the Midrash states, Hashem caused the turmoil of Yosef and his brothers to intrude upon Yaakov's peace.

R' Chaim Shmulevitz, in his *Sichos Mussar,* is also bothered by this difficulty. Surely, he asks, wanting peace to improve the quality of one's service to Hashem — which was Yaakov's only motive — is not a fault! How could there be a desire that is more "kosher"?

R' Chaim answers that the lesson here is that Hashem did not create the world for us to perform His service in peace and comfort. To the contrary, the service that Hashem desires most is that which is performed in difficult and trying circumstances, as the Mishnah states in *Avos* (5:26): *The reward is according to the difficulty.* We find also the statement of *Tanna D'Vei Eliyahu:* "One [mitzvah] performed with difficulty is more valuable than 100 performed without difficulty." Yaakov sought to serve Hashem in peace, but Hashem preferred that Yaakov serve him from the midst of hardship.

This point is illustrated by a famous incident involving the *Gra.* The *Gra* had a daughter who, tragically, died as a *kallah* shortly before her wedding. The *Gra,* in his greatness, accepted the decree of Heaven upon himself with joy. Shortly afterward, the *Gra's* mother came to him in a dream, and told him, "If you would know what has been prepared for you in Heaven as a result of your joyous acceptance of Hashem's decree, you would have danced more at the funeral than you would have danced at the wedding!"

HALACHAH OF THE DAY

A *kli rishon* (literally, *first vessel*) is a vessel that was heated directly upon a flame or other similar source of heat (e.g., an electric heating coil). Such a vessel retains its capacity to cook even after it has been removed from the source of heat. The same holds true for any liquids that have been heated in a pot upon a flame. As long as the liquids are still in the pot in which they were cooked, they too have the power of a *kli rishon,* and are considered to have the ability to cook any food item that is immersed in them. By the same token, solid foods that are in a *kli rishon* (the pot in which they were cooked) retain the power to cook anything they may come into contact with, even after having been removed from the source of heat upon which they were cooked.

The capacity of a *kli rishon* to cook is retained until such time as the pot and its contents cool below the temperature of *yad soledes bo.*

A *kli sheni* (second vessel), in the literal sense, is a vessel into which the contents of a *kli rishon* have been transferred. However, generally speaking, we use the term *kli sheni* to refer to the hot contents that have been transferred from a *kli rishon* to a *kli sheni.* While the heat of the contents of a *kli sheni* is not as intense as that of the contents of a *kli rishon,* we shall see that in regard to most foods we extend the prohibition of cooking to a *kli sheni* as well.

A *kli shelishi* (third vessel) is a vessel into which the contents of a *kli sheni* have been further transferred. Once moved to a *kli shelishi,* the contents of a pot lose most of their capacity to cook. However, we will see that there are some foods that cook so easily that they may not be placed even into a *kli shelishi.*

The heat of a *kli rishon* and its contents are considered by halachah as being very potent, and capable of cooking any uncooked item. For this reason, the laws of cooking are no different with respect to a *kli rishon* than they are with any other source of heat. One may not place any uncooked food or drink into a *kli rishon* on Shabbos, even after the *kli rishon* has been removed from the flame.

If a *kli rishon* contains hot foods or liquids, it is forbidden to bring virtually any uncooked item into contact with them. For example, one may not add uncooked seasonings into a hot pot of soup on Shabbos, even if the pot has already been removed from the flame or *blech.* This is because by placing the uncooked seasonings in the *kli rishon,* or by bringing them into contact with the hot contents of the *kli rishon,* one will be cooking the seasonings, a clear violation of the *melachah* of *bishul.*

A CLOSER LOOK AT THE SIDDUR

This week, we will continue our discussion of the seventh of the Thirteen Fundamental Principles (י״ג עיקרים) enumerated by *Rambam,* which states:

> אֲנִי מַאֲמִין בֶּאֱמוּנָה שְׁלֵמָה שֶׁנְּבוּאַת מֹשֶׁה רַבֵּנוּ עָלָיו הַשָּׁלוֹם הָיְתָה אֲמִתִּית וְשֶׁהוּא הָיָה אָב לַנְּבִיאִים לַקּוֹדְמִים לְפָנָיו וְלַבָּאִים אַחֲרָיו.
>
> *I believe with perfect faith that the nevuah of our Teacher Moshe was absolutely true, and that he was the chief of all nevi'im that preceded him and that came after him.*

Last week, we discussed the ways in which the *nevuah* of Moshe differed from that of any other *navi.* This week, we will touch upon another important difference between Moshe and all other *nevi'im* — the *source* of our belief in Moshe as a true prophet.

Rambam, in the eighth chapter of *Hil. Yesodei HaTorah,* explains at length that the basis for Klal Yisrael's acceptance of Moshe as a *navi* was different than the basis for their belief in any other *navi.* The Jews did not believe in Moshe because of any signs that he performed. For when a person believes in someone because of signs or miracles, there can still exist in his heart a doubt that perhaps the signs were accomplished through trickery or magic. Although we find stated in the Torah that Moshe performed miracles after the Jews left Egypt and in the Wilderness, he did so only when such miracles were essential. When it was necessary to defeat the Egyptians, he split the Sea and afterward caused them to be drowned in it. When the Jews needed food he prayed for the manna to descend, and when they needed water he split the rock for them. When Korach and his congregation rebelled, he prayed that they be swallowed by the earth.

Why, then, did the Jews believe in Moshe? Because of what happened at Mt. Sinai. We ourselves saw Hashem speak to Moshe at Mt. Sinai, with our own eyes; our ears (miraculously) heard the lightning and the thunderous sounds. Moshe drew near to the cloud surrounding the mountain, and Hashem spoke to him, in front of the entire nation. After Mt. Sinai, there was no room for further doubts.

Rambam explains that the Torah specifically reveals to us that the Revelation at Mt. Sinai was to be the source for knowing that Moshe's prophecy was genuine, for the verse states (*Shemos* 19:9) that Hashem told Moshe: *Behold, I will come to you in a thick cloud, so that the people will hear when I speak to you, and they will also believe in you forever.* This implies that the belief in Moshe that existed before Mt. Sinai was not a permanent, unshakable belief, but one that could be subject to doubts.

All other *nevi'im* are accepted as prophets not only because of any miracles that they might perform, but because the Torah, which was taught to us *by Moshe,* instructs us to listen to them. Thus, in a sense, the authenticity of *all* subsequent *nevi'im* stems from Moshe. [Indeed, *Rambam* explains that this is why a *navi* can never instruct us to disregard a mitzvah that we received from Moshe, for belief based on miracles cannot overcome belief based upon what we saw with our own eyes.]

It is for this reason that total belief in Moshe as a unique prophet is so critical. As the teacher of the Jewish nation, and the primary transmitter of the Torah, it is essential that his status be completely unassailable.

פרשת וישב

MONDAY

PARASHAS VAYEISHEV

A TORAH THOUGHT FOR THE DAY

וַיִּשְׁמַע רְאוּבֵן וַיַּצִּלֵהוּ מִיָּדָם וַיֹּאמֶר לֹא נַכֶּנּוּ נָפֶשׁ. וַיֹּאמֶר אֲלֵהֶם רְאוּבֵן אַל־תִּשְׁפְּכוּ־דָם הַשְׁלִיכוּ אֹתוֹ אֶל־הַבּוֹר הַזֶּה אֲשֶׁר בַּמִּדְבָּר וְיָד אַל־תִּשְׁלְחוּ־בוֹ לְמַעַן הַצִּיל אֹתוֹ מִיָּדָם לַהֲשִׁיבוֹ אֶל־אָבִיו

Reuven heard, and he rescued him from their hand; he said, "We will not strike him mortally!" And Reuven said to them, "Do not shed blood! Throw him into this pit in the wilderness, but lay no hand upon him!" — intending to rescue him from their hand, to return him to his father (*Bereishis* 37:21-22).

This verse at first glance seems somewhat strange. How can Scripture describe Reuven's suggestion as a form of rescue, if it involved throwing Yosef into a pit? The Gemara (*Shabbos* 23a) asks regarding the statement in the verse (ibid. v. 24): וְהַבּוֹר רֵק אֵין בּוֹ מָיִם, *and the pit was empty, there was no water in it.* If the pit is empty, do I not know that no water was in it? The Gemara answers that the verse hints to us that while the pit was empty of water, it was not completely empty; there were snakes and scorpions in it. Such a pit hardly seems to be a place of safety and rescue! It would appear that Reuven simply pulled Yosef away from one danger and placed him into mortal peril of another sort.

Ohr HaChaim suggests an explanation based upon the following fundamental idea: A person is entrusted with the power of free choice (*bechirah*), and thus has the ability to end another's life prematurely, even if that person was not otherwise destined to die at that time. [It should be noted that not all agree with this statement; they maintain that in such an instance, the person's attempt would fail.] But animals, even deadly ones, have no power to kill a human, unless he has been sentenced in Heaven to be killed. Thus, the verse means that Reuven saved Yosef from "their hands" — from the hands of "free choice," by putting him to the test of snakes and scorpions. He knew that if Yosef were righteous, he would not be harmed by the snakes and scorpions, for they would be powerless to hurt him.

Shiras David applies this idea to explain something that occurred when the prophet Daniel was thrown into the lions' den. The verse there states that the king, who believed that Hashem would protect Daniel from being killed by the lions, nevertheless placed a large stone at the entrance to the pit, so Daniel would not be in danger from the ministers, who hated him and wanted to kill him. The question arises: If the king was convinced that Daniel would be saved from the lions, why was he concerned that the ministers would succeed in harming him?

According to the approach of the *Ohr HaChaim,* the king's action is readily understood. People have free choice, and they are entrusted with the ability to kill even a *tzaddik* prematurely. Lions (and all other animals), however, do not have free choice, and would be unable to kill anyone whom Hashem has not already sentenced to death.

Meshech Chochmah offers another approach. He explains that punishments that come from Heaven (מִן הַשָּׁמַיִם) are meted out only to those over 20 years of age. Yosef, who was only 17, thus was not subject to punishment at the hands of Heaven. A human court, on the other hand, can judge anyone over the age of 13. Thus, Reuven felt assured that punishment from the snakes and scorpions would not be forthcoming, and he wished to remove Yosef only from the hands of the court that had been formed by his brothers.

MISHNAH OF THE DAY: SHABBOS 9:4

Continuing a subject introduced in the previous Mishnah, the following Mishnah inquires after Scriptural support for another law of Yom Kippur:

מִנַּיִן לְסִיכָה שֶׁהִיא כִּשְׁתִיָּה בְּיוֹם הַכִּפּוּרִים — *From where* do we know *that anointing is tantamount to drinking on Yom Kippur?*[1] **אַף עַל פִּי שֶׁאֵין רְאָיָה לַדָּבָר זֵכֶר לַדָּבָר** — *Although there is no* clear Scriptural *proof for the matter,* there is *an intimation to the matter,*[2] **שֶׁנֶּאֱמַר ,,וַתָּבֹא**

NOTES

1. The Mishnah (*Yoma* 8:1) teaches that eating, drinking, washing one's body, anointing one's body with oil, wearing shoes, and marital relations are all forbidden on Yom Kippur. The Tanna here seeks a Scriptural basis for considering anointing tantamount to drinking and thus forbidden on Yom Kippur. [Perforce, the comparison is a limited one, for drinking is punishable by *kares* — Divinely imposed premature death — while anointing is not (*Rav*). Moreover, according to many opinions only eating and drinking are Torah prohibitions, and the other four are only Rabbinic prohibitions. According to these opinions, the verse is cited here only as an אַסְמַכְתָּא, *a support,* to a law that is actually of Rabbinic origin (see *Meromei Sadeh*).]

2. Although there is no conclusive evidence from Scripture that anointing is deemed the equivalent of drinking, there is a verse in *Tehillim* which intimates that the two can be equated.

"כַּמַּיִם בְּקִרְבּוֹ וְכַשֶּׁמֶן בְּעַצְמוֹתָיו" — ***for it is stated: "So it will come like water into his innards and like oil into his bones."***[3]

NOTES

3. *Tehillim* 109:18. Scripture here speaks of the curse that will come upon a wicked man who flouts the will of Hashem, stating that it will penetrate into his very being. The verse compares anointing the body with oil to drinking water. This verse, however, is not conclusive evidence, because it is possible that Scripture is only comparing anointing with oil to *washing* with water, as in both cases the liquid being applied enters the body through the pores (*Tiferes Yisrael*).

GEMS FROM THE GEMARA

This Mishnah, in its consideration of one of the laws of Yom Kippur, links to the previous Mishnah's mention of the red strip of wool that was tied to the head of the goat sent to Azazel. That Mishnah expounded the verse (*Yeshayah* 1:18): *If your sins will be like crimson, they will become white as snow.*

The Gemara (89b) turns to the beginning of the above verse: *Go now, let us reason together, HASHEM will say . . .* Rava finds the wording of the verse perplexing: Why does the prophet say: *Go now . . .* and not *Come now . . .*? Moreover, why does he say: *HASHEM "will" say* instead of *HASHEM says*? Rava explains that the verse alludes to the future, when Hashem will say to the Jewish people, "Go now to your forefathers and let them rebuke you [for your transgressions]." The Jewish people will then say to Hashem, "Master of the Universe, to whom should we go? To Avraham, whom you told (*Bereishis* 15:13): *Know with certainty [that your offspring will be aliens in a land not their own, they will serve them, and they will oppress them 400 years]* — and, nevertheless, he did not ask for mercy for us?! [Should we go] to Yitzchak, who blessed Eisav and told him (ibid. 27:40): *And it will be that when you are aggrieved, you may cast off his yoke from upon your neck* — and he did not ask for mercy for us? [Should we go] to Yaakov, whom You told (ibid. 46:4): *I will descend with you to Egypt, and I will also surely bring you up* [thus hinting to three more exiles], and yet he did not ask for mercy for us?! To whom should we go now? *Let HASHEM* himself *say* [our rebuke]." Hashem will respond, "Since you have made yourselves dependent upon Me, I will tell you (*Yeshayah* 1:18): *If your sins will be like crimson, they will become white as snow.*"

The Gemara then cites an exposition in the name of R' Shmuel bar Nachmani, regarding the *Avos* and the Jewish people's future atonement. The verse (ibid. 63:16) states: *For You are our father, because Avraham does not know us and Yisrael does not recognize us. You, HASHEM, are our Father, our Redeemer, from time immemorial is Your Name.* In the future, Hashem will say to Avraham, "Your children have sinned against Me." Avraham will reply, "Master of the Universe, let them be obliterated for the sanctity of Your Name!" Unsatisfied with this reply, Hashem will say, "I will speak to Yaakov, since he experienced pain in raising his children, perhaps he will ask Me to have mercy upon them." However, Yaakov will also reply that Hashem should obliterate them for the sanctity of His Name!

Finally, Hashem will turn to Yitzchak, who will say to Him, "Master of the Universe, are they then *my* children and not *Your* children?! When they said *We will do* (נַעֲשֶׂה) before *We will hear* (נִשְׁמַע) in front of You before receiving the Torah, You called them (*Shemos* 4:22): *My son, My firstborn.* Now [that they have sinned, they are] my children and not Your children?! Furthermore, how much after all could they have sinned? How many are a man's years? 70 years. Take away the first 20 since You do not punish a person for them. [We find that when God meted out punishment to the generation that accepted the evil report of the Spies (see *Bamidbar* Chs. 13,14) and decreed that they should wander in the Wilderness for forty years, He applied this decree only to those who were already 20 years old (*Rashi*).] There are 50 years left. Take away 25, which are the nights. There are 25 left. Take away $12^1/_2$, which are [spent] praying, eating or attending to bodily needs. There are thus only $12^1/_2$ years [of potential sin] left. If You will shoulder them all, fine. But if not, then half should be on me and half on You. And if You wish to say that all of them should be on me, behold I have already sacrificed myself before You!"

After hearing Yitzchak's defense of them, the Jewish people will open their months and say: *For you [Yitzchak] are our [true] father.* He will then tell them, "Instead of lauding me, laud the Holy One, Blessed is He, [Who is your true Father]," and Yitzchak will direct their eyes to Hashem. Immediately, they will lift their eyes up above and say, *You, HASHEM, are our Father our Redeemer, from time immemorial is Your Name!*

QUESTION OF THE DAY:

Where was Reuven when Yehudah suggested that Yosef be sold?

For the answer, see page 54.

פרשת וישב

MONDAY

PARASHAS VAYEISHEV

A MUSSAR THOUGHT FOR THE DAY

In *A Torah Thought for the Day,* we mentioned the advantage mankind has over the animal kingdom in the aspect of בְּחִירָה, *free choice.* As the *Rambam* states in *Hilchos Teshuvah* (5:5): This is certain: It is not predetermined how a person will behave or act.

It is worthwhile to elaborate a bit on this important concept of free will, which the *Rambam* calls "an important principle and a pillar of all Torah and mitzvos."

He states: "Do not let the thought cross your mind, that which the foolish ones among the nations and even ignorant Jews claim, that Hashem predetermined and decreed upon every person what he will be — a righteous person or a wicked one. It is not so — for every single person can be either a *tzaddik* like Moshe Rabbeinu, or a wicked man like Yeravam. There is no one pulling him in either direction. It is each person's own choice to pick the way of life that he will follow."

He continues, stating that a person cannot defend wrongdoing with the claim that he was born with a certain nature that pulls him in the direction of evil. If it were so, says *Rambam,* how could we be commanded by the prophets to do this and not to do that, if it has already been decreed from Heaven how each person will behave? Furthermore, what sense would it make to punish anyone for his sins, or reward him for his good deeds? If everything was previously programmed, what place would there be for the whole Torah?

This concept places enormous responsibility upon each person; every individual must answer for his actions, as only we are to be blamed for any choice to do evil. But it can also be a source of comfort and encouragement to know that everyone has an equal ability to use his full potential. And one who succeeds in doing so will have merited to reach the level of Moshe, who used all his abilities to perfect himself.

HALACHAH OF THE DAY

The laws of reheating cooked and baked foods on Shabbos apply also to reheating them in a *kli rishon.* Accordingly, it is forbidden to immerse a baked item in the hot liquids of a *kli rishon,* as this violates the prohibition against cooking an item that had previously been baked.

For example, one may not pour baked croutons into a *kli rishon* of hot soup, even after it has been removed from the flame or *blech,* since the previously baked croutons will now be cooked in the heat of the *kli rishon.* [There are croutons that are deep-fried as opposed to baked. Such croutons may be added to a *kli rishon* of hot soup that has been removed from the flame or *blech.* This is because deep-frying is a form of cooking, and one may cook an item that has already been completely cooked.]

One may not add small amounts of cold water to a hot *kli rishon* of soup or other liquid. Since the heat of the *kli rishon* and its contents will overpower the coldness of the added water, the result will be the cooking of the added water in violation of the *melachah* of *bishul.* This holds true even if the added cold water had previously been cooked. For as we learned above, once a liquid has fallen to a temperature below that of *yad soledes bo,* it is prohibited to reheat it.

A container of cold food or liquid may not be inserted into a hot *kli rishon,* because the heat of the *kli rishon* will penetrate the container and cook its contents. For this reason, one may not immerse a baby's bottle in a *kli rishon* pot of hot water in order to warm it, even if the pot has been removed from the *blech.* It is important to note that this is true even if the bottle will be removed from the hot pot before it reaches the temperature of *yad soledes bo.* For as we have learned, one may not place an uncooked item in a location where it can eventually become cooked to a temperature of *yad soledes bo,* even if he will remove it before it does.

In all cases where it is forbidden to cook an item in the heat of a *kli rishon,* the prohibition remains in effect until the pot and its contents cool down to a temperature below that of *yad soledes bo.*

A CLOSER LOOK AT THE SIDDUR

וַיֹּאמֶר דָּוִד אֶל־גָּד צַר־לִי מְאֹד נִפְּלָה־נָּא בְיַד־ה׳ כִּי־רַבִּים רַחֲמָיו וּבְיַד אָדָם אַל־אֶפֹּלָה, *And David said to Gad, "I am exceedingly distressed. Let us fall into* H*ASHEM'S hand, for His mercies are abundant, but let me not fall into human hands."*

This verse, from *II Shmuel* (24:14), is the opening line of the *Tachanun* prayer. Dovid HaMelech had sinned by taking a census of the Jews in a manner contrary to that prescribed by the Torah. Hashem, through the agency of the prophet Gad, gave Dovid HaMelech a choice of three calamities, one of which he and his people would have to suffer in atonement for his sin: seven years of hunger, three months of defeat in battle, or a deadly three-day plague. Dovid chose the last, because that one would be inflicted directly by God, Whose mercy is ever present even when His wrath is aroused. His choice proved to be the correct one, for God mercifully halted the plague after a duration of only half a day.

Similarly, when saying *Tachanun,* we cast ourselves upon God's compassion. *Rabbeinu Bachya* explains that the whole idea of נְפִילַת אַפַּיִם, (literally, *falling on one's face*) is a demonstration of how little we can do by ourselves, and how much we require Hashem's abundant mercy.

Here again, we see that there is great danger in falling into the hands of humans, who have the free will to harm a person. [See *Ohr HaChaim,* cited above in *A Torah Thought for the Day.*] On the other hand, falling into the hands of Hashem, Who really possesses the power to punish a person, is more "safe" so to speak, as He has an abundance of mercy.

[Of course, even *Ohr HaChaim* concurs that no person can harm another if Hashem does not wish that person to come to harm. However, one needs a great source of merit to be saved from the evil designs of a person, who was granted the ability to carry out his free will.]

A TORAH THOUGHT FOR THE DAY

פרשת וישב

TUESDAY

PARASHAS VAYEISHEV

As is the case with all passages of the Torah, the episode of Yosef and the brothers must be learned and studied in the proper perspective. To assume, God forbid, that the disagreements between Yosef and his brothers were due simply to sibling rivalry is grossly wrong — and worse than that, denigrating to the holy *shevatim,* whose names were engraved on the breastplate of the Kohen Gadol. *Rav Yerucham Levovitz* and *Rav Elyah Lopian,* two great Torah teachers, would always emphasize this point very strongly when teaching *parshiyos* such as these.

Although to completely explain the many facets of the disagreements between Yosef and his brothers is beyond the scope of this work, we will attempt to shed some light on this difficult subject, using the words of the *Rishonim* to guide us.

To begin, we must understand why Yosef felt it necessary to relate his dreams to his brothers, and seemingly thereby ignite anger and jealousy. The *Baalei Tosfos* tell us that Yosef was a prophet, and the dreams were a prophecy that he was obligated to repeat: A prophet who conceals his prophecy is punishable by death. In his humility, however, he did not tell them that the dreams had been a prophecy. The brothers, however, who thought that Yosef was not worthy of receiving prophecy, thought that he was simply repeating a dream of no significance.

The brothers interpreted Yosef's behavior as demonstrating a pattern; they felt that he was trying to push them away from being part of the chain of tradition going back to Yitzchak and Avraham. Just as some children of Avraham and Yitzchak were disqualified from continuing Avraham's legacy, the *shevatim* thought that some of Yaakov's children would also be disqualified. They feared that Yosef was attempting to become the sole heir to the tradition of the *Avos,* while casting them aside. Thus, says the *Sforno,* they regarded Yosef as a *rodeif,* a murderous pursuer, who is punishable by death.

Another approach suggested by the *Rishonim* is that Yosef's dream of ruling over the brothers branded him as a *moreid b'malchus,* one who rebels against the king, for they knew that Yehudah was designated for *malchus.* This offense is also punishable by death.

The brothers' judgment was arrived at through due deliberation and fully in accordance with halachah (the Midrash even relates that they included Hashem in their count when reaching a verdict). They were absolutely sure that far from committing any wrongdoing, they were carrying out the will of Hashem.

This is a brief glance into the complex *parashah* of Yosef and his brothers, as taught to us by our great Sages.

פרשת וישב

TUESDAY

PARASHAS VAYEISHEV

MISHNAH OF THE DAY: SHABBOS 9:5

The following Mishnah resumes the discussion (that began above, 7:4, and continued through the eighth chapter) of the minimum amounts of various substances that one must transfer from one domain to another on the Sabbath to be liable to a *chatas:*

הַמּוֹצִיא עֵצִים כְּדֵי לְבַשֵּׁל בֵּיצָה קַלָּה — ***One who takes out wood*** is liable to a *chatas* if he takes out ***enough to cook the most easily*** cooked ***egg;***[1] תְּבָלִין כְּדֵי לְתַבֵּל בֵּיצָה קַלָּה — if he takes out ***seasoning,***[2] he is liable to a *chatas* if he takes out ***enough to season the most easily*** seasoned ***egg;***[3] וּמִצְטָרְפִין זֶה עִם זֶה — ***and*** the different kinds of seasoning ***combine with one another*** to make up the minimum amount that renders him liable to a *chatas.*[4] קְלִיפֵּי אֱגוֹזִין קְלִיפֵּי רִמּוֹנִים אִיסָטִיס וּפוּאָה — One who takes out ***nut husks,***[5] ***pomegranate peels, woad,***[6] ***or madder***[7] כְּדֵי לִצְבּוֹעַ בָּהֶן בֶּגֶד קָטָן פִּי סְבָכָה — is liable to a *chatas* if he takes out ***enough to dye the small cloth*** on ***the top of a*** woman's ***hat;***[8] מֵי רַגְלַיִם נֶתֶר וּבוֹרִית קְמוֹנְיָא וְאַשְׁלָג — if he takes out ***urine,***[9]

NOTES

1. This refers to a hen's egg, which is the egg that requires the least amount of heat to cook (Gemara 80b, in reference to Mishnah 8:5, where the same minimum amount is mentioned in reference to broken reeds). Moreover, one need not carry out enough wood to cook the entire egg; one is liable for carrying out enough wood to cook even a fig-size piece of egg (*Rav; Rashi* from Gemara loc. cit.).

2. Spices such as pepper, ginger, cassia, and the like, which are used to season foods (*Rambam Commentary*).

3. This too refers to the hen's egg (see *Rambam Commentary*), as it is the egg that requires the least amount of seasoning (*Tiferes Yisrael*).

4. Because they all serve the same purpose (*Rambam Commentary*).

5. The fresh outer green shell of the nut is used in dyeing (*Tiferes Yisrael*). [The substances listed here were all used to manufacture dyes. Thus, to be liable for carrying them out, one must take out enough to make a minimally significant amount of dye.]

6. אִיסָטִיס [Latin, *isatis tinctorial*] — *woad* — is a plant that yields a bluish dye.

7. פּוּאָה [*Rubia tinctorum*] — *madder* — is a root from which red dye is made (*Rav*).

8. The סְבָכָה, *hat* [this was a standard headdress worn by women in Talmudic times (see Gemara 57b)], was actually a netting, the top of which was capped with a small piece of colored cloth (*Rav; Rashi;* see *Tiferes Yisrael*). [Thus, the amount of dye for which one is liable need not be sufficient to color an entire hat, merely enough to color the small piece of cloth affixed to the top of the hat.]

9. In Talmudic times, urine was sometimes used as a detergent to remove difficult stains (*Tos.* 90a; see *Niddah* 9:6).

natron,[10] ***soapwort,***[11] ***saltwort,***[12] ***or ashlag,***[13] כְּדֵי לְכַבֵּס בֶּגֶד קָטָן פִּי סְבָכָה — he is liable to a *chatas* if he takes out ***enough to launder the small cloth*** on ***the top of a*** woman's ***hat.*** רַבִּי יְהוּדָה אוֹמֵר כְּדֵי לְהַעֲבִיר עַל הַכֶּתֶם — ***R' Yehudah says: Enough to pass over a stain*** to test if it is a bloodstain.[14]

NOTES

10. The translation of נֶתֶר as *natron* follows *Rashi* and *Tiferes Yisrael* [the latter has the synonymous *saltpeter*]. *Rav* understands the Mishnah to be speaking of a crystalline earth called *alum* [aluminum potassium sulfate].

11. A cleaning agent of vegetable origin (*Rav, Tiferes Yisrael* from Gemara 89b; *Sefer HaShorashim*).

12. A plant found in alkaline regions, from which a cleansing agent is made. It is dried and ground, and used to remove dirt from the hands (*Rav; Aruch*).

13. A kind of mineral substance used for cleansing. It is found in the crevices of pearls, and is removed with an iron nail (Gemara 90a). Its precise definition is unknown (*Rav*).

14. The Mishnah in *Niddah* (9:6-7) describes the procedure for testing a woman's stained garment to determine whether it is a bloodstain (which would, in certain instances, render it *tamei*). Seven cleansing agents are applied to the stain in a specific order. As each one is applied, the garment is rubbed against itself three times in an effort to remove the stain. If, after this process has been completed with each of the seven substances, the stain remains unchanged, then the stain is certainly not blood. If the stain disappears or its color changes it must be treated as menstrual blood, which renders the garment *tamei*. Of the seven cleansing agents specified for this test, four are listed in our Mishnah (*Rav*). R' Yehudah holds that the amount of each of these substances used in this cleansing procedure is enough to make one liable to a *chatas* if he takes it out on the Sabbath. It is not necessary to take out the larger amount required for dyeing. [The Gemara (80a,b) states that wherever the Mishnah discusses minimum amounts in our tractate, R' Yehudah's opinion represents a smaller amount than the one required by his disputant.]

GEMS FROM THE GEMARA

The Gemara (89b) questions the need for the Mishnah's opening ruling. We have already learned in the Mishnah above (8:5) that if one takes out a reed that was thick or cracked, and is thus not suited for making a quill, he is not liable unless he takes out enough to kindle a fire and cook an olive-size portion of the most easily cooked egg. It seems that the ruling here is redundant!

The Gemara answers that if we had been taught only that Mishnah's ruling concerning reeds, we might have thought that the ruling is unique to reeds, for reeds are not fit for any other use. This is not the case, however, when it comes to small pieces of wood. Because small pieces of wood are sturdier than reeds, they are fit for other uses; for example, a small piece of wood can be fashioned into a tooth for a key. Therefore, we might have thought that one would be liable to a *chatas* for carrying out even a very small piece of wood. Our Mishnah therefore comes to teach us that even in the case of wood chips, one is not liable unless he takes out enough to cook an olive-size portion of an easily cooked egg.

[Why indeed is this not the law? We must explain that although a piece of wood can indeed be used for making the tooth of a key, it is more commonly used for kindling, not for keys. Thus, the amount that defines its measure for liability is the amount that is used to fuel a fire for cooking. This is in accordance with the rule stated by the Gemara (78a): "Where there is both a common use and an uncommon use (for an object), the Sages followed the common use" in setting the minimum measure — even if this results in a leniency (*Ritva*).]

A MUSSAR THOUGHT FOR THE DAY

As explained earlier (see *A Torah Thought for the Day*), the dispute between Yosef and his brothers was not a matter of personal dislike, but rather a *machlokes l'sheim Shamayim,* a dispute for the sake of Heaven, where each side sincerely wishes to follow the will of Hashem.

Nevertheless, the commentators study the Torah to find the root of the brothers' error, for which the punishment was so severe. Many centuries later, the *Asarah Harugei Malchus,* the Ten Martyrs, were cruelly tortured and killed as a result of this sin (for further discussion, see *A Torah Thought for the Day* and *A Mussar Thought for the Day* to Wednesday).

Rabbeinu Bachya comments that the verse: וַיִּטְבְּלוּ אֶת־הַכֻּתֹּנֶת בַּדָּם, *and they dipped the tunic in blood* (37:31), is most revealing, because the fact that the brothers wanted to deceive Yaakov and conceal the truth about what they had done was a clear indication that something was amiss. Had they truly believed, without even a trace of doubt, that Yosef deserved to be put to death, why did they not confront Yaakov Avinu? They should have told him that although he was under the mistaken impression that Yosef was a *tzaddik,* according to the judges in a court of law carrying out the will of Hashem, they had reached a verdict to the contrary. Their tampering with the evidence was a sign that they

themselves were not 100 percent sure of their conclusion. Thus, they were indeed guilty of an incorrect act. [*R' Reuven Feinstein* finds a similar idea in Yehudah's statement to his brothers (37:26): *What gain is there if we kill our brother and cover up his blood?* That is, should we be killing him if we are afraid to own up to what we are doing?]

R' Elchanan Wasserman in *Kovetz Maamarim* says that, as we know, Hashem punishes *middah k'neged middah*, measure for measure. What, he asks, is the reason behind the blood libels, from which Jews suffered terribly throughout the ages, especially around the time of Pesach? How can such a blatant and ridiculous lie, with no facts at all to back it up, attract such strong support? He suggests that perhaps this punishment through the generations comes as part of the atonement for this first breach in brotherly love. Just as the brothers dipped the garment into blood, so too did the Jews over the years suffer from "blood" accusations.

HALACHAH OF THE DAY

While we have now discussed many cases of heating and reheating that are prohibited in a *kli rishon,* there are several items that *may* be immersed in a *kli rishon* that has been removed from the flame or *blech.*

Any solid food that has already been fully cooked in liquids may be immersed in a *kli rishon* that has been removed from the heat source. This is because, as we have already explained, there is no prohibition against recooking solid foods that have previously been cooked. For example, one may immerse a [dry] piece of cold boiled chicken in a hot pot of soup after the soup has been removed from the *blech.*

Similarly, a liquid that has previously been boiled and has not yet cooled completely, so that it is still suitable for use as a warm drink, may be immersed in a *kli rishon* (that has been removed from the *blech*) in order to reheat it. Once again, since the liquid has already been cooked and has not yet cooled down, this is deemed a case of recooking something that has already been cooked, which is permissible.

There is a question regarding the immersion in a *kli rishon* of previously cooked foods that will dissolve when immersed in liquids. An example of such a food would be instant coffee granules that have previously been cooked, and which will dissolve when immersed in the hot water of a *kli rishon.* According to some *poskim,* these foods are themselves viewed as liquids, and as such are subject to the restrictions against reheating liquids that have already completely cooled. Other *poskim* disagree with this view. In such cases, a competent Rabbinic authority should be consulted.

Items that will be unable to attain the temperature of *yad soledes bo* if immersed in a *kli rishon* may be placed in a *kli rishon* and allowed to warm up to a lesser temperature. For example, one may place a large container of food in a *kli rishon* containing a relatively small amount of hot water. Since the small amount of hot water will not be able to increase the temperature of the food to the degree of *yad soledes bo,* no violation of the *melachah* of *bishul* is being accomplished. [If the item in question can eventually reach the temperature of *yad soledes bo,* it is forbidden to place it in the *kli rishon* even for a short time, as has been explained above.]

For the same reason, one may quickly pour a large quantity of cold water into the hot water of a *kli rishon,* provided that the amount of cold water is great enough to make it impossible for the final mixture to retain the temperature of *yad soledes bo.* However, the pouring must be done quickly; otherwise, the first droplets of the added cold water will be cooked, as they will combine with the hot water and attain the temperature of *yad soledes bo.*

A CLOSER LOOK AT THE SIDDUR

In the prayer of *Lamenatzei'ach* (*Tehillim* Ch. 20), which we recite every morning after *Shemoneh Esrei* (between *Ashrei* and *U'Va LeTzion*), we find the verse: יַעַנְךָ ה׳ בְּיוֹם צָרָה יְשַׂגֶּבְךָ שֵׁם אֱלֹהֵי יַעֲקֹב, *May* H*ASHEM answer you on the day of distress; may the Name of Yaakov's God make you impregnable.*

The Gemara in *Berachos* (64a) asks: Why is Hashem identified in this verse as the God of Yaakov, and not the God of Avraham and Yitzchak? The Gemara answers: It is the owner of the pillar who must move the pillar if he wishes to place it in a building. *Rashi* (ibid.) explains that it was Yaakov who fathered the twelve *shevatim,* and it was he who was responsible for their upbringing. Thus, he is the one who must pray on their behalf.

To explain further: Although, of course, Avraham and Yitzchak were also the *Avos* of Klal Yisrael, they both had children who were not included in that lineage, and did not continue that tradition. Avraham had Yishmael, and Yitzchak had Eisav. It was only Yaakov who had the responsibility of bringing all of his children under the umbrella of Torah and mitzvos. It is he whose life was filled with travails, and who was not allowed to dwell in peace (see *A Torah Thought for the Day* to Sunday). Problems beset him from all sides — Lavan, Eisav, Yosef, Shimon, Binyamin, and Dinah. He is the one who can — and will — beg Hashem for mercy for his children.

Aruch HaShulchan (132) explains that in the *Lamenatzei'ach* prayer, we ask Hashem for פַּרְנָסָה, *sustenance.* We beseech the "God of Yaakov" to help us be able to sustain our families, and to be successful, as Yaakov was, in keeping all of our offspring true to Hashem. In line with this understanding of the prayer, he also explains the next verse, which states: יִשְׁלַח־עֶזְרְךָ מִקֹּדֶשׁ וּמִצִּיּוֹן יִסְעָדֶךָּ, *May He dispatch your help from the Sanctuary, and support you from Zion. Aruch HaShulchan* explains that all blessing comes to the world through the place of the *Beis HaMikdash,* where Hashem's *Shechinah* is most concentrated. Thus, it is appropriate to ask that our sustenance come to us from Hashem's Sanctuary.

QUESTION OF THE DAY:
How many times was Yosef sold?

For the answer, see page 54.

פרשת וישב

WEDNESDAY

PARASHAS VAYEISHEV

A TORAH THOUGHT FOR THE DAY

וַיִּמְכְּרוּ אֶת־יוֹסֵף לַיִּשְׁמְעֵאלִים בְּעֶשְׂרִים כָּסֶף
וַיָּבִיאוּ אֶת־יוֹסֵף מִצְרָיְמָה

. . . and they sold Yosef to the Yishmaelites for twenty pieces of silver; and they brought Yosef to Egypt (*Bereishis* 37:28).

The sin of *mechiras Yosef* — the brothers' sale of Yosef — has been used as a constant indictment against the Bnei Yisrael throughout history. Perhaps the most obvious punishment visited upon the Jews for this sin is described in the poignant narrative of the *Asarah Harugei Malchus,* recited on Yom Kippur and Tishah B'Av. The Ten Martyrs were cruelly killed by the Roman governor in retribution for the sin of Yosef's brothers who, he charged, despite having committed the capital crime of kidnaping, had never been held culpable. One may ask: Why did Hashem reserve the ultimate punishment for this sin until so many years later, at the time of the Second Temple's destruction? Furthermore, the Torah tells us (*Bereishis* 50:20) that Yosef did not bear a grudge against his brothers for selling him; he realized that it was Hashem's will that he be taken to Egypt, so he would be able to bring Yaakov's family there, to survive the hunger. Why did the Bnei Yisrael deserve such a terrible punishment for selling Yosef when Yosef himself did not hold his brothers responsible?

In answer to these questions, *Derashos Beis Yishai* explains that aside from the personal wrong done to Yosef, which he was able to forgive and indeed forgave, the brother's sale damaged the Bnei Yisrael's perfection, by introducing *sinas chinam* — baseless hatred — within Yaakov's family. Whereas previous challenges to Yaakov's family, such as the attacks of Lavan and Eisav, came from external enemies, the hatred that ultimately spawned *mechiras Yosef* was a threat to the Jewish people from within. Although Yosef had forgiven the brothers for selling him, the weakness of disunity that had been introduced unfortunately became part of the Jewish people. It was therefore at the time of the Second Temple's destruction — a destruction which the Gemara (*Yoma* 9b) tells us was caused by *sinas chinam* — that the punishment for the sin was meted out.

R' Dovid Cohen offers a deeper insight into why the time of the Second Temple's destruction was also the time when redress for the brothers' involvement in *mechiras Yosef* was sought. One of the unfortunate ramifications of *sinas chinam,* beyond the intrinsic bitterness that any argument brings, is that once people are separated by *machlokes* (dispute),

they are unable to work together to accomplish objectives that each is unable to achieve on his own. Instead of living a life where everybody is working for the common good, using their collective abilities to bring about results beyond their individual capabilities, each person, "unable" to work with the others, is left to spending his time focused on his own selfish goals.

Yosef's unique role among the twelve tribes was that of a leader whose mission was to unify the Jewish people, and ultimately all of humanity, combining their individual strengths to achieve a collective, greater goal in the direction of Hashem's service. The implication of rulership was the message of Yosef's prophetic dreams, where he envisioned himself uniting the brothers' talents and abilities to best serve Hashem as a cohesive whole. It was for this reason, as the Midrash explains, that Yaakov was able to successfully battle Eisav only after Yosef was born. For it is only through this trait of leadership and guidance that all the qualities found in the entirety of Creation can be channeled toward the singular direction of something greater — i.e., Hashem's service; and this ensures victory over Eisav's message of the rejection of anything greater or more important than the tangible pleasures of the physical world.

It was for this reason that the time of *sinas chinam* among the Jewish people — when Jewish infighting unfortunately ensured that nobody had a goal greater than his own personal gains — became the time when the Roman Empire, the descendants of Eisav — whose entire life is based only on temporal pleasures and selfish goals — gained ascendancy over the Jews. It was thus also at this time that the Heavenly accusation of the brothers' sale of Yosef was reawakened; Eisav's rise and the Jewish people's subsequent fall was the long-term ramification of the brothers' rejection of Yosef's capacity to channel the Bnei Yisrael's collective abilities into a unified service of Hashem in the world. The brothers — and their descendants, the Jewish people — were thus punished for their sin at this time, when the seeds that were unfortunately planted during the sale blossomed into large-scale consequences.

QUESTION OF THE DAY:

From where in the parashah can we learn that when a person is in the position to reprimand, but does not, he must take responsibility for the results of his inaction?

For the answer, see page 54.

MISHNAH OF THE DAY: SHABBOS 9:6

The following Mishnah continues to consider the minimum amounts of various substances that one must take out on the Sabbath to be liable to a *chatas:*

פִּלְפֶּלֶת כָּל שֶׁהוּא — One who takes out ***pepper*** is liable to a *chatas* if he takes out ***any amount;***[1] **וְעִטְרָן כָּל שֶׁהוּא** ***and*** one who takes out ***tar*** is also liable to a *chatas* if he takes out ***any amount.***[2] **מִינֵי בְשָׂמִים** — One who takes out ***types of spices***[3] **וּמִינֵי מַתָּכוֹת כָּל שֶׁהֵן** — ***and types of metal***[4] is also liable to a *chatas* if he takes out ***any amount.***[5] **מֵאַבְנֵי הַמִּזְבֵּחַ וּמֵעֲפַר הַמִּזְבֵּחַ** — One who takes out a fragment ***of the stones of the Altar, or*** some dirt ***of the earth of the Altar,*** **מֶקֶק סְפָרִים וּמֶקֶק מִטְפְּחוֹתֵיהֶם** — or ***the decay of scrolls, or the decay of their wrappings,***[6] **כָּל שֶׁהוּא** — is also liable if he takes out ***any amount,*** **שֶׁמַּצְנִיעִין אוֹתָן לְגוֹנְזָן** — ***for we put them away in order to place them***

NOTES

1. A person suffering from bad breath would carry pepper in his mouth as a breath sweetener (*Rav* from Gemara 90a; see also 6:5). [This does not refer to the spice that is commonly called "pepper" (*Rav; Rashi*); common pepper is called פִּלְפֵּל, *pilpeil.* פִּלְפֶּלֶת, *pilpeles,* is a different species (*Tos. Yom Tov.*).] Since even a small quantity of this spice is useful in combating bad breath, any amount is considered significant, and sufficient to render a person who takes it out *in his hand* liable to a *chatas* (*Rav* from Gemara 90a). [However, a person may go out with the pepper in his mouth, as taught in the Mishnah above, 6:5.]

2. עִטְרָן, *tar,* is mentioned in 2:2 as one of the fuels unsuitable for use in the Sabbath lamps. It was used as a remedy for migraine [hemicrania], and was effective even in minute amounts (*Rav, Rashi* from Gemara 90a).

3. Here the Mishnah is considering spices that are used primarily for fragrance, and even the most minute amount of a fragrant spice is significant (*Rav; Rashi*). On the other hand, the previous Mishnah considered spices that are used primarily to season food. Since seasoning food requires a larger amount of spice, only taking out a larger amount renders one liable to a *chatas.* If a particular spice serves both purposes, its status follows its more common use. If it is equally common for the spice to be used for both purposes, then the more stringent (i.e., smaller) amount renders one liable (*Tos. Yom Tov;* see above, 8:1).

4. A minute quantity of metal can be used to make the point of an ox-goad (*Rav* from Gemara 90a).

5. [The words כָּל שֶׁהֵן, *any amount,* apply to both spices and metals. In some texts (see *Rav and Rashi*), this phrase appears after each item.]

6. From the Gemara it is evident that מֶקֶק is actually the name of a type of worm that infests scrolls and their wraps (a bookworm). Thus, the phrase מֶקֶק סְפָרִים וּמֶקֶק מִטְפְּחוֹתֵיהֶם should be understood as: *the worm-eaten parts of scrolls and of their wrappings* (*Rashi*).

in a genizah.[7] רַבִּי יְהוּדָה אוֹמֵר — *R' Yehudah says:* אַף הַמּוֹצִיא מְשַׁמְּשֵׁי עֲבוֹדָה זָרָה כָּל שֶׁהוּא — *Also, one who takes out accessories of an idol*[8] is liable for *any amount,* שֶׁנֶּאֱמַר — *for it says:* ,,וְלֹא־יִדְבַּק בְּיָדְךָ מְאוּמָה מִן־הַחֵרֶם" — *"Nothing of that which is banned shall cleave to your hand."*[9]

NOTES

7. If holy articles such as those listed here can no longer be used, they may not be discarded as trash. Ideally, they are to be placed in a *genizah* — a special chamber that serves as a respectable resting place (*Rav; Rashi*). [When such *genizos* were filled, they were often sealed. Some of these old *genizos* have been opened years later and have yielded old manuscripts of great value. Today, however, the practice is to bury worn-out holy articles.] Since one is required by the Torah to save even the smallest pieces of such articles so as to place them in *genizah,* they are considered significant, and therefore they render a person who takes them out on the Sabbath liable to a *chatas* (*Shenos Eliyahu*).

8. [This refers to any articles used to enhance an idol.]

9. *Devarim* 13:18. In issuing the mitzvah to destroy even a minute amount of accessories of an idol, the Torah imparts to them significance (albeit a negative one), making even the most minute amount or size enough to render one liable for taking them out (*Rav; Rashi*).

GEMS FROM THE GEMARA

The Mishnah ruled that one is liable to a *chatas* for taking out any type of metal in any amount on the Sabbath. The Gemara (90a) asks: Of what use is a tiny amount of metal? As we noted in our commentary to the Mishnah, the Gemara responds, citing R' Shimon bar Yochai from a Baraisa, that even a very small piece of metal is fit to be fashioned into the tip of an ox-goad.

The Gemara then quotes a Baraisa that deals with minimum amounts of metals in a different context. In this Baraisa, the Rabbis taught that if a person says, "I take upon myself to bring iron to the Temple treasury," he may not give less than a piece of iron that measures one *amah* (cubit) long by one *amah* wide. The Gemara, in the name of Rav Yosef, explains that this amount is the minimum that had significant value for the Temple, because this was the smallest useful size. This size of metal was fit to be made into a "crow-chaser." The crow-chasers were embedded in the roof of the Temple. Each crow-chaser was a square-*amah* size iron plate; its edges were razor sharp and it was studded with nails. These crow-chasers were designed to keep crows from roosting on the Temple's roof (see *Rashi*).

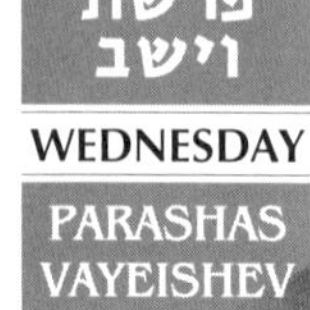

The Baraisa then teaches that if a person took upon himself to bring copper, he may not give less than an amount of copper worth at least one *ma'ah* of silver. [A *ma'ah* is one-sixth of a *dinar.* Anything less than this is not considered a significant amount, and we assume that his intention when he vowed was to pledge a significant amount of copper (*Ritva*).]

The Gemara also quotes the dissenting view of R' Eliezer, who maintains that the person must donate at least enough copper to fashion a small copper fork. Abaye explains that such forks were employed in the Temple to trim the wicks of the Menorah and to clean out its lamps.

A MUSSAR THOUGHT FOR THE DAY

As we explained in *A Torah Thought for the Day,* the punishment of the *Asarah Harugei Malchus* — The Ten Martyrs — for the brothers' sale of Yosef is one of many instances where a single action performed by one person, or a small group of people, has a very great effect many years later. While this is certainly true with respect to the *Avos* and the *shevatim,* who were the forefathers of the Jewish people, it is also true of any person. Each Jewish person is the foundation for generations of descendants to come; and any flaw, however slight, in that foundation may prove catastrophic for the building after it has been constructed. On the other hand, any positive deed performed enhances the entire structure, strengthening generations to come.

R' Yerucham Levovitz (*Daas Torah, Shemos* p. 198) finds this idea expressed in *Ramban's* comments in *Parashas Netzavim* (29:17), explaining Moshe's exhortation of the Bnei Yisrael: פֶּן־יֵשׁ בָּכֶם שֹׁרֶשׁ פֹּרֶה רֹאשׁ וְלַעֲנָה, *perhaps there is among you a root flourishing with gall and wormwood.* It is impossible, explains *Ramban,* for a people who truly believe in Hashem to bear descendants who question Him to the extent of turning to idol worship; any future lack of faith in the Jewish people, said Moshe to the assembled Jews, must have its roots in the present. Repent now, and your actions will transform future generations as well. R' Yerucham explains further, based on *Ramban's* commentary in *Parashas Lech Lecha,* that the impact each action would have on generations to come was the lifelong focus of Avraham, Yitzchak and Yaakov. The *Avos,* fully comprehending the reality of *maaseh avos siman l'banim,* attempted to live their lives in a way that would be the most beneficial for the Bnei Yisrael.

The infinite ability of every single one of man's actions to affect the world is beautifully illustrated by a story that occurred approximately 75 years ago. Rav Shimon Schwab, then a young unmarried yeshivah student, spent Shabbos at the home of the venerable *gadol hador,* the Chofetz Chaim. Over the course of the weekend, the Chofetz Chaim asked Rav Schwab, "Are you a Kohen?" Rav Schwab replied that he was not. The Chofetz Chaim asked him, "Why not?" Puzzled, Rav Schwab answered with the seemingly obvious answer — because his father was not a Kohen. The Chofetz Chaim, as if he did not realize this plainly obvious fact, continued — "And why was he not a Kohen?" Even more confused, Rav Schwab explained — because *his* father was not a Kohen! "And why was *he* in fact not a Kohen?" the Chofetz Chaim asked once again. Finally, the Chofetz Chaim looked at the young Rav Schwab and declared, "I *am* a Kohen. Do you know why? Because over 3,000 years ago, when Moshe Rabbeinu, after the *Cheit HaEigel,* proclaimed: מִי לַה׳ אֵלָי, *Whoever is to HASHEM, follow me!* (*Shemos* 32:26), my great-great-great-grandfather, along with the entire tribe of Levi, came to his side. Your ancestor did not. In reward for their dedication, the tribe of Levi was made into Hashem's emissaries. It is for this reason that, many thousands of years later, my grandfather's children are Kohanim, and will be privileged to serve in the future *Beis HaMikdash,* while the rest of the Jewish people will not. Any action of any person," concluded the Chofetz Chaim, "can incalculably influence generations to come!"

HALACHAH OF THE DAY

Hot liquids that are poured from a *kli rishon* onto a food item are viewed by halachah as possessing nearly the same cooking ability as they did when they were inside the *kli rishon.* It is therefore forbidden to pour the hot contents of a *kli rishon* onto any food that may not be immersed in a *kli rishon.*

For example, one may not pour hot soup from a *kli rishon* into a bowl containing *challah,* because the hot soup will cook the *challah,* a previously baked item. Similarly, one may not pour water from a kettle or urn into a cup containing a small amount of cold water. Once again, the hot water from the *kli rishon* will cook the cold water in the cup. For this reason, when preparing coffee or tea on Shabbos, one should take care to use a dry cup when taking water from an urn or kettle, so as not to cook the cold water droplets found in the cup. A cup that has droplets of *previously boiled* water remaining in it, however, need not be dried before use even if these drops have completely cooled.

If one desires to add hot water to the remnants of a previously cooked beverage, he may do so as long as the liquid remaining in the cup has not completely cooled off. For example, if one is drinking hot tea and desires to add more hot water to his cup, he may do so if the tea that is still in his cup remains drinkable as warm tea. If, however, it has cooled to the extent that it is no longer acceptable to him as a warm drink, he may no longer add hot water from a *kli rishon* to the cup, since by doing so he would be cooking the tea still found in his cup. [This refers only to a significant amount of liquid; droplets of tea can be ignored even if they have completely cooled, as noted in the previous paragraph.]

It is also permissible to add a small amount of hot water to a large amount of cold water, provided that the resultant mixture will definitely not attain the temperature of *yad soledes bo.*

A CLOSER LOOK AT THE SIDDUR

The most obvious mention of the brothers' sale of Yosef found in the *siddur* is the narrative, recited on Yom Kippur and Tishah B'Av, of the *Asarah Harugei Malchus,* who were killed by the Roman governor as "punishment" for this sin. However, a closer look at the Torah's account of *mechiras Yosef* gives a better understanding to a phrase in *Kabbalas Shabbos* as well. *Metzudas Tziyon,* commenting on the opening verse of the chapter in *Tehillim* that begins *Kabbalas Shabbos,* observes that while the words לְכוּ נְרַנְּנָה לַה׳, as simply understood, mean, *Let us "go" and sing to* H*ASHEM*, there is also a deeper meaning. With respect to the sale of Yosef, we find that the brothers, when they first saw Yosef approaching, said: וְעַתָּה לְכוּ וְנַהַרְגֵהוּ, *So now, "lechu" and let us kill him* (*Bereishis* 37:20). [The Midrash relates that the actual speaker was Shimon.] The word לְכוּ in this verse cannot mean "Let us go," because Yosef was coming to them, and they did not need to go anywhere! Rather, explains *Metzudas Tziyon,* לְכוּ is a term used to prompt *zerizus,* alacrity, inspiring a person or group of people to carry out a mission wholeheartedly and flawlessly.

While it is perhaps understandable why Shimon, who was trying to convince his brothers to kill their brother Yosef by throwing him into a snake-filled pit, felt that he needed to use words of encouragement to convince them to do so, it is less obvious why Dovid HaMelech, in one of the few times in *Tehillim* that this word is found, uses לְכוּ specifically in this paragraph to energize people to happily sing to Hashem, a theme which is found many times throughout *Tehillim.*

The commentaries offer several approaches that may enlighten us as to why added encouragement is needed in this opening prayer. The *Vilna Gaon* (in *Avnei Eliyahu*) explains that the exhortation of לְכוּ נְרַנְּנָה לַה' is also directed at the nations of the world, encouraging them, as well, to join the Jewish people in singing to Hashem, finally recognizing that He is the only God. Thus, it is understandable that extra encouragement is necessary. [The interpretation of this call as directed to all of the nations refers only to the opening verse. However, the *pasuk's* continuation: נָרִיעָה לְצוּר יִשְׁעֵנוּ נְקַדְּמָה פָנָיו בְּתוֹדָה, *let us call out to the Rock of our salvation; let us greet Him with thanksgiving,* calls for a higher level of praise, one that highlights gratitude for Hashem's unique and direct involvement in constantly saving the Bnei Yisrael from their enemies; as such, the call to this praise is directed only at the Jewish nation.]

R' Shamshon Raphael Hirsch offers a different explanation for the need for added *zerizus* here, noting that the previous psalm (Ch. 94) describes the sheer pain and suffering that often accompany the Jewish people in exile. Of course, we know that we really have no cause for worry because Hashem is the sole Master, Who will ultimately punish the wicked. At the same time, it is difficult, when living in such times, to realize that we ourselves have the ability to end the long exile by coming close to Hashem, and serving Him with the great joy that comes naturally from realizing what a great privilege it is to be able to serve Him. When a Jew is given encouragement and gains an awareness of his exalted purpose in life, he is able to rise above the gloom of the physical world and serve Hashem through joyful song; hence, the use of the term לְכוּ.

A TASTE OF LOMDUS

The Midrash (*Bereishis Rabbah* 84:16) accuses the brothers of transgressing the Torah prohibition against kidnaping. Included in the *Aseres HaDibros,* this capital crime is committed by abducting and selling a fellow Jew.

The Mishnah in *Sanhedrin* (85b) explains the prohibition of kidnaping in greater detail, stating: *A kidnaper is not liable* (to capital punishment) *until he brings his victim into his property. R' Yehudah says: Until he brings his victim into his property and uses him for work* [for the Torah, when describing the death penalty for a kidnaper, states (*Devarim* 24:7): *and enslaves him and sells him*].

The Gemara explains that in fact both opinions mentioned in the Mishnah agree that enslavement (הִתְעַמְּרוּת) is needed to transgress the Torah prohibition of kidnaping. The dispute in the Mishnah, explains the Gemara, is only regarding how much work the kidnaper must do with his victim in order to be liable. R' Yehudah, in stressing the need for enslavement, is saying that the victim must have been forced to work for his abductor for at least the value of a *perutah* (a small copper coin). The first opinion in the Mishnah, however, which did not mention enslavement but describes kidnaping simply as "bringing the victim into his property," does not require any minimum amount of work to be performed in order for the victim to be considered "enslaved"; any service, however minimal, that the person is forced to perform, renders the kidnaper liable once he subsequently sells the victim.

Mas'as HaMelech (to *Rambam, Hil. Geneivah* Ch. 9) explains the Gemara. While it is true that all agree that the Torah holds the kidnaper liable to the death penalty only if enslavement has occurred, a fundamental dispute exists as to why the Torah requires enslavement to occur. R' Yehudah understands the verse simply: Unlike regular theft, where a person transgresses the prohibition as soon as he takes someone else's object, the Torah includes several additional criteria beyond actual abduction that must be fulfilled to render a kidnaper liable to the death penalty; namely, taking the victim away from his home and family (*Rambam, Hil. Geneivah* 9:2), enslavement, and sale. Capital punishment for kidnaping is prescribed only for a kidnaper who fulfills each of these conditions. Thus, like all monetary minimums in the Torah, the minimum amount of enslavement needed to trigger liability is the value of a *perutah* — for any amount smaller than this is legally insubstantial.

The first opinion mentioned in the Mishnah, although it also requires enslavement, understands that enslavement is not an extra condition, separate from abduction and sale, which a kidnaper must transgress to become liable. Rather, enslavement is in fact part of abduction — that is, with respect to capital punishment, the victim is not considered to have been fully "taken" by the kidnaper until he has been forced to work for him. Enslavement, which is a kidnaper's use of his victim's capabilities for his own purposes, thus completes the abduction process begun with the physical seizure. It is for this reason that this opinion in the Mishnah maintains that even enslavement that is less than the value of a *perutah* is sufficient to obligate the kidnaper.

A TORAH THOUGHT FOR THE DAY

פרשת וישב

THURSDAY

PARASHAS VAYEISHEV

וַתַּהַר וַתֵּלֶד בֵּן וַיִּקְרָא אֶת־שְׁמוֹ עֵר.
וַתַּהַר עוֹד וַתֵּלֶד בֵּן וַתִּקְרָא אֶת־שְׁמוֹ אוֹנָן.
וַתֹּסֶף עוֹד וַתֵּלֶד בֵּן וַתִּקְרָא אֶת־שְׁמוֹ
שֵׁלָה וְהָיָה בִכְזִיב בְּלִדְתָּהּ אֹתוֹ

She conceived and bore a son and he called his name Er. She conceived again and bore a son and she called his name Onan. And yet again and she bore a son and she called his name Shelah, and it was in Chezib when she bore him (Bereishis 38:3-5).

Rashi says that כְּזִיב is the name of a place. He is then bothered by the question: Why did the Torah see fit to inform us of the location of Shelah's birth? Therefore, *Rashi* explains that the word כְּזִיב connotes *failing* or *stopping;* the Torah wishes to tell us that Yehudah's wife would no longer bear children after Shelah was born, and the local populace named the town after this fact.

Ramban asks: How was it known at the time of Shelah's birth that Yehudah's wife would bear no more children? To answer this question, *Be'er BaSadeh* suggests that perhaps she was injured during the birth of Shelah in such a manner as to prevent her from bearing children again.

However, we may still ask: Why does the Torah deem it important for us to know that a town was named after this occurrence? *Maharik* explains that Scripture is telling us of the esteem in which Yaakov's family was held by the local populace. Every detail of this prestigious family's life was carefully examined and admired.

Daas Zekeinim and other *Rishonim* cite an interesting explanation of this verse. In those days, the custom was that the father was given the right to name the first child, the mother would name the second child, and so it would continue, each parent naming every other successive child. For this reason, verse 3 states that *he* named his first son Er, while verse 4 states that *she* called the second son Onan. So when the third child was born, the naming rights actually belonged to Yehudah. Yet, verse 5 states that *she* named him Shelah! Why did Yehudah not name his third son, in line with custom? The verse tells us the answer: Yehudah was in Keziv at the time of the birth. Because Yehudah was not available to name the child, she went ahead and called him Shelah.

Ramban rejects this interpretation, stating that it does not have any "taste or scent." What need does the Torah have to tell us about a breach in some ancient custom? Furthermore, according to this interpretation, why must the verse tell us the place where Yehudah was? It would have sufficed simply to say that Yehudah was away!

[In defense of this interpretation, however, we can suggest that perhaps the Torah is teaching that this practice is a laudable one. Although it may not be a Biblical commandment, many customs and practices are derived from the Torah's relating to us how our forefathers acted and lived in ancient times.]

MISHNAH OF THE DAY: SHABBOS 9:7

The following Mishnah continues to consider the minimum amounts of various substances that one must take out on the Sabbath to be liable to a *chatas*:

הַמּוֹצִיא קוּפַּת הָרוֹכְלִין — ***One who takes out a*** spice-***peddler's box*** on the Sabbath, אַף עַל פִּי שֶׁיֵּשׁ בָּהּ מִינִין הַרְבֵּה — ***even though there are many sorts*** of spices ***inside it,*** אֵינוֹ חַיָּיב אֶלָּא חַטָּאת אַחַת — ***is not liable*** to multiple *chataos,* ***but only to one chatas.***[1] זֵרְעוֹנֵי גִינָּה — One who takes out ***garden seeds*** פָּחוֹת מִכַּגְּרוֹגֶרֶת — is liable to a *chatas* even if he takes out ***less than*** the volume of ***a dried fig.***[2] רַבִּי יְהוּדָה בֶּן בְּתֵירָה אוֹמֵר — ***R' Yehudah the son of Beseirah says:*** חֲמִשָּׁה— He is liable to a *chatas* even if he takes out only ***five*** seeds.[3]

NOTES

1. These peddlers would sell perfumes and aromatic spices to women. Their boxes contained many smaller boxes, each with its small bundle of spices. The Mishnah teaches that although the act of transferring such a box from one domain to another results in the transfer of *many different sorts* of spices, nevertheless, one is not liable to a separate *chatas* for each individual type of spice. Rather, we treat the transfer as a single act of transfer, resulting in an obligation to bring only a single *chatas* (*Rav; Rashi*).

2. Although garden seeds are edible, the minimum amount for liability for their transfer is less than the amount for other foods (which is the volume of a dried fig). This is because such seeds are commonly used both for eating and for planting — and for the purpose of planting, even a number of seeds that take up less than the volume of a dried fig are significant. Since the general rule (Gemara 78a; see the previous Mishnah) is that whenever there are two possible minimum amounts that are equally common we follow the smaller — and thus more stringent — of the two amounts, the minimum amount here is less than the size of a dried fig (*Rav; Rashi*). [Since the Mishnah does not specify how much less than the volume of a dried fig the minimum is, we assume that it is only slightly less (*Rambam Commentary; Tos. Yom Tov*).]

3. R' Yehudah ben Beseirah disputes the Tanna Kamma (*Rambam Commentary*), and holds that one is liable for taking out as few as five garden seeds. Five seeds are considered significant because that is the amount one generally plants in a garden row (*Yerushalmi*).

זֶרַע קִישׁוּאִין — One who takes out ***cucumber seeds*** שְׁנַיִם — is liable to a *chatas* even if he takes out only ***two*** seeds;[4] זֶרַע דִילוּעִין — if he takes out ***gourd seeds,*** שְׁנַיִם — he is liable to a *chatas* for taking out ***two*** seeds; זֶרַע פּוֹל הַמִּצְרִי — if he takes out ***seeds of the Egyptian bean,*** שְׁנַיִם — he is also liable for taking out ***two*** seeds. חָגָב חַי טָהוֹר — One who takes out ***a live kosher locust*** כָּל שֶׁהוּא — is liable to a *chatas* for ***any*** size;[5] מֵת — one who takes out a ***dead*** kosher locust כַּגְּרוֹגֶרֶת — is liable to a *chatas* only if he takes out a volume ***equivalent*** to the volume of ***a dried fig.***[6] צִפּוֹרֶת כְּרָמִים בֵּין חַיָּה בֵּין מֵתָה — One who takes out ***"a bird of the vineyards,"***[7] ***whether it is alive or dead,*** כָּל שֶׁהוּא — is liable to a *chatas* for ***any*** size, שֶׁמַּצְנִיעִין אוֹתָהּ לִרְפוּאָה — ***for we put them away for*** the purposes of ***healing.***[8] רַבִּי יְהוּדָה אוֹמֵר — ***R' Yehudah says:*** אַף הַמּוֹצִיא חָגָב חַי טָמֵא — ***Even one who takes out a live nonkosher locust*** כָּל שֶׁהוּא — is liable to a *chatas* for ***any*** size, שֶׁמַּצְנִיעִין אוֹתוֹ לַקָּטָן לְשַׂחוֹק בּוֹ — ***since we store*** live nonkosher locusts ***for a child to play with.***[9]

NOTES

4. The seeds of the three vegetables listed here are more valuable than those of other garden vegetables, and therefore even a very small amount of them suffices to render a person liable (*Rav; Rashi*). Both the Tanna Kamma and R' Yehudah ben Beseirah are in agreement concerning these amounts (*Rambam Commentary; Tos. Yom Tov*).

5. [I.e., even if it is smaller than the volume of a dried fig.] The reason for this is that people will store a live locust for use as a children's plaything (*Rav; Rashi*). Accordingly, even the smallest live locust is significant, and suffices to render a person liable.

6. Since it need not be slaughtered, a kosher locust that died in any manner is like any other food; therefore, its minimum amount is the equivalent of the volume of a dried fig (*Rav; Rashi*).

7. A variety of bird that was known to frequent young palms (*Rav*).

8. The flesh of the "bird of the vineyards" was eaten to increase one's mental capacity (*Rav* from Gemara 90b). Accordingly, it was subject to the principle that when something is stored for medicinal purposes even the smallest amount is significant, and suffices to render a person liable to a *chatas* (see below, Mishnah 10:1).

9. R' Yehudah holds that one may give a nonkosher locust to a child as a pet — and therefore its minimum size is the same as that for a kosher pet locust. It is his opinion that children do not eat their dead pets, but, rather, lament their death and eulogize them. The Tanna Kamma disagrees, maintaining that one would not give a nonkosher locust to a child as a pet, lest it die and the child eat it (Gemara ibid).

QUESTION OF THE DAY:

Who was the mother of Er, Onan, and Shelah?

For the answer, see page 54.

פרשת וישב

THURSDAY

PARASHAS VAYEISHEV

GEMS FROM THE GEMARA

The Mishnah taught that according to R' Yehudah, a person is liable for taking out a live nonkosher locust of any size, since people put it away for a child to play with. The Tanna Kamma disputes R' Yehudah, and holds that one is not liable for taking out a nonkosher locust of minuscule size. The Gemara (90b) explains that the Tanna Kamma holds that people do not put aside live nonkosher locusts for a child to play with, lest the child eat the locust. They therefore will not give the locust to the child, as one is forbidden to cause a minor to transgress a prohibition. Thus, people do not put away nonkosher locusts, and therefore one will not be liable for taking one out unless it has a full measure. [*Yerushalmi* gives a dog's mouthful as the minimum measure for liability for taking out nonkosher locusts.]

The Gemara then asks: If people withhold live nonkosher locusts from a child for fear that he will eat them, then they should withhold live kosher locusts as well, since they too are forbidden! For if a person eats a live locust, he violates the commandment against making one's soul abominable by eating disgusting foods. [The prohibition against eating *sheratzim* states (*Leviticus* 11:43): *Do not make your souls abominable by means of any creeping thing* (see also ibid. 20:25). Although this verse speaks only about *sheratzim,* it is expounded to teach that one must refrain from *any* food considered by most people to be disgusting (*Rashi*).]

To answer this question, the Gemara posits that the Tanna Kamma is not concerned that anyone — even children — is going to eat *live* locusts. He is concerned only that the locust might die, and the child might eat it upon its death. One therefore will not give a live nonkosher locust to a child, lest it die, and the child eat it. Hence, as people do not put away nonkosher locusts as toys, one is not liable for taking these locusts out unless he takes out a full measure according to its normal use (viz., a dog's mouthful).

The Gemara then explains why R' Yehudah is not concerned for this possibility: He holds that if the locust dies, the child will mourn it, not eat it. Hence, people do put away live nonkosher locusts to give to children, and therefore one is liable for taking one out whatever its size.

A MUSSAR THOUGHT FOR THE DAY

One of the greatest lessons the Gemara teaches us regarding how to protect another's feelings is learned from Tamar's behavior in this *parashah.* The verse tells us that she sent to her father-in-law Yehudah his staff and signet, saying only, "By the man to whom these belong I am with child." She did not confront Yehudah directly, as *Rashi* explains, because she did not want to embarrass him. She said: If he will admit his deed on his own, fine; if not, let them burn me. From here the Gemara derives (*Sotah* 10b) that it is preferable for a person to throw himself into a fiery furnace rather than to humiliate his fellow in public.

[The Gemara relates how other great sages heeded this lesson when it came to giving money to poor people. They avoided being seen by the poor man to whom the charity was being given, even if it meant jumping into a dangerous place to hide! The Gemara (*Kesubos* 67b) tells us that this once occurred with Mar Ukva, and he and his wife jumped into a furnace. A miracle took place, and the merit of *tzedakah* protected them from serious injury. Mar Ukva's wife emerged completely unscathed, while his feet got slightly scorched. The Gemara explains that her merit was greater, for she used to actually serve the poor people bread, while he only gave them money, and they had to go through the hardship of buying bread. From this Gemara we learn that the more effort one puts into his *tzedakah,* the more he is protected.]

From Tamar we learn that no accomplishment can justify hurting someone's feelings. Tamar knew that her meeting with Yehudah was not coincidence, but an intervention from God to create the seed of Mashiach, as the Midrash tells us. Indeed, the Midrash also relates that a special angel was sent to direct Yehudah to Tamar, to help in the formation of the lineage of Mashiach. But even such a great achievement was not worth causing the public humiliation of Yehudah.

Many times, says *Rav Yerucham Levovitz,* a person has a worthy agenda; he wishes to do a great mitzvah. But along the way, he is careless and hurts many people's feelings. Such actions, no matter how noble the cause, are wrong, and will not earn Hashem's approval.

We may contrast Tamar with Potiphar's wife, who, as *Rashi* says, also wished to attach herself to Yosef for the sake of Heaven (see *Rashi* to 39:1). However, the actions she took in her attempts to achieve those results — which caused such embarrassment and suffering to Yosef — were not justified by her noble intentions.

HALACHAH OF THE DAY

As we mentioned yesterday, hot liquids being poured from a *kli rishon* retain *nearly* the same cooking ability as the *kli rishon* itself. There is, though, one major difference between immersing food in a *kli rishon,* and pouring from a *kli rishon* onto foods. When food is *immersed* in a *kli rishon,* the contents of the *kli rishon* have the ability to cook the food through and through. When the contents of a *kli rishon* are *poured* onto food, their ability to cook the food is limited to the surface area of the food. There is one leniency that arises from this distinction.

We have learned previously that it is forbidden for one to heat a container of food or liquids through immersion in the contents of a *kli rishon.* It is, however, permissible for one to pour hot water from a *kli rishon* onto such a container in order to warm its contents. This is because the contents of the container cannot become cooked by the water being poured on it. Since the cooking ability of the poured water is limited to the surface of the object upon which the water is poured, the most potent heat of the water will be expended on the surface of the container; it will be unable to penetrate it in order to cook the food contained therein.

This method of heating may be used with all foods as long as the poured water is allowed to run off the surface of the container. If, however, the poured water is permitted to build up in a bowl or other container so that it eventually surrounds the container of food, this will result in the container being immersed in a *kli sheni,* which is subject to restrictions we will outline shortly.

A short summary of the laws pertaining to *kli rishon*:

- ❑ It is forbidden to place uncooked foods or cold liquids in a *kli rishon.*
- ❑ Cooked foods may be warmed in the hot liquid of a *kli rishon* that has been removed from the fire.
- ❑ It is forbidden to pour hot liquids from a *kli rishon* onto any item which may not be immersed in a *kli rishon.* However, one may pour the hot water from a *kli rishon* onto a container of food, provided that the poured water is allowed to run off after being poured over the container.
- ❑ Any item which cannot possibly attain the temperature of *yad soledes bo* through the heat of the *kli rishon* may be warmed in a *kli rishon.*

A CLOSER LOOK AT THE SIDDUR

When we celebrate a *Sheva Berachos,* we recite seven special blessings after *Bircas HaMazon.* [*Sheva Berachos* literally means "seven blessings"; these blessings give the celebration its name.] The fifth blessing begins with the words: שַׂמֵּחַ תְּשַׂמַּח רֵעִים הָאֲהוּבִים, *Gladden the beloved friends.* This is a reference to the *chassan* and *kallah,* who through marriage become loving companions to one another (*Avodas Yisrael*).

We may ask: Why is this term used to describe a *chassan* and *kallah*? "Companions" or "friends" are seemingly not adequate descriptions of the bond between husband and wife. What is the reason for referring to them in this manner?

We find the word רֵעַ used in the Torah after the selling of Yosef, with respect to the friend of Yehudah. The Torah tells us that Yehudah was demoted from his position of leadership over the brothers, for they said to him, "We heeded your command when you told us to sell Yosef. Had you said to return him to Yaakov, we would also have listened!"

At this point, Yehudah isolated himself and found a new friend, Chirah the Adulamite. The Torah (*Bereishis* 38:12) describes him as: חִירָה רֵעֵהוּ, *Chirah, [Yehudah's] friend.* During this time, Yehudah suffered the triple loss of his two children and then his wife. It is during this distressing period in his life that the Torah describes Chirah as Yehudah's friend.

As the expression goes, "a friend in need is a friend indeed." When everything is going smoothly and pleasantly, it is not the time to determine if one has a secure friendship. It is rather during rough times, when someone cannot manage on his own, and a friend gives a caring hand, that friendship is truly tested and proven.

This important message, says the *Shaarei Orah,* is being emphasized in the *Sheva Berachos,* at the onset of the young couple's new life. When *chassan* and *kallah* are starting a new life together, everything seems rosy and pleasant. But, we ask the couple to remember that their role must be one of רֵעִים הָאֲהוּבִים, *beloved friends.* There may be pressing times ahead in their lives, and difficult challenges to face, when true friendship will be put to the test. With this in mind, we express the wish that *chassan* and *kallah* will successfully overcome all the hurdles that they may face in their life together.

A TORAH THOUGHT FOR THE DAY

וַיְהִי כְּהַיּוֹם הַזֶּה וַיָּבֹא הַבַּיְתָה לַעֲשׂוֹת מְלַאכְתּוֹ
וְאֵין אִישׁ מֵאַנְשֵׁי הַבַּיִת שָׁם בַּבָּיִת

And it was on that day that he entered the house to do his work — and none of the men of the household were there in the house (*Bereishis* 39:11).

R*ashi* quotes the dispute in the Gemara (*Sotah* 36b): Rav and Shmuel argue concerning the meaning of the verse's statement that Yosef came "to do his work." One says it means his work, literally; he came to perform his regular duties. The other says it means that Yosef's resolve weakened and he came to yield to the demands of his master's wife; but he did not do so, because the image of his father's visage appeared to him.

This second opinion is difficult for us to comprehend. Can it be possible that Yosef, who is called "the righteous one, the foundation of the world," entered the house in order to sin, God forbid?

Rav Shimon Schwab explains that the "work" of a *tzaddik* is defined differently than that of most people. His work, and his needs, are always related to the service of Hashem. A *tzaddik* looks for ways to perfect his *avodas Hashem* — even going so far as to confront the *yetzer hara* and triumph over it by not giving in to its temptations. Indeed, we find in the Gemara (*Avodah Zarah* 17a) that two Amoraim were walking, and one suggested that they pass by a house of evildoers, but refrain from entering and succumbing to their temptations. By these actions they hoped to diminish the power of the evildoers.

Yosef also wanted to enter the house and overcome his *yetzer hara,* hoping that this would strengthen him in his ability to resist the temptation posed by his master's wife from that time on.

However, R' Schwab states, this route is a very dangerous one; indeed, from the Gemara we see that it can be undertaken only when two *tzaddikim* are together, so that one can encourage the other if he falters. Yosef, however, tried doing it all alone; this is alluded to in the verse, which states that *none of the men of the household were there.* The temptation was great, and he was very vulnerable. At that critical juncture, he saw a vision of his father warning him to run outside, because in such a situation he might very well fall into the clutches of the *yetzer hara.* He obeyed and was saved from sin.

In our prayers every morning, we ask that Hashem not put us into situations where we will be tested, for the risk factor is too great. Only when one is properly prepared and protected may he embark upon this dangerous route, to try and weaken the *yetzer hara.*

MISHNAH OF THE DAY: SHABBOS 10:1

פרשת וישב

FRIDAY

PARASHAS VAYEISHEV

As we have learned in previous chapters, normally a person is liable for violating the forbidden *melachah* of *transferring objects from one domain to another* on the Sabbath only if he takes out a prescribed minimum amount or size of a particular substance or item. The coming Mishnah considers circumstances under which a person is liable even for lesser amounts or sizes (*Tiferes Yisrael*):

הַמַּצְנִיעַ לְזֶרַע — ***One who put away*** a minute amount of seed ***for*** the purpose of ***planting,***[1] וּלְדוּגְמָא — ***or*** one who put away a small amount of a substance to use ***as a sample*** to show prospective customers, וְלִרְפוּאָה — ***or*** one who put away a small amount of a substance to use ***for healing,*** וְהוֹצִיאוֹ בְּשַׁבָּת — ***and*** then ***took it out on the Sabbath*** to another domain,[2] חַיָּיב בְּכָל שֶׁהוּא — ***is liable*** to a *chatas* ***for*** taking out ***any*** amount or size.[3] וְכָל אָדָם — ***But any*** other ***person*** אֵין חַיָּיב עָלָיו אֶלָּא כְּשִׁיעוּרוֹ — ***is liable only for*** taking out ***its prescribed*** minimum ***amount.***[4] חָזַר וְהִכְנִיסוֹ — Likewise, if the person who originally stored the lesser amount or size ***returned and brought it back in*** from the domain to which he took it out,[5]

NOTES

1. In all these cases, a person put away a substance for safekeeping [before the onset of the Sabbath (*Rav*)] in a quantity of less than the minimum amount of that substance that is normally required for one to be liable for taking out on the Sabbath (*Tiferes Yisrael*). For example, in the case of seeds, he stored away a single seed (see the previous Mishnah for the normal minimum number of seeds and amounts of the following substances). Subsequently, however, he forgot his original purpose in hiding away such a small amount (*Rav* from Gemara 90b).

2. I.e., forgetting his reason for putting the item away, he carried it out on the Sabbath with no special purpose in mind (*Rav* from Gemara 90b, 91a), other than the intent to transfer it from one domain to another domain (*Rashi* 90b).

3. When he put away this small amount or size of a substance, he indicated that this amount was important to him. Hence, even if he later forgets the purpose for which he put this substance away, it retains its subjective significance, and renders him liable to a *chatas* (*Rav* from Gemara 91a). This rule is interpreted literally — e.g., even if only one tiny seed is involved (*Tos. Yom Tov* from Gemara 91a).

4. I.e., if someone other than the one who put the substance away took it out, he is not liable to a *chatas*. He is not beholden to the subjective whims of one individual. Rather, he is bound by the objective minimums set forth in the preceding two chapters, which are the smallest amounts and sizes that are *commonly* put away for safekeeping (*Rav*).

5. I.e., if the person who originally put away this amount or size and then took it out on the Sabbath now recalls his original intention, changes his mind and decides not to use the seed for his original purpose, and *then* brings it back from the public domain into a private one (*Rav; Rashi*).

אֵינוֹ חַיָּיב אֶלָּא בְּשִׁיעוּרוֹ — then ***he*** too ***is liable only for*** bringing back ***its prescribed*** minimum ***amount.***[6]

NOTES

6. Since he has decided against using the seed in line with his original intention, it no longer possesses any more subjective significance to him than to anyone else. His standard for liability reverts to the default, objective amount or size. Hence, he is exempt from liability for this new transfer of the smaller amount or size (*Rashi*). [However, if after having taken the seed out with no specific intent, he recalls his original intent and wishes to put the seed away again to be used *for that purpose,* it retains its subjective significance, and he will be liable to a *chatas* for taking it back inside.]

GEMS FROM THE GEMARA

The Gemara (91a) considers variations on the case mentioned by our Mishnah: The first, presented by Rava in the name of Rav Nachman, concerns a person who took a quantity of produce the size of a dried fig out to a public domain for the purpose of eating it there, but before placing it down, changed his mind and decided to plant it instead. Or, conversely, he initially meant to plant it, but in mid-transfer changed his mind and decided to eat it. In both cases, he is liable for the *melachah* of transferring.

The Gemara asks: Isn't this obvious? If he took out the minimum amount necessary for liability, why should it matter if he changed his mind as to the purpose of the transfer? The Gemara replies that were it not for Rav Nachman's teaching, we might have thought that in order to be liable for carrying, it is necessary that both one's removal of the object from its present location and his setting it down in a new place be done with the same intent. Thus, Rav Nachman informs us that there is no such requirement.

Then Rava asks: Suppose one took a quantity of produce that was *half* the size of a dried fig out to a public domain, intending to plant it there, and in mid-transfer it [absorbed liquid and] expanded to the volume of a full dried fig, at which point he changed his mind and decided to eat it instead of planting it. Is he liable or exempt for the transfer? On the one hand, perhaps one is liable only if the requisite volume is present at all stages of the transfer. On the other hand, since if he had not decided upon a new intent before setting the item down, he would certainly have been liable on account of his original intent to plant it (for the item had the minimum measure for planting), so too now, he should remain liable.

Rava queries further: Even if we accept the second argument and hold him liable in such a case, what of a scenario in which a person took a quantity of produce the size of a dried fig out to a public domain for the purpose of eating it, and in mid-transfer it shrank in size, at which point he changed his mind and decided instead to plant it? On the one hand, had he not changed his mind and decided to plant the produce, he would not have become liable on the basis of his original intent to eat it, and, as such, he should be exempt for the transfer. On the other hand, perhaps we take into account only his current intent, and he should be liable!

Rava then takes this line of inquiry a step further. Even if we were to assume that we take only his current intent into account, and hold him liable in the previous case, what of a case in which he took out a quantity of produce that was the size of a dried fig for the purpose of eating it, and in mid-transfer it shrank in size, but then expanded again, so that when the person finally set it down, it was again the size of a fig? Do we say that once the item lost the minimum measure, even temporarily, the person cannot be held liable for the transfer? Or do we say that since at the end of the transfer the measurement was there, the fact that it was missing at one point in the middle of the transfer is not relevant? [See there for further clarification of this inquiry.]

The Gemara leaves all of these questions unresolved.

A MUSSAR THOUGHT FOR THE DAY

Many times, a person finds himself in a situation where he is unsure whether the direction in which he is heading is the path of the *yetzer tov,* or whether he is being led into the snares of the *yetzer hara.* How can one determine which road to take, and what Hashem wishes him to do?

A lesson can be taken from the actions of Yosef. We see that Yosef did not give in to the extreme pressures exerted upon him by the wife of Potiphar, and he did not allow himself to sin. However, *Rashi* (to 39:1) says that her intention at the beginning was for the sake of Heaven. Her stargazers had informed her that her family was destined to establish sons through Yosef, and she was not sure if this would come about from her or from her daughter [in the end, Yosef indeed married her daughter (see below, 41:45)]. The obvious question is: How was Yosef certain that this was not the call of the *yetzer tov*? Why was he convinced that this

was a sin? [The simple answer is, of course, that she was married at the time, and no good deed can come from committing a sin.]

Rav Sholom Shwadron used to offer an answer to this question by saying, in his classic way, "The *yetzer tov* is not a 'nudge.' " As the verse says (39:10): *And so it was, just as she coaxed Yosef day after day, so he would not listen to her.* When the message is received daily, and the opportunity to carry out the mission is easy, that is a sign that it is a message from the *yetzer hara.* The *yetzer tov,* on the other hand, states its message and then leaves; part of our challenge is to understand this message and act accordingly.

The *Gra* (Vilna Gaon) says something similar regarding the narrative of Ruth. Naomi tried to convince Ruth to return to her father's home, but the verse states that when Naomi saw that Ruth was struggling (מִתְאַמֶּצֶת) to go along with her, she ceased her efforts at dissuasion. *Gra* explains that if something comes to a person easily, without a battle and struggle, one must be concerned that it is coming from the *yetzer hara.* Once a person faces difficulty, this is a sign that it is a mitzvah that he is encountering. A person by nature is formed from dust (*yesodo mei'afar*), which means that he does not have the natural energy to do mitzvos. It takes effort to overcome this tendency, and to be able to perform mitzvos properly.

The story is told that when *Rav Chaim Volozhiner* first approached his rebbi, the Vilna Gaon, to ask if he should establish the great Volozhin Yeshivah, the *Gra* was reluctant to give his approval. A year later, when Rav Chaim mentioned this idea again in passing, the *Gra* responded with his approval and blessing. When Rav Chaim asked what had prompted the *Gra* to change his mind, he replied, "When you first approached me a year ago with this idea, I was concerned. I noticed much excitement and enthusiasm in your request, and I was worried that some *yetzer hara* was mixed in with your pure intentions. Now that you mentioned it without that extra energy, I know that it is a request approved by the *yetzer tov.* Now you will be successful!"

QUESTION OF THE DAY:

The verse states that Yosef came to the house on "that day." What was the significance of that day?

For the answer, see page 54.

HALACHAH OF THE DAY

Now that we have concluded our discussion of the laws that pertain to cooking in a *kli rishon,* we will turn our attention the the laws of a *kli sheni.*

As described above, a *kli sheni* is a vessel into which the contents of a *kli rishon* have been transferred. Generally speaking, we use the term *kli sheni* to speak of the hot contents of the vessel, rather than the vessel itself.

When hot liquids are transferred from a *kli rishon* into a *kli sheni,* the walls of the *kli sheni* begin to absorb some of the heat emanating from the liquids. For this reason, the heat of the contents of a *kli sheni* is not as intense as that of the contents of a *kli rishon.* Accordingly, the contents of the *kli sheni* are considered by our Sages as capable of cooking only those items which they classified as קַלֵּי הַבִּשּׁוּל, *easily cooked items.* These items, being especially sensitive to heat, will become cooked even through the heat of a *kli sheni,* as opposed to other items, which require a more intense source of heat to be cooked.

Over the centuries, however, our knowledge of which food items are to be classified as קַלֵּי הַבִּשּׁוּל has diminished. As a result of this ignorance, the *poskim* rule that with the exception of those items which we know for certain were considered by the Sages *not* to be classified as easily cooked, all items must be treated as if they belong to the classification of קַלֵּי הַבִּשּׁוּל, and they therefore may not be immersed in a *kli sheni.* Consequently, it is forbidden to immerse any uncooked food in a *kli sheni,* with the exception of the few items that we will specify below.

Furthermore, it follows from this ruling of the *poskim* that, generally speaking, any food which may not be immersed in the contents of a *kli rishon* may not be immersed in the contents of a *kli sheni* either.

There are, though, several leniencies which do apply to a *kli sheni,* which we will discuss tomorrow.

A CLOSER LOOK AT THE SIDDUR

As we have mentioned previously, the *Shemoneh Esrei* prayers of the Sabbath are unique in that the *Shacharis, Minchah* and *Maariv* prayers are not identical (as is the case both on weekdays and on festivals). Rather, each of the three prayers addresses a specific theme, and the central blessing of each prayer (the Sabbath *Shemoneh Esrei* prayers each contain seven blessings) changes to reflect this.

The *Shemoneh Esrei* prayer of the Friday night *Maariv* speaks of the first Sabbath, the Sabbath of Creation. With the onset of Sabbath, Creation was complete, and *menuchah,* rest, came to the world. [Indeed, *Rashi* (to *Bereishis* 2:2) comments: "What was the world lacking at the end of the sixth day? Rest! When the Sabbath came, rest came with it."]

We begin the central blessing with the words, אַתָּה קִדַּשְׁתָּ אֶת יוֹם הַשְּׁבִיעִי לִשְׁמֶךָ, *You sanctified the seventh day for Your Name's sake.* This simple statement identifies what the Sabbath is meant to be, and what it is not meant to be. Sabbath is not simply a "day of rest," meant to provide people with opportunities for leisure or to "recharge their batteries." That would make the Sabbath a *lesser* day than its counterparts in the weekly schedule — a day when nothing important need be accomplished. In this *tefillah* we state unequivocally that this is *not* the case. The Sabbath is *sanctified* — it is so much *more* than just a regular day. And we continue — it is sanctified *for Your Name's sake.* The Sabbath is a spiritual day, a day that we are to spend strengthening our bond with Hashem, so that the holiness we internalize will stay with us through the week that follows. The Sabbath is the culmination of the week, its peak rather than its valley.

The prayer continues with the words: תַּכְלִית מַעֲשֵׂה שָׁמַיִם וָאָרֶץ, *the conclusion of the creation of Heaven and earth.* Simply understood, this means that every seventh day is Sabbath to commemorate the fact that Hashem finished Creation in six days and rested (so to speak) on the seventh. *Be'er Mayim Chaim,* however, notes that the word תַּכְלִית can also mean *purpose.* Thus, he explains, we are saying that the true *purpose* of Creation is for us to draw closer to Hashem — a purpose that we can more readily accomplish during the sanctified day of the Sabbath.

A TORAH THOUGHT FOR THE DAY

וְלֹא־זָכַר שַׂר־הַמַּשְׁקִים אֶת־יוֹסֵף וַיִּשְׁכָּחֵהוּ
But the Chamberlain of the Cupbearers did not remember Yosef, and he forgot him (*Bereishis* 40:23).

The *Parashah* ends by telling us that although Yosef requested that the Chamberlain of the Cupbearers mention his plight to Pharaoh, the chamberlain in fact forgot to do so, and indeed did not remember Yosef at all until two years later, when Pharaoh dreamed his dreams and could not find an interpretation that satisfied him. *Midrash Tanchuma* states that this two-year period was added by Hashem to Yosef's sentence in jail, because he placed his trust in man, instead of having complete trust (*bitachon*) in God.

Many commentators ask: Was it not reasonable for Yosef, who had been languishing in prison for ten years for a crime he did not commit, to seize upon an avenue for possible freedom that had presented itself in such a fortuitous manner? Why was such an action not permitted to him as proper *hishtadlus,* effort, in the same way that one is permitted to work at earning a living, rather than trusting that Hashem will miraculously grant him whatever he needs?

Several approaches are suggested to resolve this question. Some commentators maintain that Yosef was indeed permitted to ask the chamberlain to remember him to Pharaoh; his only sin was that he did so *twice,* first stating, *if only you would remember me,* and then repeating, *and mention me to Pharaoh* (see verse 13). The first request was sanctioned as proper *hishtadlus;* the second was not. In a similar vein, some suggest that it was not Yosef's request per se that was incorrect, but the way that he couched it, stating that he had done nothing to deserve being thrown into prison, and implying that the accuracy of his interpretation might hinge upon whether the chamberlain actually mentioned him to Pharaoh. These statements were not necessary parts of his *hishtadlus,* and should have been omitted.

Others maintain that Yosef should have instantly recognized that the entire episode that placed the chamberlain in his care was miraculous in nature, unfolding for the express purpose of freeing him from prison. Had he recognized this, he would have realized that Hashem had already set the wheels of his liberation in motion, and that there was no reason for him to say anything at all. His failure to perceive this resulted in his request, and this shortcoming caused him to suffer the additional two years of imprisonment (*R' Moshe Feinstein*).

Yet another approach is taken by *Rabbeinu Bachya.* He maintains that Yosef indeed instantly recognized that Hashem was paving the way for his freedom, and thought that his request was the proper way to proceed. Indeed, he states, for a lesser man than Yosef, this would have been perfectly correct. But a *tzaddik* of Yosef's caliber was held to a higher standard. God expected him to trust so completely in Him, that he would not seek any human assistance at all, even where it would seem to be warranted; and it was for this minute lapse that he was punished.

MISHNAH OF THE DAY: SHABBOS 10:2

The prohibition of transferring an object from one domain to another on the Sabbath is violated when a person picks up an article in a private domain and deposits it in the public domain, or vice versa. The Mishnah now discusses a case where this process is interrupted: הַמּוֹצִיא אוֹכָלִין וּנְתָנָן עַל הָאִסְקוּפָּה — ***One who takes foodstuffs out*** of his house ***and places them on the threshold*** between his house and a public domain,[1] בֵּין שֶׁחָזַר וְהוֹצִיאָן — then no matter ***whether he*** himself ***returns and takes*** the foodstuffs ***out*** into the public domain, בֵּין שֶׁהוֹצִיאָן אַחֵר — ***or someone else takes them out,*** פָּטוּר — each one of them is ***exempt,*** מִפְּנֵי שֶׁלֹּא עָשָׂה מְלַאכְתּוֹ בְּבַת אַחַת — ***since he did not perform his labor all at once.***[2]

NOTES

1. I.e., a person took foodstuffs out of his house and went toward the public domain. However, before he reached the public domain, he placed the foodstuffs down upon the threshold between his house and the public domain. This threshold is a *karmelis*: a distinct area that is at least 4 *tefachim* (handbreadths) wide and 4 *tefachim* long, and at least 3 *tefachim* — but less than 9 *tefachim* — high (*Rav* and *Rashi* from Gemara 91b). [A threshold that is 10 or more *tefachim* high is a private domain. A threshold that is between 9 and 10 *tefachim* high is considered a part of the public domain, because passersby make use of it to adjust the burdens on their shoulders. A threshold that is less than 3 *tefachim* high is also considered a part of the public domain (*Rashi* 91b).]

2. In order to violate the forbidden *melachah* of transferring, a person must not only pick up an object in either a public or private domain and deposit it in the opposite domain (see Mishnah 1:1), but he must also do so in a single act of transfer. In our case, by first placing the object on the threshold before moving it to the other domain, he has divided his act into two separate transfers: (a) from the private domain to the threshold, and (b) from the threshold into the public domain. Thus, he is not in violation of the Biblical law, and is therefore exempt from a *chatas*.

Another law:
קוּפָּה שֶׁהִיא מְלֵאָה פֵּירוֹת — One who took ***a basket filled with produce*** from his house וּנְתָנָהּ עַל אִסְקוּפָּה הַחִיצוֹנָה — ***and placed it on the outer threshold,***[3] אַף עַל פִּי שֶׁרוֹב פֵּירוֹת מִבַּחוּץ — ***even though most of the produce*** in the basket ***is outside*** in the public domain,[4] פָּטוּר — nevertheless, since a part of the basket remains in the airspace of the private domain, the person is ***exempt*** from a *chatas*[5] עַד שֶׁיּוֹצִיא אֶת כָּל הַקּוּפָּה — ***unless he takes out the entire basket*** into the public domain all at once.[6]

NOTES

3. In this case, the person took a basket of produce from his house (a private domain) and placed it on the outermost step leading to the public domain (*Rav*). This step is less than 3 *tefachim* above the level of the public domain. Since it is that low, not enclosed by walls, and it abuts the public domain, it is considered a part of the adjacent public domain (*Tos. Yom Tov*).

4. I.e., the basket was placed so that most of it — and therefore a majority of the produce inside it — rested upon the step that is considered part of the public domain, while a small part of it — and therefore a minority of the produce — protruded back into an area that was part of the private domain.

5. An object is not considered to have been transferred from one domain to another unless it has been entirely removed from one domain and entirely placed in the other domain. Since part of this basket and the produce it contained remained in the domain from which it was taken, the person who moved the basket is not in violation of the Biblical prohibition of transferring.

6. He is not liable to a *chatas* unless he takes out the entire basket at once. Once he has put the basket down after it has been only partially taken out, he is exempt even if he subsequently moves the rest of it out as well (*Rav; Rashi*).

GEMS FROM THE GEMARA

Our Mishnah ruled that a person taking out a basket filled with produce is not liable to a *chatas* unless he takes the entire basket out at once. Putting the basket down after it has been only partially taken out exempts him even if he subsequently moves the rest of it out, too.

The reason for this exemption is that an object cannot be said to have been transported from one domain to another unless it has been removed entirely from the first domain and been placed entirely in the second. Since part of this basket still rests in its original domain, no liability for transferring from one domain to another can be imposed.

The question, however, arises as to the produce inside the basket. Since several individual fruits or vegetables may be resting in their entirety outside their original domain, why should one not be held liable for transferring these foodstuffs, even if he cannot be held liable for transferring the basket?

The Gemara (91b) offers two divergent opinions. Chizkiyah is of the opinion that this Mishnah refers only to a basket containing long produce, such as cucumbers or gourds, whose lengths reach across the entire interior of the basket. Therefore, as long as part of the basket remains within its original domain, a part of each unit of produce contained within that basket also remains in the original domain. If, however, the basket contains small units of produce such as mustard seeds (this is the example cited by the Gemara), so that the protrusion of the basket inevitably results in the complete removal of some units of that produce from their original domain, one is then liable for having transported those units of produce from one domain to another. This, despite the fact that one is not liable for having transported the basket itself.

According to this view, when the Mishnah states that the greater portion of the produce is outside, it refers to the greater portion of each individual unit.

R' Yochanan, however, maintains that the rule of the Mishnah applies to all instances, regardless of the type of produce contained in the basket. According to him, this Mishnah is teaching us the rule that: אֶגֶד כְּלִי שְׁמֵה אֶגֶד, *the bond of a vessel is regarded as a bond. Rambam* (*Hil. Shabbos* 12:11) interprets this as meaning that all the various units contained in a vessel are considered as if (legally) bound together (by that vessel), and are therefore viewed by the law as one unit. Accordingly, unless the basket has been removed entirely from its original domain, even the individual units contained within that basket, since they are "bound together" by the basket, are viewed by the halachah as being still partially in the original domain. This, despite the fact that several of these units may physically be entirely removed from their original domain. *Rambam* (ibid.) rules in accordance with the latter view; *Rav*, however, explains the Mishnah according to the first view.

QUESTION OF THE DAY:

Why was the cupbearer of Pharaoh pardoned, while the baker was executed?

For the answer, see page 54.

A MUSSAR THOUGHT FOR THE DAY

Chovos HaLevavos, in *Shaar HaBitachon,* speaks of the mind-set that is possessed by one who trusts in Hashem:

"The essential attitude of *bitachon,* trust, is the peace of mind that is possessed by one who practices it. His heart is secure in the knowledge that God, the One in Whom he places his trust, will do what is good and correct for him. But the root of this trust, and that which allows it to exist, is the unshakable conviction that God will keep His word and do as He has guaranteed; and furthermore, that God wishes to benefit every man, though He has no obligation to do so . . .

"Upon reflection, it becomes clear that God is more deserving of such trust than any other entity. God is merciful toward His creations; he never neglects them; He knows all and can never be defeated; He controls all that happens to everything and everyone; and His generosity and kindness are unlimited. All these facts are obvious to anyone who wishes to see, and all are alluded to in the Torah as well . . .

"When the true nature and extent of God's kindness becomes clear to a person, he will place his trust in God completely. He will leave the guidance of his life in God's hands, without questioning His judgment or being upset at whatever misfortune may befall him. We find this attitude expressed by King David in *Tehillim.* He reacts to good fortune by exclaiming (*Tehillim* 116:13): *I will lift up the cup of salvation, and I will call out in the Name of HASHEM!* And he reacts to evil tidings in a similar manner (ibid. vs. 3-4): *I will find sorrow and anguish, and I will call out in the Name of HASHEM . . .*

"Even when a person's mind and body are occupied in earning a livelihood, he should bear in mind that by doing so, he is fulfilling the dictate of the Creator. For we find that God created man and commanded him to work, plow and plant, as it is written (*Bereishis* 2:15): *And HASHEM/ELOHIM took the man and placed him in the Garden of Eden, to work it and to guard it.* This commandment encompasses the mandate to utilize the other creatures of the world for man's benefit and to provide him with sustenance. The Torah also enjoins man to build cities for his habitation, and to marry, be fruitful, and multiply, all of which are tasks that require attention and industry. Thus, let a person who is engaged in attaining his needs intend to do so for the sake of fulfilling God's command, and he will be rewarded for the intent, even if he is not successful in all of his endeavors."

HALACHAH OF THE DAY

As we learned yesterday, items that are not viewed by halachah as being easily cooked may be immersed in the contents of a *kli sheni.* Practically speaking, however, there are only four items that definitely fall into this category. These items are: water, oil, and sticks (not powder) of cinnamon or ginger. Since these items require more heat for their cooking than that provided by the contents of a *kli sheni,* they may be placed into a *kli sheni* even if they will thereby attain the temperature of *yad soledes bo.*

For example, one may add cold water to the hot water of a *kli sheni* even if the resultant mixture will retain a temperature higher than that of *yad soledes bo.* A common application of this ruling would be adding cold water to hot tea being served in a *kli sheni* in order to cool it down slightly. Even though the tea will remain hot and the temperature of the added water will be increased beyond *yad soledes bo,* this is nonetheless permitted.

Another leniency of the *kli sheni* pertains to previously cooked liquids. Any liquids that have been previously cooked may be reheated in a *kli sheni — even if they have already cooled completely.* [The reasoning behind this leniency is as follows: since we are not certain that all liquids are to be classified as "easily cooked" and therefore subject to cooking in a *kli sheni,* and the matter of reheating liquids that have cooled is itself an object of dispute, we adopt a lenient attitude to the question of reheating liquids in the heat of a *kli sheni.*]

Pouring the hot contents of a *kli sheni* onto food items is subject to the same restrictions as immersion in the contents of a *kli shelishi* — the rules of which we will discuss tomorrow.

A CLOSER LOOK AT THE SIDDUR

In the prayer of *U'Va LeTzion,* we cite the verse in *Yeshayah* (26:4) that states: בִּטְחוּ בַה׳ עֲדֵי־עַד כִּי בְּיָהּ ה׳ צוּר עוֹלָמִים, *Trust in HASHEM forever, for in God, HASHEM, is the strength of the worlds.* The simple meaning of this verse, as explained by the commentators to *Yeshayah,* is that Hashem is worthy of our eternal trust, for He is the source of all the strength in the Universe. He created and controls all, so it is proper to trust in Him.

The Gemara in *Menachos* (29b) finds another level of meaning in the verse. R' Ami states that in addition to being an explanation of why one should trust in Hashem, the verse is extending a promise: if one trusts in Hashem, he will be provided with a safe haven both in this world and the next. According to this exposition, the word צוּר is not to be understood as a description of Hashem, but as the *shelter* that one who trusts in Hashem will attain.

However, we must still understand why the verse uses two Names of Hashem in its statement, one of them being the somewhat uncommon Two Letter Name of יָהּ. Seemingly, the verse would read perfectly well if the second Name had been omitted! Furthermore, according to either of the above interpretations, the verse could have simply stated: *for God, HASHEM, is the strength of the worlds.* Why does the verse state בְּיָהּ, *"in" God*?

This extra letter reveals yet a third layer of meaning in the verse. The word צוּר can also be translated as *one who forms.* The Gemara (ibid.) explains that when God created the world, He did so using the powers that were contained within the words of the Torah. He created this world with the letter *hei,* and the World to Come with the letter *yud* (see the Gemara there for further elaboration). These are the two letters that comprise the Two-Letter Name of God that appears in our verse. According to this interpretation, the verse is read as follows: *Trust in HASHEM forever, for it was HASHEM Who formed the worlds with the letters "yud" and "hei."* In other words, since He is the Creator of both this world and the World to Come, it behooves us to place our trust in Him.

This last interpretation can serve to add a dimension to our trust in Hashem as well. Although we sometimes may struggle with our perception of Hashem's fairness, wondering why those who seem to be deserving suffer while the wicked prosper, we must bear in mind that Hashem is the One Who formed *both* worlds, and what seems to be unfair in this world will always be rectified in the World to Come.

ANSWERS TO QUESTIONS OF THE DAY

Sunday:

Nine years. Yosef was born after Yaakov had been in Lavan's house for fourteen years, which was eight years before Yaakov returned home; and Yosef was sold at the age of 17.

Monday:

From *Rashi* (37:29) it seems that he had returned to serve Yaakov; *Bechor Shor* suggests that it was his turn to tend the sheep while the others ate.

Tuesday:

Rashi (37:28) states that the brothers sold him to the Yishmaelites, who sold him to the Midianites, who sold him to the Egyptians. Thus, he was sold [at least] three times.

Wednesday:

When the *shevatim* regretted the sale of Yosef, they blamed Yehudah, claiming that he could have ordered them to return Yosef to Yaakov, and they would have obeyed. As a result, Yehudah's brothers removed him from his position of leadership among them (*Rashi* 38:1).

Thursday:

Her name is not mentioned in the Torah; she is identified only as the daughter of Shua, a merchant (כְּנַעֲנִי). *Abarbanel* suggests that her name was "Bas-Shua."

Friday:

The Gemara (*Sotah* 36b) states that it was a pagan festival day, when everyone would be out of the house. *Ibn Ezra* and *Ralbag* suggest that perhaps it was the anniversary of the day that Potiphar's wife began to torment him.

Shabbos:

The cupbearer was jailed because a fly was found in Pharaoh's cup. He was pardoned, since it was decided that this was not due to negligence, as a fly can fly where it pleases. The baker, however, was jailed when a pebble was found in Pharaoh's bread. Since he was negligent in not sifting the flour properly, he was executed.

פרשת מקץ

Parashas Mikeitz

פרשת מקץ

SUNDAY

PARASHAS MIKEITZ

A TORAH THOUGHT FOR THE DAY

Yesterday (see *A Torah Thought for the Day*), we discussed Yosef's request to the Chamberlain of the Cupbearers, and why he was faulted for making it. *Midrash Rabbah* opens this week's *parashah* with a discussion of this very subject, offering the following comments concerning Yosef's actions while in jail:

אַשְׁרֵי הַגֶּבֶר אֲשֶׁר־שָׂם ה׳ מִבְטַחוֹ – זו יוסף, *Praiseworthy is the man who has made* HASHEM *his trust* (*Tehillim* 40:5) — this is referring to Yosef. The Midrash continues expounding the verse:

וְלֹא־פָנָה אֶל־רְהָבִים – שֶׁעַל יְדֵי שֶׁאָמַר לְשַׂר הַמַּשְׁקִים ״כִּי־אִם זְכַרְתַּנִי . . . וְהִזְכַּרְתַּנִי״ נִיתּוֹסְפוּ לוֹ שְׁתֵּי שָׁנִים, *And turned not to the arrogant* — because Yosef requested from the שַׂר הַמַּשְׁקִים, *Chamberlain of the Cupbearers,* to think of him and mention him to Pharaoh, two more years were added to his prison term.

This Midrash is somewhat puzzling, as it seems self-contradictory. Even as it praises Yosef for trusting in Hashem, it nevertheless condemns him for seeking the help of others! What message does the Midrash want to relate to us: Yosef's perfection with respect to *bitachon,* or his lack thereof?

Beis HaLevi offers a wonderful insight. The truth is, he says, that the Torah allows and permits הִשְׁתַּדְּלוּת, *effort.* We are supposed to earn a livelihood and not rely on miracles. But at the same time, the Torah expects a person to rely on and trust in Hashem, and to believe that He and only He gives him what he needs.

How does one balance these two seemingly contradictory ideas? It all depends on the person's spiritual level. The closer a person is to perfection in his belief in Hashem, the more he is expected to rely on Hashem, and his level of *hishtadlus* must drop accordingly. Until a person reaches that level he may — and must — work, to achieve whatever he needs to function and sustain himself and his family. As his belief and trust in Hashem grow — and he must work on this mitzvah constantly, to reach ever higher levels of *bitachon* — he must adjust his level of *hishtadlus* and rely more on Hashem.

The Midrash begins by praising Yosef's great level of *bitachon.* He is the man to whom the verse in *Tehillim* refers, who places his total trust in Hashem. It is *only* for this reason that the Midrash can continue, stating that even a relatively insignificant act of *hishtadlus* — asking the cupbearer to mention his name to Pharaoh — was unbefitting his great level of *bitachon.* Yosef was therefore "punished" with a two-year extension of his sentence, to enable him to climb back to his rightful place with perfection in this *middah,* without any flaw or blemish — totally relying on Hashem. [This interpretation of the Midrash accords with the approach of *Rabbeinu Bachya,* which we discussed yesterday.]

MISHNAH OF THE DAY: SHABBOS 10:3

This Mishnah teaches that under Biblical law, one does not violate the prohibition of transferring an object from one domain to another unless he carries it in a normal manner:

הַמּוֹצִיא — ***One who takes out*** an object from one domain to another on the Sabbath, בֵּין בִּימִינוֹ בֵּין בִּשְׂמֹאלוֹ — ***whether with his right [hand] or whether with his left [hand],*** בְּתוֹךְ חֵיקוֹ אוֹ עַל כְּתֵיפָיו — ***whether in his bosom or on his shoulders,***[1] חַיָּב — ***is liable*** to a *chatas;* שֶׁכֵּן מַשָּׂא בְּנֵי קְהָת — and he is liable even for taking out an object on his shoulders, ***for such was the*** method of ***carrying*** used ***by the sons of Kehas.***[2] כִּלְאַחַר יָדוֹ — However, if he takes out the object ***backhandedly:***[3]

NOTES

1. The first three methods listed — carrying in one's right or left hand, or in one's bosom — are the common means by which people carry and transfer things, and no Scriptural support is necessary to categorize them as normal means of transport. However, the next method — carrying on the shoulder — is less common. Therefore, the Tanna will cite a Scriptural reference to prove that such carrying is normal (*Rav; Rashi*).

2. During the Jewish people's travels through the Wilderness, the Tabernacle was taken down each time they broke camp, and was reerected at the new encampment. Transporting the Tabernacle was the responsibility of the three Levite families, with the most sacred objects — the Ark, Table, Menorah and two Altars — being entrusted to the family of Kehas. Although other parts of the Tabernacle were carried on wagons, Hashem decreed that these most sacred objects could be borne only by the Leviim themselves, on their shoulders. The Mishnah derives from the Leviim's manner of transporting on the shoulder that one who transfers an object on his shoulder on the Sabbath is liable to a *chatas* (*Rav; Rashi;* see *Numbers* 7:9).

3. According to our reading, כִּלְאַחַר יָדוֹ, *backhandedly,* is not meant as a specific example of carrying in an unusual manner. Rather, it is the general term used for anything done in an unusual way. Thus the Mishnah is to be read: *if he carried backhandedly, viz., with his foot, in his mouth . . .* (*Tosafos* to 92a). On the other hand, *Rambam Commentary* and *Tosafos* read: לְאַחַר יָדוֹ, *on the back of his hand.* Accordingly, this phrase is a specific example of carrying in an unusual manner, and the Mishnah is to be read: *if he carried on the back of his hand, with his foot, in his mouth . . .* [This reading is also found in 12:5, which lists unusual manners of holding a pen for writing (*Tos. Yom Tov*).]

פרשת מקץ
SUNDAY
PARASHAS MIKEITZ

בְּרַגְלוֹ — for example, *with his foot,* בְּפִיו — *in his mouth,*[4] וּבְמַרְפְּקוֹ — *with his elbow,*[5] בְּאָזְנוֹ — *in his ear,* וּבִשְׂעָרוֹ — *in his hair,* וּבְפוּנְדָּתוֹ וּפִיהָ לְמַטָּה — *in his moneybelt with its opening* hanging *downward,*[6] בֵּין פוּנְדָּתוֹ לַחֲלוּקוֹ — *between his moneybelt and his shirt,*[7] וּבִשְׂפַת חֲלוּקוֹ — *in the hem of his shirt,* בְּמִנְעָלוֹ בְּסַנְדָּלוֹ — *in his shoe* or *in his sandal,* פָּטוּר — in all these cases, *he is exempt,* שֶׁלֹּא הוֹצִיא כְּדֶרֶךְ הַמּוֹצִיאִין — *for he did not take out* the object *in the manner of those who take things out.*[8]

NOTES

4. This applies only to carrying nonfoods in one's mouth. However, if one carries food in his mouth on the Sabbath, he is liable, since it is not unusual to carry out food in such a manner (*Tosafos; Tiferes Yisrael* from Gemara 102a).

5. I.e., he takes out an object in the crook of his arm (the inside of the elbow). Since it is unusual to carry in this manner, one is not liable for doing so. However, if one suspends a basket or other container from his elbow and takes out an object in it, he is liable, as this is a common manner of transporting objects (*Tiferes Yisrael; Tos. Yom Tov*).

6. *Rashi* describes פוּנְדָּתוֹ as a hollow belt. *Meiri* and *Ran* add that once the money was placed in the belt it was tied with a knot. Nevertheless, because such belts would tend to become undone, even when knotted, the belt would not usually be allowed to hang freely, lest the money fall out. Instead, a person would normally fasten the hollow end that held the money to his waist. If he did not wear the belt in this usual manner, but allowed the end to hang freely, he is not liable for taking out the money in the belt (cf. *Rambam Commentary*).

7. I.e., he draped an object over the moneybelt, partly between the belt and the shirt and partly over the outside of the belt. An object transported in this manner is not secure, since its weight often shifts, thereby unbalancing the object and causing it to fall. Hence, people do not usually carry objects in this manner (*Meiri, Ran*).

8. [I.e., in all the cases listed above, he is exempt, since he is taking out the object in an unusual manner.]

QUESTION OF THE DAY:

After Yosef interpreted the dreams, he also told Pharaoh to appoint someone as overseer [and Pharaoh appointed him]. Why was this suggestion not considered unnecessary hishtadlus?

For the answer, see page 108.

GEMS FROM THE GEMARA

Our Mishnah described four different cases of one who carries in a normal manner: *One who takes out, whether with his right [hand] or whether with his left [hand], whether in his bosom or on his shoulders, is liable], for such was the carrying by the sons of Kehas.*

As we learned in the Mishnah, according to *Rav* and *Rashi* the first three methods listed — carrying in one's right or left hand, or in one's bosom — are the common means by which people carry and transfer things, and no Scriptural support is necessary to categorize them as normal means of transport. The Scriptural reference to the manner in which the sons of Kehas carried the holy vessels was meant specifically to explain why the last method — carrying on the shoulder — renders a person liable, even though it is a less common manner in which to bear a burden.

Yerushalmi, however, provides a Scriptural derivation for the Mishnah's specification of each of these four body parts as being involved in the bearing of burdens. According to *Yerushalmi,* Scriptural support for each of these four methods being considered a normal method of carrying can be derived from the verse (*Bamidbar* 4:16) that speaks of the items that were carried by Elazar, the son of Aharon. The verse reads: *And the charge of Elazar the son of Aharon the Kohen was*: שֶׁמֶן הַמָּאוֹר, *the oil of lighting* (this refers to the oil that was used to light the Menorah); וּקְטֹרֶת הַסַּמִּים, *and the incense of spices* (this was the incense that was offered on the Inner Altar daily); וּמִנְחַת הַתָּמִיד, *and the daily meal-offering* (that accompanied the daily *tamid* offering); וְשֶׁמֶן הַמִּשְׁחָה, *and the oil of anointment. Yerushalmi* explains that the verse does not simply mean that Elazar was in charge of these items; rather, it means that whenever the Israelite camp would travel through the Wilderness, Elazar would carry these four items *on his person. Yerushalmi* explains that Elazar would carry all of the items at once by making use of all the manners of carrying specified in our Mishnah: He would carry the two types of oil in his two hands, the incense in his bosom, and the meal-offering upon his shoulder (*Rashi,* citing R' *Yitzchak bar Yehudah,* who quotes *Rav Hai Gaon's* version of the *Yerushalmi; Rabbeinu Chananel* and *Meiri* cite a slightly different version, while extant editions of *Yerushalmi* have still a third reading).

פרשת מקץ

SUNDAY

PARASHAS MIKEITZ

A MUSSAR THOUGHT FOR THE DAY

In *A Torah Thought for the Day,* we noted that the *middah* of *bitachon,* trust in Hashem, depends on a person's level of connection to Hashem. *Chovos HaLevavos* states that every person is vulnerable, and instinctively places his trust in some superior power upon which he feels he can rely. This is part of human nature. If a person gets caught up in his physical surroundings, he automatically will place his trust in other people or powers, and be distracted from relying on Hashem.

What is the true meaning of *bitachon*? The *Chazon Ish* writes in his *Sefer Emunah U'Bitachon* that many people make a common mistake. They think *bitachon* means that one must trust that everything will definitely be good, and that if one has any doubts concerning the outcome of any matter, he is lacking *bitachon.* This, writes the *Chazon Ish,* is a gross error, and an incorrect description of *bitachon.* Anything that will take place in the future, unless it has been forecast by a *navi,* is unknown and unpredictable.

The true description of *bitachon* is the belief that there is no coincidence in this world, and that everything that transpires occurs with Hashem's approval and instruction.

When a person finds himself in a situation which appears dangerous according to the natural way of the world, and he is powerless to help himself, he must overcome his fear by realizing that the One Who controls everything in this world can cause a positive outcome just as easily as a negative one. This is called *bitachon.*

Chazon Ish states that just as there are levels (מַדְרֵגוֹת) in other *middos,* such as mercy, humility, etc., there are many levels of *bitachon.* As long as one possesses even a small trace of *bitachon,* he is not excluded from the group of believers, and will merit ultimate redemption. It is only when someone is devoid of all trust and belief in Hashem that he is considered a כּוֹפֵר, *heretic.*

HALACHAH OF THE DAY

Hot foods or liquids transferred out of a *kli sheni* into another vessel are now referred to as being in a *kli shelishi,* a third vessel. Once transferred into a *kli shelishi,* hot liquids no longer retain the capacity to cook most foods. It is, therefore, generally permissible to immerse any foods — whether raw or cooked — in a *kli shelishi* on Shabbos, even if the temperature of the contents of the *kli* exceeds *yad soledes bo.*

There are, however, foods so sensitive to heat that they can become cooked even through the weak heat of a *kli shelishi.* These foods are: eggs, extremely salty fish, and, according to some *poskim,* tea leaves. Since these items are very easily cooked, it is forbidden for one to either immerse them in a *kli shelishi,* or to pour the hot contents of a *kli sheni* over them. [It should be noted that *Rav Moshe Feinstein* ruled that it is permissible for one to immerse a tea bag in a *kli shelishi.*] Indeed, such items are so sensitive to heat that they may not be heated in any vessel at all — even a fifth or sixth vessel — as long as the contents exceed the temperature of *yad soledes bo.*

Let us now turn to a discussion regarding the adding of spices to hot foods on Shabbos. As we have learned previously, hot solid foods in a *kli rishon* maintain the ability to cook foods that come into contact with them, just as hot liquids do. It is therefore forbidden to add any uncooked seasoning to hot food in a *kli rishon.* Dry seasonings that have been precooked, such as sugar or salt, may be added to hot solid foods in a *kli rishon,* since there is no prohibition against recooking solid foods. Liquid condiments (such as ketchup or mustard), however, may not be added to a hot *kli rishon,* since even if they have been previously cooked during their production they are still subject to the prohibition against recooking liquids that have completely cooled.

The law regarding adding spices to hot solid foods found in a *kli sheni* or *shelishi* is more complex. As we explained above, cooking becomes increasingly permissible as foods are transferred from one vessel to another, because the walls of each subsequent vessel absorb some of the heat from the food being placed inside of them. There is a question among the *poskim* as to whether this logic applies to both liquids as well as solids, or only to liquids. As we shall see tomorrow, the answer to this question determines the halachic outcome in the case under discussion.

A CLOSER LOOK AT THE SIDDUR

Yesterday, we discussed a verse found at the end of the prayer of *U'Va LeTzion.* Today, we will look at the entire section of that prayer, and put our discussion of *bitachon* into greater perspective.

Aruch HaShulchan (Ch. 132) explains that earlier in the *U'Va LeTzion* prayer, we declare the purpose of our creation: בָּרוּךְ הוּא אֱלֹהֵינוּ שֶׁבְּרָאָנוּ לִכְבוֹדוֹ . . . וְנָתַן לָנוּ תּוֹרַת אֱמֶת, *Blessed is He, our God, Who created us for His glory . . . and gave us the Torah of truth.* We follow by asking for Hashem's help to study the Torah with the proper motives (הוּא יִפְתַּח לִבֵּנוּ בְּתוֹרָתוֹ), and ask Him to grant us success in passing on this vital mission to our children (see *Mishnah Berurah* 47:10). We then ask for His assistance and guidance in enabling us to keep all the laws of the Torah (שֶׁנִּשְׁמֹר חֻקֶּיךָ). Following this, we recite the verses that speak about *bitachon. Aruch HaShulchan* explains the transition from Torah to *bitachon*: We must strengthen our belief that although it is necessary for us to leave the *beis hamidrash* and go out to earn a livelihood, we must constantly remind ourselves that Hashem is really the One Who sustains us. All of our *hishtadlus* and effort is useless if Hashem does not approve. It is only with His blessing that we will have what we need.

In this vein, *Aruch HaShulchan* also explains the connection to the final verse that we recite: ה׳ חָפֵץ לְמַעַן צִדְקוֹ יַגְדִּיל תּוֹרָה וְיַאְדִּיר, *HASHEM desired, for the sake of [Israel's] righteousness, that the Torah be made great and glorious.* Here we are excusing our actions, so to speak. Although we are going out to work in order to bring food for our family, which is our obligation, we do realize what is the main goal in this world; we understand the difference between what is called חַיֵּי עוֹלָם, *eternal life,* and what is called חַיֵּי שָׁעָה, *temporary life.* The true "desire of Hashem" is to glorify and enhance the Torah. The permission granted to us to work is only secondary to our primary obligation to study and glorify the Torah. And even if we are very limited in the time we have to study Torah, says the *Aruch HaShulchan,* at the very least we must make sure that our children study Torah, and that we steadfastly support Torah scholars who are fulfilling Hashem's desire.

A TORAH THOUGHT FOR THE DAY

פרשת מקץ

MONDAY

PARASHAS MIKEITZ

וַיִּשְׁלַח פַּרְעֹה וַיִּקְרָא אֶת־יוֹסֵף וַיְרִיצֻהוּ מִן־הַבּוֹר וַיְגַלַּח וַיְחַלֵּף שִׂמְלֹתָיו וַיָּבֹא אֶל־פַּרְעֹה

So Pharaoh sent and summoned Yosef, and they rushed him from the pit. He shaved his hair and changed his clothes and he came to Pharaoh (*Bereishis* 41:14).

Rashi notes that Yosef made these preparations מִפְּנֵי כְּבוֹד הַמַּלְכוּת, *out of respect for royalty.* The commentaries explain that *Rashi* is referring to the Gemara in *Rosh Hashanah,* which states that Yosef was released from prison on Rosh Hashanah. Thus, he should have been forbidden to shave or cut his hair. *Rashi* therefore had to explain that out of honor for the king, one may transgress a Rabbinical prohibition (called a שְׁבוּת), such as having one's hair cut by a non-Jew. But if not for this dispensation, Yosef would not have allowed them to shave him on that day.

A difficulty still remains, however. The Gemara tells us that from the day Yosef separated from his brothers, he accepted upon himself to keep all the laws of *nezirus. A nazir* is forbidden to shave his hair, and may not be shaved even by someone else who is not a *nazir.* This is a Biblical prohibition, which כְּבוֹד מַלְכוּת would not override (see *Taz, Yoreh Deah* 181).

Rav Shternbuch offers the following suggestion. It may well be that Yosef intended his *nezirus* to be in force only as long as he was in a situation of separation. Once Yosef saw a ray of light and the beginning of his redemption, he was not obligated to keep those laws, and was therefore allowed to shave and cut his hair, as he was no longer a *nazir.*

This idea may be used to resolve a similar difficulty later in the *parashah. Rashi* says (43:34) on the words וַיִּשְׁתּוּ וַיִּשְׁכְּרוּ עִמּוֹ, *they* (Yosef's brothers) *drank and they imbibed with him*: "From the day that they sold him, they did not drink wine nor did he drink wine. But that day they drank."

Now, we do not know that the brothers accepted *nezirus* upon themselves; rather, it may be that they refrained from drinking wine because of the pain they had caused their father. But Yosef was certainly a *nazir!* Why then was he permitted to drink wine during the meal? (see *Shabbos* 139a).

This difficulty, too, is resolved if we say that Yosef's *nezirus* was in force only as long as the end of the separation was not in sight. Although Yosef was not yet reunited with his father, once he saw that this possibility was imminent, the *nezirus* was ended, and he was allowed to drink.

MISHNAH OF THE DAY: SHABBOS 10:4

The following Mishnah discusses situations where one intended to perform a prohibited transfer in a certain way, but due to happenstance, he ended up performing the transfer in a different way:

הַמִּתְכַּוֵּין לְהוֹצִיא לְפָנָיו — ***One who intended to take out*** an object, while maintaining the object ***in front of himself,***[1] וּבָא לוֹ לְאַחֲרָיו — but the object shifted in mid-transfer, ***and came behind him,***[2] פָּטוּר — ***is exempt*** from a *chatas.*[3] לְאַחֲרָיו — Conversely, if he intended to take out an object ***behind himself,*** וּבָא לוֹ לְפָנָיו — but the object shifted in mid-transfer, ***and came in front of him,*** חַיָּיב — ***he is liable*** to a *chatas.*[4] בֶּאֱמֶת אָמְרוּ — ***In truth, they said:***[5] הָאִשָּׁה הַחוֹגֶרֶת בְּסִינָר — ***A woman girded with an apron,***[6] who hangs an object from it and transports it outside, בֵּין מִלְּפָנֶיהָ וּבֵין מִלְּאַחֲרֶיהָ — no matter ***whether*** the object shifted ***in front of her or behind her,*** חַיֶּיבֶת — ***is liable,*** שֶׁכֵּן רָאוּי

NOTES

1. For example, he tied money in his cloak in such a manner that it would hang in front of him, thus enabling him to watch it closely (*Rav; Rashi*).

2. Thus, rather than remaining in front of him where he could safeguard it closely, the money is now in back of him, where he cannot watch it closely (*Rav* from Gemara 92b).

3. Since the way in which he completed the transfer was actually inferior (in the extent of his ability to safeguard the money) to the way in which he intended to perform the transfer, we treat the case as one in which his intent was not fulfilled. He is therefore exempt. This case is similar to מִתְעַסֵּק, *one who commits a sin absentmindedly* (*Rashi*). Both the ruling exempting the person who commits a sin absentmindedly and the ruling in our Mishnah exempting the person whose burden shifted, emerge from the principle: מְלֶאכֶת מַחֲשֶׁבֶת אָסְרָה תוֹרָה, *only a calculated labor was prohibited by the Torah.* Among other things, this implies that a person cannot be held liable unless his intention in regard to the forbidden labor in question was actually fulfilled.

4. In this case, his original intent was to maintain the money behind him, where he cannot safeguard it closely. However, by the time he actually completed the transfer, the money was in front of him — i.e., in a place where he was able to watch it closely (*Rav* from Gemara 92b). Since the way in which he completed the transfer was superior to the way in which he intended to perform the transfer, we treat the case as one in which his intent was fulfilled. He is therefore liable (*Rav; Tiferes Yisrael*).

5. The expression בֶּאֱמֶת אָמְרוּ, *in truth they said,* generally introduces a statement that is universally accepted as law, whether of Biblical or Rabbinic origin (*Rav, Terumos* 2:1; see above, 1:3). It is also occasionally used to preface a הֲלָכָה לְמֹשֶׁה מִסִּינַי, *an Oral Law taught to Moshe at Sinai* (*Rambam Commentary;* see *Rashi* to *Nazir* 54b, and *Rav* to *Terumos* 2:1).

6. In translating the word סִינָר as *apron,* we have followed *Tiferes Yisrael. Rashi* characterizes סִינָר as a short underskirt worn for purposes of modesty. Others translate it as *belt* or *girdle* (*Rambam Commentary;* see also *Meiri*).

לִהְיוֹת חוֹזֵר — ***for it is common*** for an apron ***to shift around.***[7]

רַבִּי יְהוּדָה אוֹמֵר — ***R' Yehudah says:*** **אַף מְקַבְּלֵי פִּתָקִין** — ***Also letter carriers*** are liable to a *chatas* when the object they are carrying shifts behind them or in front of them.[8]

NOTES

7. Since an apron is very likely to shift its position, a woman knows in advance that it may slip behind her. Therefore, her intent from the outset must have been to carry it either way (*Rav; Rashi*).

8. Mailmen (*Meiri*), couriers (*Rambam; Rav*), or court officials (*Tos.*) would hang pouches or tubes from their belts or from a loop around their necks to carry messages or documents. As they walked or ran, these containers would shift from front to back. Since they know in advance that it is very likely that their pouches or tubes will slip, their intent from the outset must have been to carry them either way, and therefore they are liable in any event.

GEMS FROM THE GEMARA

A Baraisa, cited by the Gemara (92b), teaches that if one carries out coins in his moneybelt with its opening fastened above, near his waist, he is liable. But in a case in which the opening is hanging downward, where the money could more easily fall out, there is disagreement: R' Yehudah holds him liable, while the Sages rule he is exempt. [R' Yehudah holds that although this is not a secure way of carrying coins, it is not so significantly different from the norm as to be deemed aberrant. The Sages, however, deem this a completely unusual method of transfer, and therefore they exempt the perpetrator (*Rashi*).]

The Baraisa records an exchange between the disputants:

R' Yehudah said to the Sages: Would you not agree that in a case where one tied an object behind him and it remained behind him, that the person is liable, even though he transported the object in an insecure way? If so, apply the same ruling to one whose moneybelt was hanging downward! The Sages responded to him: And would you not agree that when one places an object on the back of his hand or foot and transports it that way, he is exempt? If so, apply the same ruling to one whose moneybelt was hanging downwards!

Summing up their debate, R' Yehudah concludes: I stated one point to support my view, and in response, they stated one point to support their view. I have not found a rejoinder against their point, and they have not found a rejoinder against my point.

The Gemara analyzes the implications of the Baraisa:

From the fact that R' Yehudah said to the Sages: Would you not agree in a case where the object was tied behind him and it remained there, that he is liable, can it not be inferred that indeed, the Sages *do not* agree with him and would exempt the perpetrator in that case? If so, it would seem that there is a dispute between R' Yehudah and the Sages over whether one is liable in the case where the object remained tied behind the person!

The Gemara rejects this analysis, for according to this reasoning, we should infer from the fact that the Sages said to R' Yehudah: Would you not agree in a case where one places an object on the back of his hand or foot, etc., that R' Yehudah does *not* agree in that case, and he holds the perpetrator liable. Yet this conclusion is untenable, for it was explicitly taught in a Baraisa that one who places an item on the back of his hand or foot and transports it, is exempt according to everyone.

In light of this, the Gemara provides a new analysis of the respective positions of R' Yehudah and the Sages: In the case where one ties an object behind him and it remains behind him, both R' Yehudah and the Sages agree that the perpetrator is liable. Likewise, in the case where one transports an object on the back of his hand or foot, everyone agrees he is exempt. R' Yehudah and the Sages disagree only concerning the case of one who transports coins in his moneybelt with its opening hanging downward. R' Yehudah compares this to a situation where one tied an object behind him and it remained behind him, and he therefore rules in favor of liability, whereas the Sages compare this to a situation where one placed an object on the back of his hand or foot, and they therefore rule in favor of exemption.

[R' Yehudah sees both of these scenarios as cases where one provides a minimal degree of security for the item being transported, while in the Sages' view, carrying something inside a moneybelt hanging downward provides less protection than hanging an object on the back of one's cloak. In the latter case, the item is not *well* protected, but it is at least protected somewhat (e.g., from thieves). With a moneybelt hanging downward, though, there is no protection whatsoever, for the coins can simply fall out and become lost of their own accord (*Rashi*).]

QUESTION OF THE DAY:

Where else do we find that wearing unkempt or improper clothing is forbidden before a king?

For the answer, see page 108.

A MUSSAR THOUGHT FOR THE DAY

פרשת מקץ

MONDAY

PARASHAS MIKEITZ

On the words וַיְרִצֻהוּ מִן־הַבּוֹר, *they rushed him from the pit,* we find a fascinating *Sforno.* He says the reason for the haste here is that all salvations from Hashem happen instantly. As soon as the appropriate time comes, there can be no delay. The same thing occurred upon the redemption of Egypt — the Jews had no time to let their dough rise, as they left in haste; thus, the dough was baked into matzah. *Sforno* writes that we find this written concerning the ultimate arrival of Mashiach as well: "Suddenly, he (Mashiach) will come to the *Mikdash.*"

Although Yosef had been punished by having his prison sentence lengthened by two years (see *A Torah Thought for the Day,* Sunday), when the time came for him to be released, not a second was lost.

The Midrash on the words מִקֵּץ שְׁנָתַיִם, *at the end of the two years,* states: קֵץ שָׂם לַחֹשֶׁךְ, *Hashem places an end to darkness.* Every tragedy, pain, or illness is put in place for an exact length of time — it will not afflict the intended recipient for even one second longer than that time.

The Gemara in *Avodah Zarah* (55b) explains that sicknesses are called (*Devarim* 28:59) נֶאֱמָנִים, *loyal,* for every sickness must take an oath to be a loyal messenger; it must enter the person at an exact time and exit at an exact time, as a result of the ministrations of a specific doctor, and through the use of a specific medicine.

This lesson was part of the preparation for Bnei Yisrael's *galus* (exile). We can derive encouragement from Yosef, secure in the knowledge that any situation that we may encounter, as dark as it may seem, has a קֵץ, *a limit.* And when the time and place for redemption arrive, not a second will be wasted. יְשׁוּעַת ה׳ כְּהֶרֶף עַיִן, *God's salvation [occurs] in the blink of an eye.* Nothing holds Him back from releasing us from any situation.

HALACHAH OF THE DAY

As we alluded to yesterday, there are many *poskim* who rule that the distinctions made by halachah between *kli rishon, sheni,* and *shelishi* apply only when the contents under discussion are liquids. However, when dealing with solids, it is the opinion of these *poskim* that since solid foods do not lose their heat to the walls of their containers as readily as do liquids, transferring them from container to container has no effect on their ability to cook. As long as they maintain a temperature equal to or exceeding *yad soledes bo,* we must view them as if they are contained in a *kli rishon,* and follow all of the guidelines brought forth by this determination. [The definition of "solid foods" in the context of this discussion includes foods such as meat, chicken, and *kugel* that are not accompanied with much liquid, as well as foods that are clumped together, such as a dry *cholent.*]

While other *poskim* dispute this ruling and hold that the rules of *kli sheni* and *kli shelishi* apply equally to solids as well as liquids, in practice the rules that apply to solid foods are as follows:

With regard to uncooked spices, we follow the more stringent view, which always applies the rules of *kli rishon* to solid foods. Accordingly, one must refrain from seasoning any hot solid foods with uncooked spices whether they are in a pot just removed from the flame (*kli rishon*), on a serving platter (*kli sheni*), or even if they have already been taken from the platter and placed on a plate (*kli shelishi*). As long as the food is *yad soledes bo,* it may not be spiced with uncooked spices.

With regard to precooked liquid condiments, such as ketchup, one may follow the more lenient view that the rules of *kli sheni* and *shelishi* apply to solid foods as well. Therefore, one may pour precooked condiments onto dry solid foods in a *kli sheni.*

A CLOSER LOOK AT THE SIDDUR

At the end of each day's *Shacharis* (*Mussaf* on Shabbos according to *Nusach Ashkenaz*), we find the שִׁיר שֶׁל יוֹם, *Song of the Day,* a psalm specially chosen to be recited by the Leviim in the Temple. These psalms were incorporated into the daily prayers as a memorial to the *Beis HaMikdash.* In Thursday's Song of the Day, we find the verse: עֵדוּת בִּיהוֹסֵף שָׂמוֹ בְּצֵאתוֹ עַל־אֶרֶץ מִצְרָיִם שְׂפַת לֹא־יָדַעְתִּי אֶשְׁמָע, *He imposed it as a testimony for Yehosef (Yosef), when he went forth over the land of Egypt — I understood a language I never knew.*

This entire verse is based on the life of Yosef. The Gemara in *Rosh Hashanah* (10b) teaches that Yosef was released from prison and appointed as viceroy of Egypt on Rosh Hashanah. In honor of this event, Hashem ordained the mitzvah of *shofar* on Rosh Hashanah as a testimony — a reminder of Yosef's freedom.

In order to qualify as a ruler under Egyptian law, Yosef had to be able to speak all the languages — a requirement that was miraculously fulfilled when the angel Gavriel came and taught them to him. Thus,

Yosef exclaimed: "I understood a language I never knew!" This is how *Rashi* explains the verse.

Rabbeinu Bachya offers a beautiful homiletic interpretation of the verse. He notes that we find some discrepancies between Pharaoh's actual dream and the way it was repeated to Yosef. The verse states that in the dream itself, Pharaoh was standing *on* the water of the river. However, when Pharaoh repeated the dream to Yosef, he said: הִנְנִי עֹמֵד עַל־שְׂפַת הַיְאֹר, *Behold, I was standing upon "the bank"* (שְׂפַת) *of the river.*

Chasam Sofer explains that Pharaoh's vision that he was standing on "the water" was a reference to the blessing that Pharaoh would receive from Yaakov, that the Nile would rise up when he would come to its banks. Pharaoh, who did not understand this particular of his dream, was afraid to mention it lest Yosef dismiss the entire dream as insignificant. Pharaoh therefore changed this detail to make the dream sound more convincing, and said that he stood by the bank of the river.

Pardes Yosef, citing a Midrash, states that Pharaoh deliberately changed the dream by adding the word שְׂפַת, *the bank of [the river],* to test Yosef. When Yosef, through *ruach hakodesh,* detected the extra word שְׂפַת, then Pharaoh knew that he was an אִישׁ אֲשֶׁר רוּחַ אֱלֹהִים בּוֹ, *a man in whom is the spirit of God.*

Rabbeinu Bachya finds an allusion to this in our verse. Which testimony or proof did Pharaoh depend upon to appoint Yosef as a ruler in Egypt? The fact that Yosef told him, "שְׂפַת" לֹא־יָדַעְתִּי אֶשְׁמָע — "I do not know the interpretation of the word שְׂפַת (*the bank of*), because it was not part of the dream!" This proved to Pharaoh that Yosef's interpretation was correct, and based on *ruach hakodesh.*

A TORAH THOUGHT FOR THE DAY

וְאֶת־בִּנְיָמִין אֲחִי יוֹסֵף לֹא־שָׁלַח יַעֲקֹב
אֶת־אֶחָיו כִּי אָמַר פֶּן־יִקְרָאֶנּוּ אָסוֹן
But Binyamin, Yosef's brother,
Yaakov did not send along with his brothers,
for he said: "Lest disaster befall him"
(*Bereishis* 42:4).

R*ashi* asks: "Could a disaster not befall him at home? From here we see that the שָׂטָן, *the Accuser,* prosecutes at a time of peril."

It is clear that even initially there was a need for Binyamin to go down with the other brothers, and the only reason Yaakov did not send him was because of the fear of danger en route. The Midrash explains that it was necessary for all eleven brothers to go for the food, for Yosef had made a decree that no slave could buy food — only actual householders could come, and only one donkey-load was allowed per household. Thus, each one of the tribes had to purchase food for his own family. Nevertheless, because Yaakov feared danger for Binyamin, he remained at home, and they made do with less food.

The question may be asked: Why was Yaakov concerned about Binyamin more than any of the others? Weren't they all under the same danger? *Targum Yonasan* on this verse says that Yaakov feared most for Binyamin because he was the youngest, and thus the most vulnerable. *Shiras David* points out that in truth there is a simpler explanation, which *Rashi* himself offers later in the *parashah.* When Yaakov was later pressured to send Binyamin to gain Shimon's release, he still refused, as it says in the verse (42:38): *My son will not go down with you, for his brother is dead and he alone has remained; should disaster befall him on the journey which you shall take, then you will have brought down my old age in sorrow to the grave. Rashi* explains this (44:29) as follows: When Binyamin is next to me, I am consoled through him over his mother and over his brother. If he were to die, it would seem to me that the three of them died on the same day.

In defense of *Targum Yonasan, Shiras David* suggests that Yaakov advanced this stronger reason only when it was necessary to rescue Shimon. Initially, however, Yaakov objected only on the basis of "*lest a disaster befall him*"; and *Targum Yonasan* therefore explains why disaster was more of a danger with respect to Binyamin.

MISHNAH OF THE DAY: SHABBOS 10:5

This Mishnah teaches that under Biblical law, one does not violate the prohibition of transferring an object that he is able to carry by himself unless he carries it alone:

הַמּוֹצִיא כִּכָּר לִרְשׁוּת הָרַבִּים — ***One who takes out a loaf*** of bread from a private domain ***into a public domain*** **חַיָּיב** — ***is liable*** to a *chatas.*[1] **הוֹצִיאוּהוּ שְׁנַיִם** — However, ***if two*** people ***took*** the loaf ***out*** together, **פְּטוּרִין** — ***they are*** both ***exempt.***[2] **לֹא יָכוֹל אֶחָד לְהוֹצִיאוֹ** — On the other hand, if each ***one*** of the two ***cannot take out*** something by himself,[3] **וְהוֹצִיאוּהוּ שְׁנַיִם** — ***and*** the ***two took it out*** together, **חַיָּיבִין** — ***they are*** both ***liable;***[4] **וְרַבִּי שִׁמְעוֹן פּוֹטֵר** — ***but R' Shimon exempts them.***[5]

NOTES

1. This ruling is obvious, and is stated here only as an introduction to the following case (*Ritva; Meiri*).

2. Since no assistance is required to carry out a loaf of bread, the assistance of the second person serves merely to detract from the amount of labor being performed by the first. Both are therefore exempt. This rule is derived from the verse (*Vayikra* 4:27): וְאִם־נֶפֶשׁ אַחַת תֶּחֱטָא בִשְׁגָגָה . . . בַּעֲשֹׂתָהּ אַחַת מִמִּצְוֹת ה׳ אֲשֶׁר לֹא־תֵעָשֶׂינָה וְאָשֵׁם, *And should one person* [lit., *soul*] *sin inadvertently . . . by his performing one of the commandments of* H*ASHEM* *which may not be done and [so] be guilty.* [This is the first verse of a section describing the laws that pertain to an individual's *chatas.*] By stating *by his performing,* the Torah implies that in order to be liable to a *chatas,* a person must perform the entire act, to the extent of which he is capable, himself.

3. For example, two people carried out a beam that was too heavy for either of them to carry alone (*Rambam, Hil. Shabbos* 1:16).

4. As explained above, the verse exempts one who performs less than the entire act of the sin. However, the Torah meant only to exempt two people who were each capable of performing the act alone, since their partnership is not a normal manner in which to perform this act. On the other hand, in the case of an act that can be performed only by two people in partnership, their partnership *is* the normal manner of performance, and therefore they are both liable for *chataos* (*Rashi*).

5. Both the Tanna Kamma and R' Shimon expound the three singular expressions in the verse: (a) נֶפֶשׁ . . . תֶּחֱטָא — *should "a person" sin;* (b) אַחַת תֶּחֱטָא — *should "one" sin;* and (c) בַּעֲשֹׂתָהּ — *by "his"* [lit., *its*] *doing.* By exempting a sin committed by more than one person from a *chatas* three times, the Torah indicates that the exemption applies to three scenarios. The first scenario is the one in which each person consecutively performs only a part of the forbidden labor — i.e., one performs the *akirah* and another performs the *hanachah* (see Mishnah 1:1). The second scenario is the one at the beginning of our Mishnah (e.g., the loaf of bread carried by two people). The third scenario is the subject of this disagreement between the first Tanna of our Mishnah and R' Shimon. R' Shimon maintains that the third expression comes to exempt two people who perform in partnership a forbidden labor that neither could do himself. On the other hand, the Tanna Kamma maintains that the third expression comes to

The Mishnah discusses liability for carrying out objects that are mere accessories of other objects:

הַמּוֹצִיא אוֹכָלִין פָּחוֹת מִכַּשִּׁיעוּר בִּכְלִי — ***One who takes out*** from one domain to another ***less than the prescribed amount of foodstuffs,***[6] and the foodstuffs are ***in a container,*** פָּטוּר אַף עַל הַכְּלִי — ***is exempt*** for the entire act, ***even for*** taking out ***the container,*** שֶׁהַכְּלִי טְפֵלָה לוֹ — ***because the container is subordinate to*** the food.[7]

אֶת הַחַי בְּמִטָּה — Likewise, if he takes out ***a live person on a bed*** פָּטוּר אַף עַל הַמִּטָּה — ***he is exempt*** for the entire act, ***even for*** taking out ***the bed,*** שֶׁהַמִּטָּה טְפֵלָה לוֹ — ***because the bed is subordinate to*** the person.[8]

A contrasting case:

אֶת הַמֵּת בְּמִטָּה — However, one who takes out ***a corpse on a bed*** חַיָּיב — ***is liable.***[9]

The Mishnah concludes:

וְכֵן כְּזַיִת מִן הַמֵּת — ***And similarly,*** one who takes out a ***an olive-size*** portion ***of a corpse,*** וּכְזַיִת מִן הַנְּבֵלָה — ***or an olive-size*** portion ***of an animal's carcass,*** וְכַעֲדָשָׁה מִן הַשֶּׁרֶץ — ***or a lentil-size*** portion ***of a***

NOTES

exempt a person who commits a sin as a result of a mistaken ruling of the Sanhedrin — which is treated as not being *his* sin — i.e., it is not his responsibility, and therefore he is exempt from a *chatas* (Gemara 93a; see *Horayos* 1:1).

6. I.e., less than the volume of a dried fig, the minimum amount of food that a person must transfer to become liable for a *chatas.*

7. Thus, not only is he exempt for taking out the food, since it was less than the prescribed measurement, but he is also exempt for taking out the container. This is because the container was not transported for its own sake, but merely as a means to transport the foodstuff. In these circumstances, the container has no inherent importance. It is merely an accessory. Hence, it is treated as subordinate to the foodstuff — and since there is no liability for taking out the primary substance (the foodstuff), there can be no liability for taking out the subordinate substance (the container). However, if he also intended to transport the container for its own sake from domain to domain, he is liable for taking out the container (Gemara 93b).

8. The Gemara explains that one does not violate the Biblical prohibition of transferring when he takes out a live person, due to the fact that the person being carried aids in his own transport, in that he holds on and instinctively balances himself, thus lightening his burden for the person transporting him (see *Rashi*). This exception is based on the principle: חַי נוֹשֵׂא אֶת עַצְמוֹ, *a living creature carries itself.* Since the person taking out the bed is exempt for taking out the person, he is also exempt for taking out the bed, as the bed is merely an accessory to that person (as long as it is not being transported for its own sake).

9. In this case, the principle of *a living creature carries itself* obviously does not apply. The corpse is treated as any other inanimate object, and the person who takes out the bed is liable to a *chatas.*

dead *sheretz,*[10] חַיָּיב — *is liable.*[11] וְרַבִּי שִׁמְעוֹן פּוֹטֵר — *But R' Shimon exempts him.*[12]

NOTES

10. One of eight species of creeping animals whose carcasses convey *tumah* (see *Vayikra* 11:29-30 and the Mishnah below, 14:1).

11. The amounts listed here are the minimum amounts of each creature that convey *tumah* to a person touching them (see ibid. 22:5 with *Rashi*). When one transports these things to another domain, he accomplishes the objective of removing an object that can transmit *tumah* to him. The transfer is thus regarded as significant enough to render him liable to a *chatas* (*Rav; Rashi*).

12. All these cases are examples of מְלָאכָה שֶׁאֵינָהּ צְרִיכָה לְגוּפָהּ, *a labor not needed for its defined purpose* (see below). It is R' Shimon's position throughout our tractate that one who performs a forbidden labor in such a manner is exempt from bringing a *chatas* (the act is prohibited by Rabbinic decree, however). The Tanna Kamma of our Mishnah, presumed to be R' Yehudah (*Tosafos* 94a), maintains that even *a labor not needed for its defined purpose* is a Biblically prohibited act.

[In determining the *defined purpose* of various *melachos,* R' Shimon refers to the linkage of the laws of the Sabbath to the construction of the Mishkan. According to *Rashi* (here and elsewhere throughout the tractate), the salient point is that in the Mishkan all the acts of labor were done to achieve an inherently higher order of design; they were not performed merely as a response to some external difficulty. Thus, to be liable to a *chatas,* we must also perform the forbidden labor to achieve a higher order of design: A labor performed only in reaction to an undesirable condition — either to prevent it or to rectify it — is not an inherently creative act and one is therefore not liable for it.

An example of this is the case of the corpse in our Mishnah: One who takes out a corpse is not involved in achieving some "higher order." Rather, he merely seeks to rectify an unwanted situation — e.g., he wishes to avoid contracting *tumah* from the corpse. The labor therefore is not being done for its "defined purpose," and, hence, according to R' Shimon, the perpetrator is exempt. (For an expanded discussion of this issue, see above, Mishnah 2:5.)]

GEMS FROM THE GEMARA

We saw in our Mishnah that one does not violate the forbidden labor of transferring objects from one domain to another on the Sabbath by carrying live people who are capable of such movement under their own power. [This exemption is only from a *chatas* — the transfer is Rabbinically prohibited (*Shulchan Aruch* 308:41; *Mishnah Berurah* 308:154).] This exception is based on the principle: חַי נוֹשֵׂא אֶת עַצְמוֹ, *a living creature carries itself.*

Tosafos, citing *R' Yitzchak,* explain the basis of this rule in the following manner: The forbidden labors of the Sabbath are those labors which were performed in the construction of the Mishkan. At no time during the building of the Mishkan were live creatures carried. Only three animals were needed; rams, *techashim* [whose hides were used for the topmost roof-coverings (*Shemos* 26:14) and the carrying cases of the vessels (*Bamidbar* 4:6-14)], and the *chilazon* [whose blood was the basis of the *techeiles,* a blue dye used for the curtains and covers of the Mishkan]. The first two walked on their own, and had to be carried only after their slaughter. The *chilazon* was punctured immediately upon being removed from the water, for any delay would affect the quality of the dye. Thus, in the Torah there is no source to prohibit the carrying of a living creature (*Tos.* 94a).

Korban Nesanel (in note §6 to this chapter), followed by *Tiferes Yisrael,* finds difficulty with *Tosafos'* conclusion, according to which no distinction should be drawn between man and beast. Yet the Gemara (94a) clearly teaches that the Sages apply the principle "a living creature carries itself" only to man, and not to animals (although this distinction is indeed disputed by R' Nassan, who holds that even the carrying of animals is exempted).

Korban Nesanel explains that since derivatives from the construction of the Mishkan need not be precisely as they were in the Mishkan, the lack of a clear source prohibiting the carrying of a living creature would not suffice to permit it. We need a logical differentiation as well. The obvious distinguishing characteristic of the transportation of a live person is that he aids in his own transport by holding on and by tensing his muscles so as to distribute his weight equally. [This is most clearly seen from the fact that a person can lift a child of a given weight though he would find great difficulty in lifting an inanimate object of equal "dead" weight.] An animal, however, does not assist when it is being carried; to the contrary, it resists being held. Therefore, concludes *Korban Nesanel,* we can understand why only the carrying of a person may be exempted by the lack of a clear source for it in the construction of the Mishkan, while the carrying of an animal is equated with the carrying of inanimate objects.

QUESTION OF THE DAY:

When the brothers went down to Egypt, how did they enter, and why?

For the answer, see page 108.

A MUSSAR THOUGHT FOR THE DAY

פרשת מקץ

TUESDAY

PARASHAS MIKEITZ

In *A Torah Thought for the Day* we noted *Rashi's* comment that the שָׂטָן, *the Accuser,* prosecutes at a time of peril. The commentators question this concept. Why is it that when a person is in danger, that is an opportune time for the שָׂטָן to prosecute?

Maharsha (to *Rosh Hashanah* 16a) explains this while answering another question. If, on Rosh Hashanah, the Day of Judgment, everything that will take place the following year is preplanned and judged, how can the Accuser change the results? The decree was issued on Rosh Hashanah, and it should be a closed case!

Maharsha explains that when a person finds himself in peril or danger, he needs more merits to be saved. This can cause his Rosh Hashanah judgment to need reevaluation, for it was issued without taking such unusual occurrences into account. If a person is in a situation where he is more likely to be harmed, he must use up more of his merits; thus, a new מִשְׁפָּט, *judgment,* must be issued, and this gives the שָׂטָן new opportunities to prosecute.

The Gemara tells us in *Rosh Hashanah* that three things cause a person's sins to be remembered. One of them is standing under a leaning wall, because the danger of its collapse can cause a new judgment, which will result in Heaven studying his merits again.

The Gemara in *Shabbos* (32a) spells this out very clearly: "A person should not stand in a place of danger and expect a miracle to save him, because perhaps a miracle will not occur. And even if a miracle does take place, his merits are deducted for this miracle."

The less a person places himself in dangerous situations, the more merits he will retain, and he will be able to live his life according to the judgment that took place on Rosh Hashanah.

HALACHAH OF THE DAY

When a ladle is used to serve soup from a *kli rishon,* i.e., a pot removed from the flame, into a bowl, there is a question as to the halachic status of the ladle. Some *poskim* are of the opinion that the pot is a *kli rishon,* the ladle used to remove the soup from the pot qualifies as a *kli sheni,* and the bowl into which the soup is served is therefore a *kli shelishi.* According to these *poskim,* since the bowl into which the soup has been served is a *kli shelishi,* one may immerse any item — raw or cooked — into the hot bowl of soup (as long as it is not one of the easily cooked items mentioned earlier).

While this opinion would seem to follow the basic premise of the different stages of *kli rishon, sheni* etc., there are other *poskim* who disagree, and take the position that since the ladle is *submerged* into the heat of the *kli rishon,* it too receives the status of *kli rishon* — thus, the bowl is not considered a *kli shelishi* but rather a *kli sheni.* If the bowl from which the soup is being consumed is a *kli sheni,* it would be forbidden for one to immerse in the hot soup any raw items, or even any items that have been previously baked rather than cooked, such as *challah* or matzah.

In practice, the following rules should be observed:

With regard to uncooked spices, the ladle should be treated as a *kli rishon,* and the bowl as a *kli sheni.* Therefore, before adding any uncooked seasoning to a bowl of soup, one must either first transfer the soup to another *kli,* so it will be a *kli shelishi,* or wait until the soup cools to a temperature below *yad soledes bo.*

With regard to items that have been previously baked, we may consider the ladle a *kli sheni,* thus making the bowl a *kli shelishi.* Accordingly, one may add pieces of matzah or baked croutons to soup that was placed in a bowl with a ladle. One may also pour soup from the ladle directly onto a baked item, since pouring from a *kli sheni* falls under the rule of *kli shelishi.*

It is important to note that the above guidelines apply *only if the ladle is left out of the pot between the serving of multiple bowls of soup.* If, however, the ladle is left in the soup for an extended period of time, or if it is immersed in the *kli rishon* many times in rapid succession, *all poskim* agree that the ladle is then to be considered a *kli rishon,* resulting in the bowl having the status of a *kli sheni.*

It should also be noted that the question regarding the status of the ladle is most often irrelevant with respect to the use of pre-cooked spices such as salt, which may be added to a *kli sheni* according to all opinions.

A CLOSER LOOK AT THE SIDDUR

יְהִי רָצוֹן מִלְּפָנֶיךָ ה׳ אֱלֹהֵינוּ . . . שֶׁתּוֹלִיכֵנוּ לְשָׁלוֹם, וְתַצְעִידֵנוּ לְשָׁלוֹם, וְתַדְרִיכֵנוּ לְשָׁלוֹם. וְתַגִּיעֵנוּ לִמְחוֹז חֶפְצֵנוּ לְחַיִּים וּלְשִׂמְחָה וּלְשָׁלוֹם, וְתַצִּילֵנוּ מִכַּף כָּל אוֹיֵב וְאוֹרֵב וְלִסְטִים וְחַיּוֹת רָעוֹת בַּדֶּרֶךְ.

May it be Your will, HASHEM . . . that You lead us toward peace, emplace our footsteps toward peace, guide us toward peace, and make us reach our desired destination for life, gladness, and peace. May You rescue us from the hand of every foe, ambush, bandits, and evil animals along the way . . . (*Tefillas HaDerech*).

Someone who sets out on a journey must pray that he will complete it safely. This applies even if there is no reason to expect danger. As we discussed earlier (see *A Torah Thought for the Day*), every journey is considered a time of peril (as the Gemara tells us, כָּל הַדְּרָכִים בְּחֶזְקַת סַכָּנָה, *all roads are rendered a place where danger can occur*), and a special prayer to protect oneself from danger was instituted.

The Gemara in *Berachos* (29b) cites several different versions of this prayer, recited by different Sages. It is interesting to note that even Eliyahu instructed Rav Yehudah to say this prayer upon leaving a city, telling him: "When you set out on a journey, ask permission from your Creator to leave" (*Rashi*). From this wording, we see that *Tefillas HaDerech* is not merely a prayer to have a successful trip; rather, it is a request for permission from Hashem to take the trip.

Once one views this prayer in such a light, he will obviously only go to those places that he believes will meet with Hashem's approval. Furthermore, he will take his whole trip with Hashem in mind. As the *Shelah HaKadosh* comments concerning the verse (*Bamidbar* 9:23): עַל־פִּי ה׳ יַחֲנוּ וְעַל־פִּי ה׳ יִסָּעוּ, *According to the word of HASHEM they would encamp, and according to the word of HASHEM they would journey*: Wherever a person goes, it should be with Hashem's Name on his lips. *Shelah* uses this verse as a basis to exhort people to accustom themselves to use the phrases: "אִם יִרְצֶה ה׳, *God willing,*" and "בְּעֶזְרַת ה׳, *with the help of God.*"

Tefillas HaDerech is thus not simply a regular prayer, but a request to be granted permission to travel. However, it is nevertheless automatically a request for protection as well, for one who travels with Hashem's approval will surely be protected from any peril he may encounter.

A TORAH THOUGHT FOR THE DAY

וַיֹּאמְרוּ אִישׁ אֶל־אָחִיו אֲבָל אֲשֵׁמִים אֲנַחְנוּ
עַל־אָחִינוּ אֲשֶׁר רָאִינוּ צָרַת נַפְשׁוֹ בְּהִתְחַנְנוֹ אֵלֵינוּ
וְלֹא שָׁמָעְנוּ עַל־כֵּן בָּאָה אֵלֵינוּ הַצָּרָה הַזֹּאת

They then said to one another,
"Indeed, we are guilty concerning our brother,
inasmuch as we saw his heartfelt anguish
when he pleaded with us and we did not listen.
That is why this anguish has come upon us"
(*Bereishis* 42:21).

The verse tells us that Yosef's brothers expressed their anguish and feelings of guilt not for selling him into slavery, as one would expect, but for ignoring his pleas for mercy.

Ramban explains that the brothers regarded the cruelty they showed Yosef as a greater sin — deserving a greater punishment — than the sin of the sale itself. For he was, after all, their brother, their flesh and blood; he had been begging and falling to their feet, and they had not had mercy on him.

Ramban asks: If the brother's ignoring of Yosef's pleas was such a crucial detail, why was it not mentioned when the Torah tells us of the sale? He offers two possibilities: (1) It is well-known and natural that a person will beg his brothers for mercy when they intend to harm him; thus, the Torah saw no need to state the obvious. (2) The Torah was brief in describing their sin, out of respect for the brothers.

Sforno also notes that the brothers only regretted not having mercy on Yosef when he was pleading for his life, but they did not regret the actual sale. This was because as far as the sale was concerned, the brothers had determined that Yosef was halachically deemed a *rodeif,* who was trying to kill them. They were therefore justified in selling him to remove the threat. However, their cruelty was uncalled for, and they reasoned that this was the cause of their present predicament.

From here, says *Rav Yerucham* of Mir, we see the purity of character of the holy *shevatim.* Only those far removed from Torah would err and see the brothers as lacking in morals and acting impulsively in selling their brother. God forbid! We see here the exact opposite — they had no doubt whatsoever that the sale was legitimate, and they faulted themselves only for not being merciful to their own flesh and blood.

[*Rabbeinu Bachya* takes a completely different approach to this verse.

He says the fact that the Torah does not mention their guilt about the sale is proof to the opinion that the brothers themselves *never sold Yosef;* in his opinion, this was done by the Midianites who pulled him from the pit (see *Bereishis* 37:28). Thus, they felt guilt only for throwing him into the pit and ignoring his pleas.]

MISHNAH OF THE DAY: SHABBOS 10:6

Although the balance of Chapters 10 and 11 deal with the forbidden labor of transferring from one domain to another, the following Mishnah, which deals with *tolados* of various *avos,* is added here because, like the end of the previous Mishnah, it too considers מְלָאכָה שֶׁאֵינָהּ צְרִיכָה לְגוּפָהּ, *a labor not needed for its defined purpose.*

הַנּוֹטֵל צִפָּרְנָיו זו בְּזו או בְּשִׁנָּיו — ***One who removes his fingernails one with the other, or with his teeth;***[1] **וְכֵן שְׂעָרוֹ** — ***and similarly*** one who removes ***his hair*** in such a manner, i.e. he plucks the hair of his head with his hand, **וְכֵן שְׂפָמוֹ** — ***and similarly*** the hair of ***his mustache,*** **וְכֵן זְקָנוֹ** — ***and similarly*** the hair of ***his beard;*** **וְכֵן הַגּוֹדֶלֶת** — ***and similarly one who braids*** her hair, **וְכֵן הַכּוֹחֶלֶת** — ***and similarly one who paints*** her eyes, **וְכֵן הַפּוֹקֶסֶת** — ***and similarly one who fixes*** her hair; **רַבִּי אֱלִיעֶזֶר מְחַיֵּיב** — ***R' Eliezer holds*** that person ***liable*** to a *chatas,*[2] **וַחֲכָמִים אוֹסְרִין מִשּׁוּם שְׁבוּת** — ***while the Sages prohibit*** each of these acts ***by Rabbinic decree.***[3]

NOTES

1. I.e., either a person used the edge of one of his fingernails as a blade to remove the part of another nail, or bit off a part of his nail.

2. R' Eliezer rules that the person who cuts either his fingernails or his hair is performing a *toladah* of shearing (*Tos. Yom Tov*). He rules that the person who braids or parts her hair is performing a *toladah* of building, while painting the eyes is *a toladah* of writing (*Rav* from Gemara 94b) — since using a brush to apply makeup is tantamount to writing with a pen (*Rashi*). Alternatively, by painting her eyes she is liable for dyeing (*Tos. Yom Tov; Tiferes Yisrael*).

3. The Sages exempt from a *chatas* a person who commits any of the acts mentioned above, because he did not perform the act in the usual manner of that particular labor (*Rav; Tiferes Yisrael* from Gemara 94b). Moreover, in order to be liable for cutting nails or hair, one must have a need for the nails or the hair which he cuts off. Otherwise, his act is *a labor not performed for its designated purpose,* and is exempt (*Tos.* 94b). Nevertheless, since the manner in which these activities are performed very closely resembles the manner in which they would constitute violations of actual Torah law, the Sages decreed them prohibited (*Meiri*). [A Sabbath prohibition by Rabbinic decree is called a שְׁבוּת — literally, *rest.*]

The Mishnah goes on to discuss the rule for things growing in a flowerpot:

הַתּוֹלֵשׁ מֵעָצִיץ נָקוּב — ***One who plucks*** a plant ***from a perforated flowerpot*** on the Sabbath חַיָּיב — ***is liable*** to a *chatas;*[4] וְשֶׁאֵינוֹ נָקוּב — ***but*** if he plucks it ***from an unperforated*** flowerpot פָּטוּר — ***he is exempt*** from a *chatas.*[5] וְרַבִּי שִׁמְעוֹן פּוֹטֵר בָּזֶה וּבָזֶה — ***R' Shimon, however, exempts him in both this*** case ***and that*** case; i.e., whether he plucks it from a perforated flowerpot or an unperforated one.[6]

NOTES

4. Since the flowerpot is perforated, the plant growing in it is regarded as growing from the ground. Plucking it out is therefore a *toladah* of *harvesting.* This applies even if the hole is on the side of the flowerpot — as long as it is large enough for a small root to fit through it (*Rav* from Gemara 95b; *Rashi; Rambam, Hil. Shabbos* 8:3).

5. Since the flowerpot is not perforated, the plant cannot derive its nourishment from the ground. It is therefore not regarded as attached to the earth. One who plucks such a plant is, therefore, exempt from a *chatas.* Nevertheless, plucking this plant is prohibited by Rabbinic decree (*Beis Yosef* 336, *Shulchan Aruch* 336:7).

6. R' Shimon does not regard a perforated flowerpot as attached to the earth. Hence, a person who plucks a plant from this flowerpot is exempt from a *chatas* (*Rav*).

GEMS FROM THE GEMARA

Halachah distinguishes between a plant growing in a perforated flowerpot, and one growing in a non-perforated flowerpot. Since a perforated pot can draw some sustenance from the ground by absorption through its perforation — even if it is not sitting directly on the ground — it is considered attached to the ground. On the other hand, an unperforated pot, even if it is sitting directly on the ground, is not considered attached to the ground. Hence, many laws regarding growing plants (viz., *terumah, maaser, sheviis,* etc. — particularly those that are contingent on a plant growing in the land of Israel), do not apply to plants that are growing out of soil in a non-perforated flowerpot or container, but only to plants growing in a perforated pot.

This distinction is important with regard to the Scripturally forbidden labor of harvesting on the Sabbath. To be liable to a *chatas* for this labor, one must detach a plant that is in some way connected to the ground (e.g., through a stalk or a tree). Hence, this forbidden labor applies only to plants in a perforated pot.

The Gemara (84b) states that there is one type of pot that does not need to be perforated for a plant growing within it to be treated as growing from the ground. Its identity, however, is subject to a difference of opinion. *Rashi* (*Gittin* 7b) states that an earthenware pot, even without a hole, is dealt with as a perforated pot. Accordingly, our Mishnah, which differentiates between perforated and unperforated pots, is discussing either wooden or metal pots. *Tosafos* (ibid. and in *Menachos* 85a), however, identify the exception as being wooden, *not* earthenware, pots. According to this explanation, our Mishnah is discussing either an earthenware or a metal pot. *Shulchan Aruch* (*Orach Chaim* 336:8) states that we adopt the stringencies of both opinions. [There is a third opinion, quoted in the name of *Rabbeinu Tam,* that states that a wooden pot, even if it is perforated, is dealt with as an unperforated pot!]

In any event, even detaching a plant from an unperforated pot is prohibited by Rabbinical decree (*Shulchan Aruch* loc. cit.).

A MUSSAR THOUGHT FOR THE DAY

We discussed above (see *A Torah Thought for the Day*) how the brothers regretted only their lack of sympathy toward their brother Yosef. They did not show any remorse for the actual sale, as they felt that their decision was totally justified according to their understanding of Torah law and Yosef's actions toward them.

Taam VeDaas says that this teaches us a very important lesson that we must apply in our daily behavior. There are many situations where we are expected to act in a certain way, or to take a strong stand with respect to certain issues. Sometimes we must even punish someone physically or monetarily. In rare cases, such as when someone is a *rodeif* who is trying to kill someone, one must even kill him. But the Torah still expects the person not to lose the fine *middah* of caring and feeling bad for that person even while doing so.

This was the fine line that the holy *shevatim* failed to walk. They did not regret selling Yosef, for that was fully justified. It was the caring and sympathy that was missing.

We find that Hashem Himself exhibited this *middah* when the Egyptians were swept away into the *Yam Suf.* Bnei Yisrael suffered terribly under Egyptian rule and oppression, and their oppressors were certainly deserving of severe punishment. Nevertheless, when it came time to drown the Egyptians, the angels were not allowed to sing *shirah,* as Hashem told them, "The creations of my hand — the Egyptians — are drowning in the sea, and you are singing *shirah*?!"

We see that the Torah (*Vayikra* 19:18) applies the rule of וְאָהַבְתָּ לְרֵעֲךָ כָּמוֹךָ, *You shall love your friend as yourself,* even when it comes to killing a person who transgressed a terrible sin punishable by the death penalty. The Gemara tells us that court-ordered death sentences are carried out as quickly as possible, so as not to prolong the criminal's pain, and also to maintain his dignity.

How much more does the Torah expect from us in our relationships with people who are not sinners and are not deserving of any punishment!

HALACHAH OF THE DAY

Having discussed the general rules that govern the complex laws of the *melachah* of *bishul,* we will now turn our attention to applying these rules to some common household situations.

It is common practice to warm up a baby's bottle by either immersing it in a container of hot water, or by running hot water over the bottle. If the bottle in question contains a liquid that has been pasteurized, such as milk or most commercially available apple juices, one may immerse the bottle in a *kli sheni.* This is because, as we have already learned, one may reheat pre-cooked liquids that have completely cooled in the heat of a *kli sheni.*

It is also permissible to pour hot water from a *kli rishon* onto the bottle in order to reheat the liquids inside. This is because, as we have seen, the cooking power of the water poured from the *kli rishon* extends only to the surface upon which it is poured — in this case the surface of the baby's bottle, which is not subject to the *melachah* of *bishul.*

If, however, the bottle contains a non-pasteurized liquid, it is necessary to immerse the bottle in a *kli shelishi* to avoid violating the prohibition of *bishul.*

Cooked noodles may be added to a pot of hot soup that has been removed from the flame. Since the noodles have already been completely cooked, there is no prohibition against reheating them in a *kli rishon.*

Croutons that have been baked may not be added to either a pot of soup (a *kli rishon*), or into a bowl that has the status of a *kli sheni.* Since the croutons have been baked and not cooked, we do not permit them to be cooked in the heat of a *kli rishon* or *sheni* on Shabbos. However, if a ladle was used to serve the soup into the bowl, it is permissible to place croutons in the bowl, since in such cases we view the ladle as a *kli sheni.* [As we noted earlier, croutons that have been deep-fried and not baked may be added directly to the pot or bowl.]

It is permissible to add cold water to a hot beverage in a cup (a *kli sheni*) in order to cool it off, even if the drink will remain hotter than *yad soledes bo.* Since water is known by us to be an item which is not easily cooked, it may be immersed in the heat of a *kli sheni.* This may not be done in a *kli rishon.*

Coffee may be prepared on Shabbos in the following manner: Hot water should be poured from the kettle or urn (the *kli rishon*) into a dry cup (a *kli sheni*). It is important that the cup be dry, otherwise the droplets of water found in the cup will become cooked through the heat of the hot water coming from the *kli rishon.* (If the droplets of water are remnants of water that had been previously boiled, one is not obligated to dry the cup before pouring the hot water into it.) One may then add instant coffee, sugar, and milk (all of which have been previously cooked) into the *kli sheni.* [It should be noted that there are those who adapt a more stringent practice, transferring the hot water to a *kli shelishi* before adding the additional ingredients.]

A CLOSER LOOK AT THE SIDDUR

The *Rambam* in *Hilchos Teshuvah* (2:8) says that the proper text for וִדּוּי, *Viduy* (Confession), begins with the words אֲבָל חָטָאנוּ, which he calls the main part of וִדּוּי. It means, *but indeed, we did sin.*

Whenever we recite וִדּוּי (*Nusach Sefard* — daily; *Nusach Ashkenaz* — on a fast day) we also begin with the words, אֲבָל אֲנַחְנוּ וַאֲבוֹתֵינוּ חָטָאנוּ, *but indeed, we and our forefathers have sinned.*

Why are these words such an essential part of *Viduy*?

We see that Yosef's brothers used similar similar words when they confessed their sin. They said אֲבָל אֲשֵׁמִים אֲנַחְנוּ, *Indeed, we are guilty* (42:21). *Targum* translates the word אֲבָל as בְּקוּשְׁטָא, *in truth.* How is this to be understood?

Reb Leib Chasman explains that the first step in any *viduy* or repentance is the person's realization that he has actually sinned. Any justification or excuse for his actions will only impede his true feelings of regret and guilt.

When someone declares that אֲבָל, *in truth,* he has sinned, and admits

to himself that this is the whole truth, without any room for rationalization, he is well on his way to repentance. This is the key to real confession — one must realize fully that he has sinned, without any reservation.

R' Leib notes further that the opening line of the אָבִינוּ מַלְכֵּנוּ prayer also contains the words חָטָאנוּ לְפָנֶיךָ, *We have sinned before You.* If this admission is missing, then the entire prayer is lacking in sincerity.

The *shevatim* had experienced no regrets up to this point. For twenty-two years they had no reason to say *Viduy* on what they did, even after seeing the pain that their actions had caused Yaakov. They were secure in their decision, and had no cause for remorse. Now, for the first time, they received a message from Above that there was something being held against them. Immediately, they realized the truth, and stated, "We have sinned and are guilty, and this is the truth — אֲבָל אֲשֵׁמִים אֲנַחְנוּ."

QUESTION OF THE DAY:

Why did Pharaoh call Yosef, "Tzafnas Pane'ach"?

For the answer, see page 108.

A TORAH THOUGHT FOR THE DAY

אָנֹכִי אֶעֶרְבֶנּוּ מִיָּדִי תְּבַקְשֶׁנּוּ אִם־לֹא הֲבִיאֹתִיו אֵלֶיךָ וְהִצַּגְתִּיו לְפָנֶיךָ וְחָטָאתִי לְךָ כָּל־הַיָּמִים

I will personally guarantee him; of my own hand you can demand him. If I do not bring him back to you and stand him before you, then I will have sinned to you for all time (*Bereishis* 43:9-11).

In an earlier verse, we find that Reuven also offered to guarantee Binyamin's safe return, even stating that his two sons' lives would be forfeit if Binyamin did not return (see 42:37). The commentaries wonder why, after rejecting Reuven's previous offer, Yaakov accepted Yehudah's apparently similar acceptance of responsibility, and agreed to send Binyamin to Egypt under his care. What was the difference between these two proposals?

R' Berel Soloveitchik explains that in truth, both offers were identical. However, Yehudah's statement to Yaakov came after the worsening of the famine; indeed, the Torah states: וְהָרָעָב כָּבֵד בָּאָרֶץ, *The famine was severe in the land* (43:1), before telling us about Yehudah's proposal. Even though Yaakov truly did not wish to send Binyamin to Egypt under any circumstances, he realized that he no longer had the luxury of refusing Yehudah's offer, as he had previously refused Reuven's. Since the entire family was at risk of starvation, Yaakov understood that there was no longer a choice; Binyamin had to be sent. [See *Bereishis Rabbah* 91:6 for a full account of the conversation between Yehudah and Yaakov.]

Other commentaries, such as *Beis HaLevi,* disagree, maintaining that Yehudah's offer to Yaakov was in fact a superior proposal; the reason that Yaakov agreed to send Binyamin with Yehudah was because a different level of commitment for Binyamin's safety was being offered. When Reuven undertook to return Binyamin safely home to Yaakov, he was offering to do his utmost to fulfill his father's wish that Binyamin not be harmed. Yehudah, however, went further. He did not simply offer to fulfill Yaakov's wish to protect and return Binyamin; rather, he staked his entire future — in both this world and the next — on Binyamin's safe return home. Yehudah thus implied that he would not only guard Binyamin for Yaakov's sake; rather, Binyamin would be protected for his — Yehudah's — own benefit. [See *A Taste of Lomdus* for the halachic ramifications of Yehudah's guarantee.]

Be'er Yosef offers an interesting explanation of why Yehudah's personal guarantee would be more reassuring to Yaakov, based on the *Yerushalmi* (*Shabbos* 6:9). He explains that the reason for Yaakov's unwillingness to send Binyamin on this journey to Egypt was that Yaakov had learned from experience that his family was placed in particular danger whenever they were traveling. Rachel died while traveling, Yosef was lost when on a mission for his father, and most recently, Shimon, when sent on a journey to the Egyptian ruler, had been arrested. Accordingly, Yaakov feared that even if Reuven would be protecting Binyamin, this would be insufficient to shield him from the poor *mazal* that followed Yaakov during travel. Yehudah's response to this specific reluctance of his father was the statement that Binyamin was being sent on *Yehudah's* behalf, not on Yaakov's. Yehudah said to Yaakov: I and my children have never had a history of accidents on the road. Thus, Binyamin will be safe if sent under my responsibility.

MISHNAH OF THE DAY: SHABBOS 11:1

In the previous chapters, we studied the laws governing the forbidden labor of transferring via carrying an object from domain to domain. The following Mishnah considers the laws governing transferring by *throwing* from domain to domain. This form of transfer is a *toladah* of the forbidden labor of transferring by carrying something out (*Tiferes Yisrael*). [Although the result of *throwing* is the same as *carrying*, it is, nevertheless, considered a *toladah* since in the construction of the Mishkan, things were either carried or handed over, but never thrown (*Meiri*).]

הַזּוֹרֵק מֵרְשׁוּת הַיָּחִיד לִרְשׁוּת הָרַבִּים — ***One who throws*** an object ***from a private domain to a public domain*** on the Sabbath, **מֵרְשׁוּת הָרַבִּים לִרְשׁוּת הַיָּחִיד** — or ***from a public domain to a private domain,*** **חַיָּיב** — ***is liable*** to a *chatas*.[1]

מֵרְשׁוּת הַיָּחִיד לִרְשׁוּת הַיָּחִיד — If he throws the object ***from*** one ***private domain to*** another ***private domain,*** **וּרְשׁוּת הָרַבִּים בָּאֶמְצַע** — ***and there is a public domain between*** the two private domains, **רַבִּי עֲקִיבָא מְחַיֵּיב** — ***R' Akiva holds*** him ***liable*** to a *chatas*[2] **וַחֲכָמִים**

NOTES

1. [As we shall see below, the thrown object in question traverses the airspace of the public domain at a height of less than 10 *tefachim* (handbreadths).]

2. R' Akiva's ruling is based on the principle of קְלוּטָה כְּמִי שֶׁהֻנְּחָה, *[something] encompassed is considered as if placed at rest;* i.e., when an object enters the airspace of the public domain, it is encompassed by that domain and "caught" in it (hereafter referred to as *kelutah,* "caught"). Accordingly, it is legally treated as having come to rest

פּוֹטְרִין — *while the Sages exempt* him.[3]

NOTES

there. The one who threw it is therefore guilty of throwing into the public domain. However, this is true only if the object traversed the public domain within 10 *tefachim* of the ground, since the public domain extends only to that height. If the object traversed the public domain at a greater height he is exempt, since the airspace above 10 *tefachim* is an exempt region. Even R' Akiva agrees that the principle of *kelutah* does not apply to the airspace more than 10 *tefachim* above a public domain (*Rav* from Gemara 97a; *Rashi* to Gemara 4b).

3. The Sages do not subscribe to the principle of *kelutah*. Consequently, the thrown object is not regarded as having come to rest in the public domain. Since the object never came to rest in the public domain, the only transfer that occurred was from one private domain to another, for which there is no liability (*Rav*). [There is a difference of opinion in the Gemara (97a) as to whether the Sages agree that the principle of *kelutah* does apply in regard to an object within 3 *tefachim* of the ground (see *Rashba* ad loc.; cf. *Rambam Commentary* and *Maggid Mishneh, Hil. Shabbos* 13:16 according to Rava, 100a).]

GEMS FROM THE GEMARA

We learned in the Mishnah that if a person throws an object from one private domain to another private domain, and there was a public domain between the two private domains, R' Akiva holds him liable to a *chatas,* based on the principle of קְלוּטָה כְּמִי שֶׁהֻנְּחָה, *[something] encompassed is considered as if placed at rest.*

In theory, it would seem that the person who performed this forbidden labor should be liable for *two chatas* offerings: one for the transfer from the first private domain to the public domain, and another for the transfer from that public domain to the second private domain. There is, however, another factor to consider. As we saw in Mishnah 1:1, for a person to be considered in violation of the Torah prohibition of "transferring," his act must consist of three components:

(a) עֲקִירָה — *akirah* (lit., *uprooting*): removing the object from its place in one domain;

(b) the transfer of an object from domain to domain;

(c) הַנָּחָה *hanachah*: setting the object down in a place in another domain.

The Gemara (4a) quotes various Tannaic opinions as to whether the *akirah* and *hanachah* have to be from and upon a surface of at least 4 *tefachim* (handbreadths) by 4 *tefachim* in order to incur Scriptural liability to a *chatas.* [Transfers from and to smaller surfaces are prohibited Rabbinically in any event.]

On the other hand, the principle of *kelutah* merely treats a flying object as a stationary one; it does not render the air in which the object is considered to be at "rest" a surface of 4 square *tefachim.* Since R' Akiva renders one liable for throwing through a public domain, by dint of the principle of *kelutah,* he obviously does not require that the *hanachah* be on such a surface. Nevertheless, suggests the Gemara, perhaps R' Akiva does require such a surface for the *akirah;* i.e., although one may be liable for transferring without setting the object down on a surface of less than 4 square *tefachim,* he is not liable unless he originally lifted that object from an actual surface of at least 4 square *tefachim. Rashi,* taking this suggestion to be a definite assertion, cites as its source the fact that R' Akiva does not, in our Mishnah, render the thrower liable to two *chatas* offerings. According to *Rashi,* the reason for this is that the second transfer — i.e., from the virtual place of rest in the airspace of the public domain to the surface of the second private domain — does not result from an *akirah* from an actual surface of 4 square *tefachim.* Consequently, one can be held liable only for the first transfer — i.e., from the actual 4-*tefachim* square surface of the first private domain from which he picked up the object prior to throwing it, to the virtual place of rest in the airspace of the public domain (*Rashi* 4b).

Tosafos (loc. cit.), however, assert that the Gemara's suggestion remains a suggestion only. Consequently, it is possible that even for *akirah* R' Akiva does not require a 4-*tefachim* square surface. This would seem to lead to a double liability in our Mishnah. It is certainly possible that according to R' Akiva he actually is liable twice (the fact that the Mishnah does not say so clearly is not necessarily proof to the contrary, as *Tosafos* proves from other places). *Ran,* however, suggests that the Mishnah obligates him only to bring one *chatas* because the two violations that he committed were performed in one period of forgetfulness, and two violations of a single *melachah* within the same period of forgetfulness render a person liable to only one *chatas* (see above, Mishnah 7:1).

QUESTION OF THE DAY:

Why did Yehudah emphasize in his guarantee to Yaakov that he would return Binyamin "and stand him up before you" (43:9)?

For the answer, see page 109.

A MUSSAR THOUGHT FOR THE DAY

We mentioned in *A Torah Thought for the Day* that according to *Beis HaLevi,* one of the reasons Yaakov accepted Yehudah's proposal of becoming a guarantor to safely return Binyamin was that once Yehudah accepted this responsibility, he was not only protecting Binyamin for Yaakov's sake; he had the added incentive of saving himself — including his share in *Olam Haba* — as well. *R' Eliyahu Meir Bloch* and *Avnei Nezer* both explain that although Yehudah (or Reuven) would have undoubtedly done his best to protect Binyamin in any case, it is an inherent part of human nature that a person will do only as much as he thinks he can achieve. Understanding this, Yehudah wanted to motivate himself to do the most that could possibly be done to protect and return Binyamin to his father, and the best way to do this was to make his own fate dependent on Binyamin's safe return. Yehudah recognized that by making this pledge, he would actuate the deep motivation that a person can have only for himself and his own benefit, and channel these drives toward protecting Binyamin.

The idea of channeling a person's natural tendency to benefit himself, and using it to help other people as well, is a theme discussed by *R' Shimon Shkop* in the introduction to his *Shaarei Yosher.* By man's very nature, explains R' Shimon, each person is most interested in himself and his own gains. However, since we know that a lifestyle that is lived selfishly is wrong — as is obvious from the countless times that the Torah repeats the need to do *chesed* — it would seem that a person's mission in life is to conquer this selfish outlook and concentrate on doing good for others.

Now, it would be possible to conclude that in a perfect world, a person should *never* think about himself or what he needs; instead of spending his life working on advancing himself, he should spend all his time and resources helping others. However, R' Shimon Shkop observes that this perspective, too, is incorrect. The love for one's self and one's own accomplishments is an inherent part of man, and the Torah does not expect or direct a person to go against this natural trait. Indeed, the Gemara states that if two people are stranded in the desert and one of them has enough water for only one person to survive and make it to safety, he is not allowed to share it with his friend, for חַיֶּיךָ קוֹדְמִין לְחַיֵּי חֲבֵרְךָ, *preserving your own life takes precedence over saving your friend's.* This demonstrates that a person is required to take his own needs into consideration before thinking about others. Thus, one must walk a

middle path — tending to his own needs but seeing that others are provided for as well.

R' Shimon notes that one can reach this level by realizing that benefiting others truly *is* the same as benefiting oneself. To explain: A truly selfish person is one who cares only about himself. He will therefore spend his time eating, hoarding his money, or engaging in other hedonistic activities. Another person, who realizes that man is more than a body, will perform mitzvos to benefit his *neshamah.* He is still selfish, but he realizes that a higher benefit comes from actions that are loftier than base pleasures.

A slightly less selfish person will give to his wife and children. The reason he shares with them, however, is not necessarily because he is a "giver"; rather, it is because he realizes that these people are an extension of himself, and he will be fulfilled only if they are happy. A person who is on an even higher level experiences this relationship with his entire community, and feels a personal deficiency if the community is lacking. And one who is truly unselfish feels a connection to every Jew, and will assist anyone who is in need. He realizes that the innate connection between one Jew and the next means that they are like two parts of the body, and any pain or want that one person feels impedes his fellow man as well.

A person who succeeds in channeling his tendency to benefit himself into a drive to help others will help them to a greater degree than one who performs *chesed* out of pity. Instead of looking at his actions of kindness as a luxury, such a person will do anything that can be done for others with the same drive and devotion as he would for himself, for he realizes that the other person's happiness is in truth to his own benefit as well.

HALACHAH OF THE DAY

We have learned that certain cooked foods may be reheated on Shabbos. These are: fully cooked dry foods as well as fully cooked liquids that have not completely cooled and may yet be considered suitable as warm drinks. However, while it is true that these foods and beverages may be reheated on Shabbos, there are restrictions which apply to the method of reheating that may be used.

Even in cases where it is permissible to reheat items on Shabbos, it is forbidden to do so by placing them directly over a flame or any other heat source normally used for cooking. This prohibition was enacted by the Sages because the placement of any food items on a flame — even those to which the *melachah* of *bishul* does not apply — so closely resembles the act of cooking that the Sages feared it would eventually lead to a transgression of the *melachah* of *bishul.*

For this reason, it is forbidden to place even cooked foods on a flame, electric range, or in an oven on Shabbos in order to warm them. [The laws that apply to a *blech* (the metal sheet often used to cover a flame on the Sabbath) will be discussed later on.] There are, however, other methods of rewarming foods that are unconventional, these methods do not fall under the Rabbinic prohibition and are therefore permitted.

- ❑ It is permissible to reheat fully cooked foods by placing them on top of a pot that is on the flame or *blech.* This is permitted only if the lower pot contains food; an empty pot may not be used.
- ❑ Fully cooked foods may be placed *near* a flame in order to reheat them.
- ❑ One may immerse fully cooked foods in a *kli rishon* that has been removed from the fire in order to rewarm them. [If the food is a baked item, it may be placed only in a dry *kli rishon.* If the *kli rishon* contains liquids, immersing a baked item in them would not be permitted, since this would be a case of cooking an item that has been previously baked; this is forbidden, as we have learned earlier.]
- ❑ A hot plate that is generally not used for cooking but only for keeping food warm, which has only one non-adjustable temperature setting, may be used for reheating fully cooked foods. [Needless to say, the hot plate must be connected and turned on prior to the onset of Shabbos.] A hot plate with an adjustable temperature setting is considered to be a device used for cooking. Its use is therefore seen as a conventional method of cooking, and is therefore forbidden by the previously mentioned Rabbinic decree.

A CLOSER LOOK AT THE SIDDUR

The thirteenth blessing of the weekday *Shemoneh Esrei* is the prayer of *Al HaTzaddikim* (*Regarding the righteous . . .*), in which we ask Hashem to protect and benefit the righteous among the Jewish nation. *Yaaros Devash* explains that the reason for this special request is because it is only in the merit of the righteous in each generation that blessing and prosperity are granted to the world.

An understanding of how the mitzvos performed by the righteous impact the rest of the generation may be gained from *Yalkut Shimoni's*

פרשת מקץ
THURSDAY
PARASHAS MIKEITZ

explanation of the opening verse of *Parashas Nitzavim.* As his final exhortation of the Bnei Yisrael drew to a close, Moshe stated: אַתֶּם נִצָּבִים הַיּוֹם כֻּלְּכֶם לִפְנֵי ה׳ אֱלֹהֵיכֶם רָאשֵׁיכֶם שִׁבְטֵיכֶם זִקְנֵיכֶם וְשֹׁטְרֵיכֶם כֹּל אִישׁ יִשְׂרָאֵל, *You are standing here today, all of you, before HASHEM, your God: the heads of your tribes, your elders, and your officers — all the men of Israel* (*Devarim* 29:9). *Yalkut Shimoni* wonders why, if Moses was in fact speaking to *all the men of Israel,* did he single out *the heads of your tribes, your elders, and your officers*? The *Yalkut* explains that all of the Jewish people enjoy a relationship of *arvus* — that is, they act as guarantors for one another. Even if much of the generation is wicked, a few righteous people are able to provide merit for the masses.

R' Aharon Kotler (based on *Tomer Devorah*) explains that just as a guarantor unites himself with the borrower, and thus assures that even if the borrower defaults, all financial obligations will be met, the Jewish people's unity means that even if some of them do not meet their obligations to Hashem, the nation as a whole remains uplifted, and will continue to be blessed, by virtue of the few who continue to serve Hashem properly. [Of course, the benefits of this relationship will help the nation prosper only in *Olam Hazeh;* every individual still must answer for his or her actions in the ultimate Judgment in *Olam Haba.*]

Teaching this message, Moshe equated the leaders, elders and righteous to the rest of the nation, understanding that even in times of general wrongdoing, when most of the Jewish people "default" on their responsibilities to Hashem, the guarantors who continue performing Hashem's will — the *tzaddikim* — are able to single-handedly ensure that, through their merit, Hashem's blessings will continue to be realized. It is for the welfare of these guarantors that we pray three times daily, pleading with Hashem to bless and protect the righteous and the devout, the elders and the teachers, and the righteous converts. For this reason, we close the prayer with the request, וְשִׂים חֶלְקֵנוּ עִמָּהֶם לְעוֹלָם, *and always place our portion with them,* so we may benefit fully from Hashem's bounty.

A TASTE OF LOMDUS

The Gemara in *Bava Basra* (173b) attempts to find a Scriptural source for the law that a person who promises verbally to be an *areiv,* guarantor, for a debt is in fact legally responsible to repay the debt in the event that the borrower defaults. Without an explicit source, explains *Rashbam,* there is no reason why an *areiv's* oral assurances to

repay should be legally binding; a person can obligate himself financially only through performing a legal *kinyan,* such as signing a document, or concretizing his commitment though a handshake or other form of formalized agreement. The Gemara cites Yehudah's declaration of responsibility to Yaakov to bring Binyamin home safely — אָנֹכִי אֶעֶרְבֶנּוּ מִיָּדִי תְּבַקְשֶׁנּוּ, *I will personally guarantee him; of my own hand you can demand him* (*Bereishis* 43:9) — to demonstrate that a guarantor is in fact obligated to carry out his word; if an *areiv's* promise was meaningless, Yaakov would not have accepted the proposal.

The Gemara, however, deflects the proof, explaining that Yehudah was not an ordinary *guarantor;* rather, his offer to return Binyamin safely was a higher level of assurance, akin to the type of guarantor known as an *areiv kablan* (literally, *a guarantor who receives).* [The difference between these two types of guarantors can be seen by *Rambam's* contrasting (in *Hilchos Malveh VeLoveh* 25:2-5) the guidelines that a lender must follow when collecting payment from an ordinary *areiv,* with those applicable when dealing with an *areiv kablan.* Although even an ordinary *areiv* agrees to assume responsibility if the debtor does not pay, the lender must first approach the debtor for payment. It is only if the debtor is in fact unwilling or unable to repay his debt that the lender may approach the *areiv* for payment. An *areiv kablan,* states *Rambam,* is different — while the lender is allowed to approach the debtor first if he wishes to do so, this is not necessary; he may approach the *areiv kablan* as soon as the loan is due, without needing to approach the borrower at all.]

Having established that there are in fact two separate types of guarantors, the Gemara concludes that Yaakov's acceptance of Yehudah's offer of responsibility would indeed demonstrate that one who agrees to be an *areiv kablan* accepts legal accountability without the need for further *kinyan;* it does *not* prove, however, that an ordinary *areiv* accepts his responsibility with mere words alone. Ultimately, the Gemara is forced to turn to a different, unrelated Scriptural source to demonstrate that an ordinary *areiv,* based on his promise alone, is legally obligated to pay the debt if the debtor defaults.

R' Shmuel Rozovsky points out that the difference between an *areiv* and an *areiv kablan* is not simply procedural. Nor is it only a question of how much responsibility — primary or secondary — the guarantor wishes to assume in paying the borrower's debt. Rather, each type of guarantor in fact has a different relationship with the lender. An ordinary *areiv* is a person who promises the lender that the debtor's financial obligations will be met, even though he personally has nothing to do

with this transaction — he is not borrowing the money, nor is he lending it to the debtor. If the person who borrowed the money in fact defaults, the *areiv* is responsible to meet *the borrower's* obligations. An *areiv kablan,* however, is different. He does not assure the lender that the debtor will pay or that he will pay on the debtor's behalf; rather, serving as an *areiv kablan* makes this apparently unconnected person an actual *legal recipient of the loan.* It is as if the lender agreed to give the *areiv kablan* a loan, and instead of receiving the money directly, the *kablan* tells the lender to give it to somebody else — the "borrower." [While in truth the borrower initiated the loan and received the money, from a legal standpoint two separate transactions are occurring; the lender is lending money to the *areiv kablan,* who in turn gives a loan to the "borrower." Since the lender gave the borrower money only because the *areiv kablan* designated this person as the one to whom the loan should be given, the obligation to the lender is the *areiv kablan's,* and the lender may therefore approach him directly when seeking repayment.]

With this definition in mind, it is understandable why the Gemara does not accept Yehudah's *areiv kablan* guarantee to return Binyamin as a source that demonstrates that a regular *areiv* is also responsible. Yehudah did not agree to arrange that *others* would bring Binyamin back from Egypt; Yehudah was the only one who would be responsible to Yaakov. Thus, it is true that we can learn from Yehudah that a person who undertakes to return or repay a sum of money that *he* received (or someone else received on his behalf), can obligate himself to repay even without performing a *kinyan.* But nothing in Yehudah's action shows that a person can verbally obligate himself to repay in the case of an *areiv* who receives nothing himself.

A TORAH THOUGHT FOR THE DAY

פרשת מקץ

FRIDAY

PARASHAS MIKEITZ

וַיֹּאמֶר גַּם־עַתָּה כְדִבְרֵיכֶם כֶּן־הוּא אֲשֶׁר יִמָּצֵא
אִתּוֹ יִהְיֶה־לִּי עָבֶד וְאַתֶּם תִּהְיוּ נְקִיִּם

And he said, "Now too, as you say, so it is; the one with whom it is found shall be my slave, but [the rest of] you shall be exonerated" (*Bereishis* 44:10).

This verse requires explanation. When the brothers protested their innocence, they exclaimed that any one of them found with the goblet should be killed, while *all* of them would be slaves if one was found to be guilty. Seemingly, Yosef's steward agreed, saying, "As you say, so it is," but he then continued with a *different* proposal: The guilty one would be a slave, while the others would be free!

Rashi, addressing this difficulty, understands the words "as you say, so it is" not as a statement of what would *actually* happen, but as a statement of what *should* be. Thus, the steward replied, "In truth, you are correct in that all of you should be punished if one of you is guilty; for if a stolen object is found in the possession of one among a group of ten, all are arrested. But I will treat you more mercifully than the strict letter of the law, and punish only the guilty one."

Several commentators find *Rashi's* explanation problematic, because the halachah is that when a stolen object is found in one's possession, he is the only one liable, and those with him are *not* punished! How, then, can the steward have said that the brothers' proposal reflected the correct judgment?

In light of this difficulty, *Ramban* suggests other ways to understand the steward's opening statement. In one approach, he understands the steward to be expressing his belief that all the protestations of the brothers as to their innocence were genuine. Thus, he began, "Even now, I will accept that as you say (that you have not conspired to do this deed), so it is." Thus, you will not all be punished if the goblet is found among you, as you suggested. Rather, only the culprit will be punished.

In defense of *Rashi, Parashas Derachim* suggests that while halachah indeed holds only the thief found in a group liable, Noahide laws would indeed hold the entire group liable, and it was to these laws that the steward referred. *Sforno,* in a similar vein, explains the steward to have meant that because the crime had been committed against the royal viceroy, the punishment proposed by the brothers would indeed have been fitting; nevertheless, he was willing to be merciful.

For another possible explanation of *Rashi's* meaning, see *A Mussar Thought for the Day.*

פרשת מקץ

FRIDAY

PARASHAS MIKEITZ

MISHNAH OF THE DAY: SHABBOS 11:2

The following Mishnah elaborates the position taken by the Sages in the previous Mishnah:

כֵּיצַד — *How so?*[1] שְׁתֵּי גְזוּזְטְרָאוֹת זוֹ כְּנֶגֶד זוֹ בִּרְשׁוּת הָרַבִּים — If there are ***two balconies,***[2] ***one opposite the other, in a public domain,***[3] הַמּוֹשִׁיט וְהַזּוֹרֵק מִזּוֹ לָזוֹ פָּטוּר — ***one who hands over or throws*** an object ***from this*** balcony ***to that*** balcony across the public domain ***is exempt*** from a *chatas.*[4] הָיוּ שְׁתֵּיהֶן בִּדְיוֹטָא אַחַת — But if ***both*** balconies ***were in one upper story,*** i.e., on the same side of the public domain,[5] הַמּוֹשִׁיט חַיָּיב וְהַזּוֹרֵק פָּטוּר — then ***one who hands over*** an object from one balcony to the other ***is liable,***[6] ***whereas***

NOTES

1. I.e., in what manner of transferring from one private domain to another via a public domain do the Sages (whose view was cited in the precious Mishnah) exempt a person from a *chatas*? (*Rav; Rashi*).

2. These balconies are unwalled, and are formed by planks laid across beams that are protruding from the wall of the house (*Rav; Rashi*).

3. I.e., the balconies extend toward each other from buildings on opposite sides of a street that is a public domain. Each balcony is at least 10 *tefachim* (handbreadths) above the ground of the public domain, and is at least 4 *tefachim* long by 4 *tefachim* wide; thus, each one is a private domain (*Rav; Rashi*).

4. The person is exempt from a *chatas* because this form of transfer is not similar to the form of transfer practiced in regard to the Mishkan. During the Jewish people's travels in the Wilderness, the Mishkan was repeatedly dismantled, transported and subsequently re-erected. The boards that made up the walls of the Mishkan were transported on wagons. When they were to be loaded on the wagons, four wagons would line up in two pairs — one pair behind the other — in the public domain outside the Mishkan. As we shall see below, the Leviim would first hoist the boards from the ground to each of the front wagons, and then pass them from the front wagons to the wagons behind them, until they were full. Each of these wagons had walls 10 *tefachim* high and was therefore a private domain. Thus, we find in the Mishkan an instance in which objects were handed over from one private domain (the front wagon) to another (the rear wagon) over a public domain (the gap between the front and rear wagons). However, this transfer took place only along the length of the public domain (from the front to the rear wagon) but never across its width (from one front wagon to the other). Furthermore, the boards were handed over, never thrown. Since we find no instance of throwing or handing over from one private domain to another across the *width* of a public domain in regard to the Mishkan, the person transferring along the width of a public domain is exempt from a *chatas* (*Rav; Rashi; Meiri*).

5. In this case, both balconies extend from the same wall of a building along the same side of the public domain, with a strip of the public domain below the gap between them (*Rav; Ramban, Rashi*).

6. I.e., one who hands an object over from one balcony to another is liable to a *chatas* — even though the object does not technically pass through the public domain at all,

one who throws the object from one balcony to the other ***is exempt,***[7] שֶׁכָּךְ הָיְתָה עֲבוֹדַת הַלְוִיִּם — ***because this was the*** manner of ***work of the Leviim:*** שְׁתֵּי עֲגָלוֹת זוֹ אַחַר זוֹ בִּרְשׁוּת הָרַבִּים — There would be ***two wagons one behind the other in the public domain,*** מוֹשִׁיטִין הַקְּרָשִׁים מִזּוֹ לָזוֹ — and ***they would hand over the*** Mishkan ***boards from this*** wagon ***to the other,*** אֲבָל לֹא זוֹרְקִין — ***but they would not throw*** the boards.[8]

The Mishnah discusses other cases of transfer between a private and a public domain:

חוּלְיַת הַבּוֹר — In the case of ***the bank of a cistern*** in a public domain,[9] וְהַסֶּלַע — ***or a rock*** in a public domain, שֶׁהֵן גְּבוֹהִין עֲשָׂרָה — ***that are ten tefachim high*** וְרָחְבָּן אַרְבָּעָה — ***and four tefachim wide,***[10] הַנּוֹטֵל מֵהֶן — ***one who takes*** an object ***from them*** and places it in the public domain, וְהַנּוֹתֵן עַל גַּבָּן — ***or one who*** lifts an object from the public domain and ***places it upon them,*** חַיָּיב — ***is liable*** for transferring an object from a public domain to a private domain. פָּחוֹת מִכֵּן — But if the dimensions of the bank or rock are ***less than that,*** פָּטוּר — ***he is exempt,*** since the bank or rock is then not a private domain.

NOTES

only through the exempt area above the 10-*tefachim* limit of the public domain — since this was the manner in which this labor was performed in regard to the Mishkan (*Tiferes Yisrael*).

7. As we have learned, and as the Mishnah proceeds to explain, the Leviim would hand over the boards from one private domain to another along the length of the public domain, but they would not throw them. Since we do not find any instance of throwing from one private domain to another over the public domain in regard to the Mishkan, a person who does so is exempt from a *chatas* (*Rav; Rashi*).

8. They would not throw the boards because of their weight (*Rav; Rashi; Meiri*).

9. When a cistern was constructed, the earth dug out was placed around it as a wall, forming a bank around the opening (*Rav; Rashi*).

10. These are the minimum dimensions of a private domain. Though this rule would seem to be obvious, the Mishnah teaches us that the height of the cistern's bank and the depth of the cistern's walls may be counted together to provide the necessary minimum height of 10 *tefachim* (*Rav*).

QUESTION OF THE DAY:

Why did the curse that the brothers placed upon whomever would be found with the goblet have no effect on Binyamin?

For the answer, see page 109.

פרשת מקץ

FRIDAY

PARASHAS MIKEITZ

GEMS FROM THE GEMARA

The Mishnah opened by stating that one who transfers between private and public domains on the Sabbath by means of *throwing* is liable to a *chatas.* This prompts the Gemara (96b) to inquire: We know that "throwing" an object from the private to public domain is a derivative (*toladah*) of the primary forbidden labor of "taking out" from the private to public domain. [Throwing is clearly a *toladah* rather than a primary forbidden labor (*av*) in its own right, as the Mishnah above (7:3) does not list it among the thirty-nine *avos* (primary forbidden labors). And it is necessarily a *toladah* of "taking out," since it is more similar to "taking out" than to any of the other *avos* (*Rashi*).] But where is "taking out" itself written in the Torah?

R' Yochanan answers that it is derived from the verse (*Shemos* 36:6): *And Moshe commanded, and they sounded the proclamation in the camp saying, "Man and woman shall not do more work [of contribution] toward the gift for the Sanctuary!" And the people were restrained from bringing.* At the time, Moshe was in the Levite camp, which served as a gathering place for all the Jews, and was thus legally considered a public domain. By issuing this proclamation, Moshe, in effect, was saying to the Jews: "Do not take out and bring materials from your private domain to the public domain of the Levite camp."

The Gemara asks: But how do we know that this proclamation took place on the Sabbath, and it was because of the prohibition against carrying on the Sabbath that Moshe commanded them to desist? Perhaps it took place on a weekday, and Moshe commanded them to desist from bringing more because the work of contribution was complete (i.e., the materials already collected were sufficient), as it says in the very next verse: *And the work [of contribution] was sufficient*!

The Gemara answers that R' Yochanan infers that the verse alludes to the Sabbath through the common use of the word *"sounding"* here and in a verse dealing with Yom Kippur (*Vayikra* 25:9): *And you shall "sound" a broken blast on the shofar.* The exegetical tool of *gezeirah shavah* ("common expression") leads us to understand that just as there the verse concerns a day on which labor is forbidden — e.g., Yom Kippur — so too here the verse concerns a day on which labor is forbidden — viz., the Sabbath.

A MUSSAR THOUGHT FOR THE DAY

פרשת מקץ

FRIDAY

PARASHAS MIKEITZ

R' *Moshe Feinstein* (*Darash Moshe,* vol. 1) cites *Rashi's* comment that if a thief is found within a group of ten, all of them are liable. He asks: How could *Rashi* have written this, when we know that the halachah in such a case is that only the thief is liable?

R' Moshe answers that *Rashi* did not mean to say that the other members of the group would be *monetarily* liable, for indeed that is not the case. Rather, *Rashi's* meaning is that the entire group is *culpable,* as the fact that a thief is in their midst points to a deficiency in all of them. [Indeed, *Rashi* does not write that all of them are חַיָּבִים, *liable,* but rather that all of them are נִתְפָּשִׂים, which can be translated as *held to account.*] For if it were clear that every other member of the group was repulsed by the idea of thievery, no member of the group would be able to bring himself to steal, as the knowledge that the others would regard him with revulsion if they were to discover his thievery would provide a powerful deterrent to theft. When one member of a group is found to have stolen, this points to a laxity among the entire group with regard to theft. R' Moshe adds that in truth, the other members of the group are *deserving* of punishment for this laxity; however, Hashem is merciful, and punishes only the one who actually commits the crime.

R' Moshe notes that Dovid HaMelech had to flee Eretz Yisrael and go to Paran to escape Shaul only after the *navi* Shmuel died (see *I Shmuel* 25:1). While Shmuel was alive, Dovid did not fear Shaul, for when he felt threatened he would simply travel to Shmuel. In Shmuel's presence, no one was capable of doing anything improper, as his influence was so powerful that nobody would even *think* of acting incorrectly in his proximity. After he died, however, this safeguard was lost, and so Dovid was forced to flee.

This lesson points clearly to the value of surrounding oneself with companions who uphold the Torah and its ways; for if a person's friends are virtuous, he will be prevented from acting improperly, due to his fear of their disapproval.

HALACHAH OF THE DAY

It is forbidden to place uncooked food on an open flame before Shabbos so that it will stay on the flame and cook on Shabbos. The Sages enacted this prohibition because they felt that if it were permissible to maintain uncooked food on a flame on Shabbos, one might come to adjust the flame on Shabbos in order to speed the cooking process. Such adjustment would be in violation of both the *melachah* of *bishul* and the *melachah* of *maavir,* kindling.

However, when enacting this prohibition, the Sages established it only for situations where it is reasonable to suspect that one may come to adjust the flame. In instances where such action is unlikely, one is permitted to allow uncooked food that was placed on the flame before Shabbos, to remain on the flame and cook on Shabbos.

In Talmudic times, most cooking was done in ovens filled with hot coals. The Sages at that time outlined two procedures for eliminating the likelihood that one would come to stir the hot embers of the coals on Shabbos in order to speed the cooking of the food in the oven. These two procedures are known as גְּרִיפָה, *removing the coals,* and קְטִימָה, *covering the coals.*

If the hot coals were removed from the oven prior to the onset of Shabbos, the Sages permitted leaving uncooked food in the oven to be cooked through the heat retained by the walls of the oven. The reason for this is simple — if there are no coals, they cannot be stirred.

The Sages also permitted leaving food in the oven if the hot coals are covered with ash. Since by covering the coals with ash one diminishes their heat output, such covering is indicative of the fact that the owner is not concerned about how fast the cooking will be accomplished. This in turn makes it unlikely that he will stir the embers of the coals in order to produce more heat.

It is in this last method of cooking allowed by the Sages — קְטִימָה, *the covering of the coals* — that the origins of the commonly used *blech* is to be found. By covering the flame with the metal *blech,* the heat of the flame is dispersed and diminished. The *blech* further serves as a reminder that it is Shabbos, and that one may therefore not raise the flame. Some *poskim* rule that as an added stringency, the knobs that control the flame should also be covered.

[It must be noted that only the guidelines that have been laid out by the *poskim* may be used in order to allow the placing of uncooked food on the *blech* for cooking on Shabbos. One may not create his own method of making the raising of the flame unlikely.]

Now that we understand the origins of the *blech,* we can begin to discuss the laws that pertain to it. We will begin this discussion tomorrow.

A CLOSER LOOK AT THE SIDDUR

This week, we discuss the eighth of the Thirteen Fundamental Principles (י״ג עיקרים) enumerated by *Rambam,* which states:

אֲנִי מַאֲמִין בֶּאֱמוּנָה שְׁלֵמָה שֶׁכָּל הַתּוֹרָה הַמְּצוּיָה עַתָּה בְיָדֵינוּ הִיא הַנְּתוּנָה לְמֹשֶׁה רַבֵּנוּ עָלָיו הַשָּׁלוֹם.

I believe with perfect faith that the entire Torah now in our hands is the same one that was given to Moshe, our Teacher, peace be upon him.

This principle actually embodies two separate truths: (1) that the entire Torah, both Written and Oral, was God-given and not conceived by man; and (2) that the Torah was transmitted faithfully through the generations by our leaders, from Sinai to this very day. Today, we will discuss the first of these truths.

It is of course a cornerstone of our faith that Hashem gave the Torah to the Jews through Moshe at Mt. Sinai. What must be stressed, however, is that this does not refer only to the Ten Commandments, or even only to the Five Books of the Pentateuch. Hashem transmitted to Moshe *the entire Written and Oral Torah,* including all of the laws that are not explicitly written in the Torah, but were derived through hermeneutic rules of exegesis. All the laws that we follow, including the complex laws of *shechitah* (ritual slaughter of animals), *succah, tefillin* and the like, though they are not to be found in the Written Torah, are of Divine origin, and were transmitted to Moshe at Sinai. [The corollary to this, of course, is the fact that the Torah can never be changed, as it is Divine and thus perfect. This is the subject of the ninth principle, which we will discuss further along.]

Moreover, the Written Torah is unlike any other book or document, in that it has no errors, nor does it contain any editorial comments. *Every word* of the Written Torah is completely accurate, and there is no part of it that can be said to be more "important" or sanctified than another part. *Rambam,* in his *Commentary to the Mishnah,* notes that even those verses in the Torah that are simply lists of names (e.g. *Bereishis* 10:6: *the sons of Cham were Kush, Mitrayim, Phut, and Canaan*) are as holy as the verses of the Ten Commandments. All are Hashem's Word. There is nothing in the Torah that was added, or that is incidental or trivial.

This principle is fundamental to our faith because the Torah is literally the blueprint of our very existence. It instructs us as to what we must do, say, eat, hear, see, and even think. It governs every aspect of our lives, from birth to burial. Thus, establishment of its sacrosanct status is absolutely essential.

We will continue our discussion of this principle next week.

A TORAH THOUGHT FOR THE DAY

וַיְחַפֵּשׂ בַּגָּדוֹל הֵחֵל וּבַקָּטֹן כִּלָּה
וַיִּמָּצֵא הַגָּבִיעַ בְּאַמְתַּחַת בִּנְיָמִן

And he searched; he began with the oldest and ended with the youngest. And the goblet was found in the sack of Binyamin (*Bereishis* 44:12).

R*ashi* notes that although the steward obviously knew that the goblet was in Binyamin's sack, he purposely started from the sack of the oldest, so they would not realize that he knew where it was to be found. The Midrash, however, makes a seemingly puzzling comment here. On the words, *he began with the oldest,* the Midrash states: *The oldest — this is Shimon.* The question is obvious — Reuven was the oldest, not Shimon! Why does the Midrash single out Shimon as the one whose sack was searched first?

Maharil Diskin offers a brilliant solution. He notes that when the steward first approached the brothers, accusing them of theft, they countered with the argument described in the verse (44:8-9): *The money we found in the mouths of our sacks* (the first time they left Egypt) *we brought back to you from the land of Canaan. How then could we steal from your master's house any silver or gold? Rashi* comments that this argument is one of several examples of a *kal vachomer* (an *a fortiori* argument) found in the Torah. Asks *Maharil Diskin:* Why would the Torah cite their argument as an example of a *kal vachomer,* when in this case the *kal vachomer* was not effective? After all, the steward did not accept their argument, and he went ahead and searched anyway!

Maharil Diskin explains that in truth the steward *did* accept their *kal vachomer,* and did not search the sacks of those who had returned with money found on the earlier trip. However, not all of the *shevatim* had returned money. Binyamin had not been with the *shevatim* on the first trip, and Shimon had not returned any money either — for he had remained in Egypt the entire time. The steward therefore replied to the brothers: I accept your *kal vachomer,* but there are still two sacks that must be searched. He began with the oldest — that of Shimon — and ended with Binyamin's. But he searched only those two sacks, because all of the others had been cleared by the *kal vachomer.* Thus, the difficulty with *Rashi* is resolved, and the reason that the Midrash identifies the *oldest* as Shimon is clear.

MISHNAH OF THE DAY: SHABBOS 11:3

פרשת מקץ

SHABBOS

PARASHAS MIKEITZ

The following Mishnah discusses the law of throwing in regard to the forbidden *melachah* of transferring 4 *amos* [cubits] in a public domain. Although there is no Scriptural reference to this prohibition, it is forbidden as a הֲלָכָה לְמֹשֶׁה מִסִּינַי, *an Oral Law [taught] to Moshe at Sinai* — a law that Hashem gave to Moshe at Mt. Sinai concurrently with the Scriptural laws, but which remained verbal, and was not written in the Torah (Gemara 96b).

הַזּוֹרֵק אַרְבַּע אַמּוֹת בַּכּוֹתֶל — ***One who throws*** an object ***four amos*** in a public domain ***against a wall:***[1] לְמַעְלָה מֵעֲשָׂרָה טְפָחִים — If it adheres to the wall at a point more than ***ten tefachim above*** the ground, כְּזוֹרֵק בָּאֲוִיר — ***it is as though he threw it in the air*** and he is exempt.[2] לְמַטָּה מֵעֲשָׂרָה — But if it adheres to the wall at a point that is ***below ten tefachim*** above the ground, כְּזוֹרֵק בָּאָרֶץ — ***it is as though he threw it on the ground*** and he is liable to a *chatas.*[3] הַזּוֹרֵק בָּאָרֶץ אַרְבַּע אַמּוֹת חַיָּיב — ***One who throws*** an object in a public domain ***four amos onto the ground is liable.*** זָרַק לְתוֹךְ אַרְבַּע אַמּוֹת — If ***he threw*** an object ***to*** a point ***within four amos*** of himself,[4] וְנִתְגַּלְגֵּל חוּץ לְאַרְבַּע אַמּוֹת — ***but it rolled*** to a point ***beyond four amos,*** פָּטוּר — ***he is exempt.***[5]

NOTES

1. A person who was standing in a public domain threw an object a distance of 4 *amos,* and the object came to rest by adhering to a wall abutting the public domain. This is possible in the case of a sticky object, such as a thick ripe fig (*Rav* from Gemara 100a).

2. The object came to a rest in the airspace at a height of more than 10 *tefachim* [handbreadths] over a public domain, which is an exempt area. Consequently, the person who threw the object is exempt from a *chatas* (*Rav*).

3. Since the airspace of a public domain is regarded as a public domain up to a height of 10 *tefachim,* the Mishnah states that it is as if the object came to rest on the ground of the public domain. [Even though when one throws a fig exactly 4 *amos* the bulk of the fig is within the 4 *amos,* he is nevertheless liable. Since he does not intend to leave the fig permanently stuck to the wall, its bulk does not detract from the 4-*amah* requirement (*Rav; Rashi;* cf. *Tosafos*).]

4. In this case, the person threw the object with the intention that it come to rest within 4 *amos;* thus, he did not intend to perform an act for which he would be liable (*Rav*).

5. Since he had no intention of performing this forbidden labor, he is exempt (*Rav; Rambam Commentary*). [Although a person is generally liable to a *chatas* for desecrating the Sabbath inadvertently, this refers to a case where he *intended* to perform the act, but was unaware that it is prohibited, either because he forgot that it was a forbidden labor or that the day was the Sabbath. In our case, however, he performed the act unintentionally, with no intention of throwing the article over a distance of 4 *amos;* thus, he is exempt.]

חוץ לְאַרְבַּע אַמּוֹת — If he threw the object ***beyond four amos*** **וְנִתְגַּלְגֵּל לְתוֹךְ אַרְבַּע אַמּוֹת** — ***but it rolled*** back ***to within four amos,*** **חַיָּיב** — ***he is liable.***[6]

NOTES

6. In this case, the person threw the object with the intent that it go beyond 4 *amos* — which it did. However, the object then rolled back to a point within 4 *amos*. Nevertheless, the object did momentarily come to a rest at a spot beyond 4 *amos*. Since it rested beyond 4 *amos*, even momentarily, the person is liable to a *chatas*. The subsequent roll of the object to within 4 *amos* cannot undo that liability.

GEMS FROM THE GEMARA

The Gemara (96b), seeking the source for the laws of our Mishnah, inquires: From where do we know that one who throws an object a distance of 4 *amos* [cubits] in the public domain is liable?

Initially, the Gemara, in the name of R' Yoshiyah, answers that the weavers of the curtains would throw their needles to each other. [The construction of the Mishkan, which included the production of many curtains, was performed in the public domain (*Rabbeinu Chananel*).] Thus, we find the Mishkan precedent — the basis of all the forbidden labors — of a curtain-weaver throwing his needle a distance of 4 *amos* in the public domain.

The Gemara, however, rejects this answer, as weavers use a loom for their work, not needles! The Gemara then revises this answer, suggesting that the precedent is that the sewers of the curtains would throw their needles to each other. But the Gemara asks: Perhaps the sewers would sit close to one another? [If so, they did not have to throw the needles at all, but could simply hand them to one another (*Rashi*).]

The Gemara defends its answer, asserting that they could not sit near one another, for they would then hit and prick each other with the needles when drawing them back to tighten the stitches.

The Gemara then asks: Granted that they did not sit close by, but perhaps they sat within 4 *amos* of one another?

Rav Chisda therefore explains that the precedent for "throwing 4 *amos*" is that the weavers of the curtains would throw their shuttles across the width of the curtains as they were being woven on the looms. However, after a series of questions concerning this derivation, the Gemara finally asks: Even if we would grant that the proposed source is a valid precedent for "*throwing* 4 *amos* in the public domain," from where do we know that one who personally *carries* an object 4 *amos* in the public domain is liable?

The Gemara therefore concludes that all manners of transferring an object 4 *amos* in the public domain (i.e., whether by means of carrying or throwing) are Biblically forbidden through an oral tradition transmitted to Moshe at Sinai (as was explained in our commentary to this Mishnah).

A MUSSAR THOUGHT FOR THE DAY

The Midrash relates that when the goblet was found in Binyamin's sack, the *shevatim* pounced upon Binyamin, taunting him, "Thief, the son of a woman who was also a thief! You have brought disgrace upon us by stealing, just as your mother disgraced our father by stealing the *terafim* (idols) from Lavan" (see above, 31:34). According to another Midrashic account, the *shevatim* actually began beating Binyamin, until he swore to them by the life of his father that he had committed no crime.

Two powerful lessons may be gleaned from this Midrash. One lesson is that even the holy *shevatim* were ready to instantly accept that their brother Binyamin was a thief. Why was this so? The Gemara (*Bava Basra* 17a) tells us that Binyamin was one of only four supremely righteous individuals who never sinned, and died only because it had been so decreed as a result of the sin of Adam HaRishon. Surely, then, he had never been guilty of any thievery before! However, they looked at Binyamin and saw not a *tzaddik,* but the brother of Yosef. Their hatred for Yosef blinded them to the fact that Binyamin surely had not stolen the goblet. If even the *shevatim* could make such a mistake due to their enmity, how much more so must each of us be on guard not to allow our dislike of people to blind us to their true character!

A second lesson can be learned from the end of the Midrash, which details the reward Binyamin received for enduring those undeserved blows. In compensation for the blows that the brothers rained upon Binyamin's shoulders, Hashem decreed that the *Shechinah* would rest "between [Binyamin's] shoulders" (see *Devarim* 33:12) — that is, that the *Beis HaMikdash* would be built in his portion of Eretz Yisrael. It thus emerges that due to their unfounded accusation of Binyamin, the brothers lost the opportunity to be the hosts of the *Shechinah.* This, too, should serve to caution a person never to be hasty in judgment of another — for the cost of making incorrect accusations may be high indeed.

HALACHAH OF THE DAY

Let us now begin to introduce the *blech* and its laws into our discussion of reheating foods on Shabbos. For halachic purposes, we divide the surface of the *blech* into three distinct areas: the area of the *blech* that is directly above the flame, the area near the flame invested with sufficient heat to raise the temperature of food placed there to the point of *yad soledes bo,* and the perimeter of the *blech,* where food cannot become heated to such a high temperature. As we shall see, each of these different areas has its own unique law.

Cooked foods which were not on the *blech* prior to the onset of Shabbos may not be placed either directly above the flame, or on the section of the *blech* capable of heating to *yad soledes bo* on Shabbos. This is because, as we explained previously, even though the food has already been cooked, the Sages forbade the placement of even cooked foods on the flame on Shabbos. It is, however, permissible to place cooked foods on the perimeter area of the *blech,* provided that it is cool to the extent that the food cannot reach the temperature of *yad soledes bo* even if it is left there until the end of Shabbos. Since this part of the *blech* is not suitable for cooking, the Rabbinic decree does not apply.

It is common that at the onset of Shabbos there are many pots on the *blech,* each one nearer or farther from the flame depending on when they will be served, or how hot they are required to be. In light of the different laws governing the various parts of the *blech,* it is of critical import that one understand and familiarize himself with the details of how pots may be moved around the *blech* in a permissible fashion.

Foods that were left on the *blech* before Shabbos in a non-*yad soledes bo* area may not be moved into the *yad soledes bo* area on Shabbos. Since at the onset of Shabbos they were found in an area not suitable for cooking, moving them to the *yad soledes bo* part of the *blech* would be akin to placing them on the flame for the first time on Shabbos — something that is certainly forbidden.

Fully cooked foods that were left in the *yad soledes bo* zone before Shabbos may be moved to an area directly above the flame on Shabbos.

Cooked foods that were left directly above the flame, or within the *yad soledes bo* area before Shabbos, and were subsequently moved to the non-*yad soledes bo* area during Shabbos, may be returned to the *yad soledes bo* area, as well as to the area directly above the flame, on Shabbos, as long as they are still warm.

A CLOSER LOOK AT THE SIDDUR

Let us continue our study of the central blessing of the Friday night *Shemoneh Esrei.*

After describing the Sabbath as the culmination of Creation, we continue with the phrase, וּבֵרַכְתּוֹ מִכָּל הַיָּמִים וְקִדַּשְׁתּוֹ מִכָּל הַזְּמַנִּים וְכֵן כָּתוּב בְּתוֹרָתֶךָ, *and He blessed it of all the days, and sanctified it of all the times — and so it is written in Your Torah.* This is a reference to the verse (*Bereishis* 2:3, which we recite both in *Shemoneh Esrei* and in the Friday night *Kiddush*) which speaks of Hashem's sanctifying of the first Sabbath, upon the conclusion of Creation: *And HASHEM blessed the seventh day, and He sanctified it.*

Rashi (ibid.) explains that both the *blessing* and the *sanctification* mentioned here refer to the miracle of the manna, which fed the Jews in the Wilderness after they left Egypt. The manna fell every weekday morning, but on Friday, a double portion fell, and on the Sabbath, none fell at all. *Rashi* explains that Hashem *blessed* the Sabbath by assuring that whatever was needed for the Sabbath was provided on the previous day, and *sanctified* the Sabbath by stopping the flow of manna on the Sabbath day.

Ohr HaChaim (ibid.) notes that the way of the world requires us to labor to attain our physical needs, but on the Sabbath, we are commanded to refrain from such labor. Yet, we are commanded to eat three festive meals on the Sabbath, and honor it with fine foods and delicacies. Although this seems to be counterintuitive, it is not. Hashem *blessed* the Sabbath with abundance, and assured us that He will provide that which is necessary for the Sabbath, as he did with the manna in the Wilderness. [Indeed, the Gemara in *Beitzah* (16a) tells us that money one spends to honor the Sabbath does not come from the income granted him each year on Rosh Hashanah; Hashem ensures that one is compensated for any extra expenditure.] Moreover, Hashem *sanctified* the Sabbath, making it a time where mundane considerations of one's livelihood should not take center stage. Rather, the Sabbath is a spiritual time, allowing us to bask in Hashem's closeness. Thus, far from being a liability to our work, the sanctity of the Sabbath is actually the source from which we can draw blessing for success in our activities during the weekdays.

[It is noteworthy that our prayer speaks of the Sabbath being blessed of all *days,* and being sanctified above all *times* (זְמַנִּים) — a distinction that is not found in the verse cited. *Shiras David* sees this as an allusion to the fact that Sabbath is more sanctified than even the festivals (which

are called זְמַנִּים, *times,* because the dates on which they would actually fall were fixed by the Jewish courts, before the advent of the fixed calendar we follow today). Indeed, there is a Midrashic view that it was only on the Sabbath that the manna did not descend, but that it indeed did fall on the festivals (see *Tosafos* to *Beitzah* 2b, who records a dispute between Midrashim regarding this).]

QUESTION OF THE DAY:

Why did the brothers tear their clothes when the goblet was found in Binyamin's sack?

For the answer, see page 109.

ANSWERS TO QUESTIONS OF THE DAY

Sunday:

Ohr HaChaim explains that Yosef told Pharaoh that the only reason he was shown the future was so that he would be able to prevent disaster by appointing an overseer. Thus, the suggestion was part of the interpretation of the dreams.

Monday:

In *Megillas Esther* (4:2) we are told that Esther sent Mordechai proper clothing to wear *for it was forbidden to enter the King's gate while wearing sackcloth.* (See *Sforno* to *Bereishis* 41:14.)

Tuesday:

Each of the brothers entered through a different gate. The commentators offer several reasons — so they would not be subject to an *ayin hara,* so they could search for Yosef, or so that they would be able to buy food separately and thus come away with more.

Wednesday:

The name literally means "revealer of hidden things," and testified to Yosef's ability to interpret dreams. [This name change also helped to hide Yosef's true identity from his brothers — for no one knew him as Yosef (*Zohar*).]

Thursday:

These words were meant to reassure Yaakov that Yehudah would return Binyamin *alive,* and capable of standing up on his own two feet.

Friday:

Moshav Zekeinim suggests that since Binyamin had not taken the goblet, and knew nothing of it, it was not considered to be *with him,* and therefore the curse did not apply to him.

Shabbos:

The Midrash states that they were being punished measure for measure with having to rend their garments, because they were responsible for Yaakov's tearing his clothes in grief when he was shown Yosef's cloak and asked to identify it.

פרשת ויגש

Parashas Vayigash

A TORAH THOUGHT FOR THE DAY

וַיֹּאמֶר יוֹסֵף אֶל־אֶחָיו אֲנִי יוֹסֵף הַעוֹד אָבִי חָי
וְלֹא־יָכְלוּ אֶחָיו לַעֲנוֹת אֹתוֹ כִּי נִבְהֲלוּ מִפָּנָיו

And Yosef said to his brothers, "I am Yosef! Is my father still alive?" And his brothers were unable to answer him, for they were astounded before him (*Bereishis* 45:3).

Yosef's question is somewhat difficult to understand. The entire discussion he had just had with Yehudah centered around the danger to Yaakov that would result if Binyamin were not returned safely — obviously, then, Yaakov was alive! Moreover, as soon as the brothers had descended to Egypt the second time, Yosef had inquired after his father's welfare — and the brothers obviously had not seen Yaakov since then. What new information did Yosef seek to elicit from his brothers? And finally, we never find an answer to this question in the verse. If the question was so important, why was no answer recorded?

Beis HaLevi explains that Yosef's declaration was in truth not a question that required an answer, but rather a reproof. In this vein, he cites the famous Midrash that states regarding Yosef's comment: " 'Woe is to us from the Day of Judgment. Woe is to us from the Day of Reproof!' If Yosef, who was of the youngest of the tribes, offered reproof to his brothers and they were unable to answer, when Hashem reproves each of us according to our deeds, how much more so will we be unable to answer!" Now, where do we find that Yosef reproved his brothers? The only thing he said to them was, "I am Yosef — is my father still alive?" But in truth, this was the most compelling reproof possible. Yosef said to his brothers, "You tell me that that you must return with Binyamin because you are concerned for Yaakov's well-being. And why were you not concerned when you took me and sold me as a slave? Has he managed to survive that grief? Then he can survive this as well!" This exposure of the brothers' hypocrisy left them with no answer to Yosef, as their own actions proved that they had no defense against his accusation.

This, continues *Beis HaLevi,* is why the Midrash tells us that we must be so fearful of the Day of Judgment. Hashem will deal with each of us in the same way that Yosef dealt with his brothers, by pointing out the inherent hypocrisy *in our own actions.* For example — a person will come before the Heavenly Court, and the accuser will charge that he did not give sufficient charity. The person will attempt to defend himself by claiming that it was difficult to earn a living, and he gave as much as he could — a defense that should at least mitigate the offense. [*Beis HaLevi* points out, however, that this defense is not a perfect one, because the Gemara in *Gittin* (7a) advises someone having difficulty in earning a livelihood to *increase* his charity, rather than decrease it.] But Hashem will confront the accused, and provide him with a list of all the worthless items that he *did* spend money to acquire, and ask, "If you could afford those items, could you have not given more charity?" And there will be no answer . . .

This is what the Midrash means when it says that Hashem will reprove each person *according to his deeds.* Our own lives will provide the truth about what we really think and how we make our decisions; and we will be responsible for our actions.

For another explanation of the nature of Yosef's reproof, see *A Mussar Thought for the Day.*

MISHNAH OF THE DAY: SHABBOS 11:4

The following Mishnah discusses the status of various bodies of water with regard to the forbidden labor of transferring:

הַזּוֹרֵק בַּיָּם אַרְבַּע אַמּוֹת פָּטוּר — ***One who throws*** an object ***four amos [cubits] in the sea is exempt*** from liability to a *chatas.*[1] **אִם הָיָה רְקָק מַיִם וּרְשׁוּת הָרַבִּים מְהַלֶּכֶת בּוֹ** — But ***if there was a puddle of muddy water with the public domain passing through it,***[2] **הַזּוֹרֵק לְתוֹכוֹ**

NOTES

1. Our Mishnah teaches that a sea cannot be considered a public domain, no matter how many people travel upon it. Since travel on the sea is difficult in comparison to a road, it cannot be considered a public domain (*Magen Avraham* 345:11, based on *Eruvin* 22b).

Moreover, although the sea is more than 10 *tefachim* deep and surrounded by banks or shorelines, it is not considered a private domain. *Meiri* explains that this is because an area as vast as a sea cannot be considered enclosed, even if the banks are sufficiently steep to create a private domain. This follows the opinion of *Ritva* (in the name of *Ramban, Eruvin* 22b) that walls only enclose an area and render it a private domain if a person standing between them *realizes* that he is in an enclosure. Once walls enclose so vast an area that a person no longer perceives himself as being enclosed, the walls are disregarded (see *Mishnah Berurah* 345:48 and *Beur Halachah* 346:1,3; cf. *Magen Avraham* 345:14). Hence, the sea's status is that of a *karmelis* — an area that is neither a private domain nor a public domain. Therefore, throwing an object 4 *amos* in the sea (or transferring from sea to shore or vice versa — see next Mishnah) is forbidden only by Rabbinic decree.

2. I.e., people, while traveling through the public domain, go through this puddle (*Rav; Rambam Commentary; Rashi* to 8b and 100b). [Though this rule is true for any type of water, the Tanna refers to a puddle of muddy water because that is the normal condition of a body of water found in the middle of a street (*Tiferes Yisrael*).]

אַרְבַּע אַמּוֹת חַיָּיב — *one who throws* an object a distance of *four amos in it is liable,* because the pool is considered part of the public domain.[3] וְכַמָּה הוּא רְקַק מַיִם — *And how much is a shallow puddle?* I.e., how deep can it be and still be a public domain? פָּחוֹת מֵעֲשָׂרָה טְפָחִים — *Less than ten tefachim* deep.[4] רְקַק מַיִם וּרְשׁוּת הָרַבִּים מְהַלֶּכֶת בּוֹ — *A shallow puddle of water through which the public domain passes,* הַזּוֹרֵק בְּתוֹכוֹ אַרְבַּע אַמּוֹת חַיָּיב — *one who throws* an object a distance of *four amos into it is liable.*[5]

NOTES

3. Since the puddle does not interrupt the flow of traffic, it too is regarded as part of the public domain (Gemara 100b).

4. Only if the puddle is less than 10 *tefachim* deep is it considered a public domain. However, if the water is 10 *tefachim* deep, its status is the same as the sea — viz., a *karmelis* — and a person who throws an object a distance of 4 *amos* in it is not liable to a *chatas* (*Rambam, Hil. Shabbos* 14:24).

5. Although this ruling is identical to the one stated earlier in the Mishnah, the Gemara (100b) explains that the repetition is added to teach one of several lessons. Two of the lessons are: (1) that even if the puddle is wider than 4 *amos,* making traveling through it more cumbersome than going around it, it is nevertheless still considered a part of the public domain, since people do travel through it; (2) that even if the puddle is narrow, and many people skip over it rather than walk through it, it is still a public domain, since some people do walk through it.

GEMS FROM THE GEMARA

Our Mishnah continues the discussion of the Biblical prohibition against transferring an object 4 *amos* in the public domain. The Gemara concluded earlier that the prohibition was given verbally to Moses at Mt. Sinai (see *Gems from the Gemara* to the previous Mishnah), and now (96b) discusses a Biblical passage that might deal with a violation of this prohibition. *Numbers* 15:32-36 records the incident of the person who was executed for "gathering wood on the Sabbath day," but does not identify which forbidden labor he performed in the course of his gathering of the wood. Rav Yehudah says in the name of Shmuel that the man had neither detached the wood from its source of growth [which would have constituted קוֹצֵר, *harvesting*] nor had he literally "gathered" it into a bundle [which would have constituted מְעַמֵּר, *gathering together*], but he had simply lifted a pile of detached wood and carried it 4 *amos* in the public domain (see *Rashi*). The Gemara also presents other explanations of the precise *melachah* violated by the gatherer.

The Gemara then digresses to a discussion concerning the identity of the gatherer, and cites a Baraisa presenting the view of R' Akiva — that the gatherer was Tzelophchad [a Jew who died during the sojourn in the Wilderness and was inherited by his five daughters (see *Numbers* 26:23,27:1 ff.)]. Although the Torah does not identify him explicitly, R' Akiva establishes his identity through the derivation of a *gezeirah shavah.* The Gemara then cites the continuation of the Baraisa, in which R' Yehudah ben Beseira rebukes R' Akiva, saying: "Akiva! Either way you are destined to give an accounting for what you have just expounded! If it is indeed true, as you state, that the gatherer was Tzelophchad, you have sinned, because the Torah concealed his identity and you reveal it! And if you are not correct in your identification of Tzelophchad as the gatherer, then you are guilty of maligning that righteous man!"

[It should be noted however, that according to *Tosafos* (*Bava Basra* 119b), Tzelophchad was a righteous man, who willingly martyred himself by desecrating the Sabbath, to demonstrate to the Jews that even those condemned to remain in the Wilderness for the rest of their lives after the sin of the *meraglim* (Spies) were still obligated to keep the laws of the Torah.]

A MUSSAR THOUGHT FOR THE DAY

R' *Chaim Shmulevitz,* in his *Sichos Mussar* (5732:13), also cites the Midrash (from the version found in *Yalkut*) that warns that we will be unable to reply to Heavenly reproof, just as Yosef's brothers had no response to him. However, while *Beis HaLevi* sees the key to Yosef's reproof in the words, *"Is my father still alive?,"* R' Chaim says that the reproof was actually just the words, "*I am Yosef*!"

What was the shattering reproof contained in this declaration? R' Chaim, in explaining, makes the point that the essence of reproof is not criticizing a person — it is simply making a person see the mistake he has made. And, once a person understands that he was mistaken, he has accepted the reproof.

When Yosef said to his brothers, "I am Yosef," he meant: I am your younger brother, whom you sold into slavery. And now I stand before you as a royal viceroy, ruler over all of Egypt, in fulfillment of all the dreams that I dreamed. You sold me so that the dreams would *not* be fulfilled (see *Bereishis* 37:20, where the brothers said: *let us kill him . . . and we will see what will become of his dreams!*). And yet, what happened was the exact opposite — your selling me *brought about* the fulfillment of those dreams. This should prove to you how wrong you were in your judgment of me — I was not simply "a dreamer" (see ibid. v. 19). And just as you misjudged my dreams, you misjudged me as well, for I never bore you any ill will. And the holy *shevatim,* confronted with the sudden realization that their entire treatment of Yosef had been based on a terrible misjudgment, had no reply.

The Midrash tells us that this is the scenario that awaits us on the Day of Judgment. Many times a person will perform an action or make a statement that he himself knows is questionable or even somewhat dubious, and he will justify it by reasoning that the end justifies the means. But what will happen when Hashem shows him that the end he has been striving to achieve is built on error, and he has no basis to justify those statements and deeds? He will be filled with shame and remorse, without answer before the Heavenly Court.

[R' Chaim adds that a person can escape this pitfall by always remembering that it is not his job to bring about desired ends by improper means — Hashem has the ability to bring about whatever ends He desires *without* needing people to do the wrong thing to make these come about. Thus, every action should be judged on its own merits, and if it is incorrect it must be avoided.]

HALACHAH OF THE DAY

We have learned previously that stirring the not-yet-fully cooked contents of a pot is a violation of the *melachah* of *bishul.* The reason we gave for this ruling is that stirring tends to accelerate the cooking process, and is therefore a forbidden activity on Shabbos.

The prohibition against stirring extends as well to fully cooked foods that are located directly over the flame. Accordingly, one may not stir any food — fully cooked or not — located directly over the flame, even if the flame is covered by a *blech.*

The commentators advance several reasons to explain why the prohibition against stirring applies even to foods that are fully cooked. One explanation is that some ingredients, while appearing to be fully cooked, may have actually clumped together, so that their centers have not yet been exposed to the heat. By stirring the contents of the pot, the clumps may be broken apart, resulting in these parts of the food becoming cooked for the first time. Another explanation is that since it may not always be easy to discern whether the contents of a pot are indeed fully cooked, the Sages decided to prohibit even the stirring of a fully cooked pot, in order to insure that one will not inadvertently stir foods that have not yet become fully cooked, and thus violate the Biblical prohibition of *bishul.*

There is, however, a halachic difference between stirring fully cooked foods and stirring foods that are not yet fully cooked. Foods that are not yet fully cooked may not be stirred even after they have been removed from the *blech,* as long as they remain heated to the level of *yad soledes bo.* The prohibition against stirring fully cooked foods extends only to food that is directly over a flame. If the pot is lifted off the flame, or even if the pot is moved to a portion of the *blech* not located directly over the flame, the cooked food may be stirred.

Water and other pure liquids that have been fully cooked are exempted from this prohibition. Thus, if these liquids were boiled, they may be stirred even while over a flame, as long as they remain warm. Once they have cooled, however, these liquids are once again subject to all the restrictions of *bishul,* and may no longer be stirred.

A CLOSER LOOK AT THE SIDDUR

This week, we will continue to discuss the eighth of the Thirteen Fundamental Principles (י״ג עיקרים) enumerated by *Rambam,* which states:

> אֲנִי מַאֲמִין בֶּאֱמוּנָה שְׁלֵמָה שֶׁכָּל הַתּוֹרָה הַמְּצוּיָה עַתָּה בְּיָדֵינוּ הִיא הַנְּתוּנָה לְמֹשֶׁה רַבֵּנוּ עָלָיו הַשָּׁלוֹם.
>
> *I believe with perfect faith that the entire Torah now in our hands is the same one that was given to Moshe, our Teacher, peace be upon him.*

This week, we will address the second point inherent in this principle: that the Torah was transmitted faithfully through the generations, from Sinai to this very day. This truth is a necessary complement to the first point, which we discussed last week — that all of the Torah was given to us by Hashem. For of what value would it be to believe that the Torah was God-given, if we did not know that the God-given Torah had survived to be passed down to us? Obviously then, the belief that the Torah we now possess is the original Torah given to Moshe is fundamental to our faith.

It must be stressed that we do not claim that the Torah was given to a single man in an unwitnessed Divine or prophetic revelation, as is the case with other faiths; there were *millions of people* present when Hashem gave us the Torah, and Moshe taught the Torah to *all* of Israel. Hundreds of thousands of fathers told their children of the miraculous events at Sinai, and the laws and precepts of the Torah were passed down through the ages in an unbroken chain of *mesorah* forged by generations of Jews to whom the Torah was life itself. Thus, we *know* that the Torah we now possess is the same Torah that was given at Sinai — for it has never passed out of our hands, never fallen into disuse. It is not an antique, a relic, or a curiosity — it is the soul of the Jewish nation, by which we live and endure.

This is true not only of the Written Torah, but of the Oral Torah as well. The two are inseparable — for many of the commandments of the Written Torah lack definition without the clarification of the Oral Law. The details of such precepts as *shechitah* (ritual slaughter) or *milah* (circumcision) are not spelled out in the Written Torah; we require the elucidation of the Written Torah to explain them. And these explanations, too, were given to Moshe at Sinai.

QUESTION OF THE DAY:

Why, when stating "I am Yosef!" for a second time (45:4), did Yosef add the words, "your brother"?

For the answer, see page 168.

A TORAH THOUGHT FOR THE DAY

וַיִּפֹּל עַל־צַוְּארֵי בִנְיָמִן־אָחִיו וַיֵּבְךְּ וּבִנְיָמִן בָּכָה עַל־צַוָּארָיו
Then he fell upon his brother Binyamin's neck and wept; and Binyamin wept upon his neck (*Bereishis* 45:14).

This verse is stated immediately after Yosef had revealed his identity to the brothers, assuring them of his brotherly love, and offering them a safe and prosperous haven in Egypt.

Although one might easily interpret this sobbing as an outpouring of emotion at the conclusion of the emotional revelation, *Rashi* and *Targum Yonasan* say differently. They cite the Midrash stating that Yosef cried because he saw that in the future, both Temples, which would be built in the portion of Binyamin, would be destroyed. In like manner, Binyamin saw that the Mishkan Shiloh (the precursor of the Temple), which would be built on Yosef's territory, would be destroyed, and so he too cried.

Sifsei Chachamim explains that the word צַוָּאר is a symbol of the Temple, based on the verse in *Shir HaShirim* (7:5) that says: צַוָּארֵךְ כְּמִגְדַּל הַשֵּׁן, which is expounded as a reference to the Temple. By using the word צַוָּאר in this verse, as opposed to simply stating וַיֵּבְךְּ עֲלֵהֶם, *and he wept upon them,* as is stated (v. 15) when speaking of the brothers, the Torah indicates that a special message is to be derived.

One must ask why these visions of destruction descended upon Yosef and Binyamin at this juncture. The *Peirush Yonasan* (on *Targum Yonasan ben Uziel*) maintains that since Yosef was engaged in relocating his father and family to Egypt, and saw with *ruach hakodesh* that they would ultimately be enslaved there (see *Targum Yonasan* to v. 15), he projected further into the future and saw the later exiles as well. The tragic destruction of the Temples, as the prelude to those exiles, caused Yosef to cry.

The *Ksav Sofer* explains this Midrash as the culmination of Yosef's monologue, rather than an interjection. Upon reflection, he says, one can see that the source of the dispute between Yosef and his brothers arose from Yosef having related to Yaakov those actions of his brothers which he had considered sinful. They perceived his "tattling" as hatred for them, and a conspiracy to cause a rift between them and their father, while enhancing his own status with Yaakov. Yosef's intentions, however, were honorable, as he sought to have their father admonish them and have them cease that behavior.

One of the main purposes of Yosef's narrative, says *Ksav Sofer,* was to demonstrate to the brothers, and have them recognize, their fallacy.

According to this approach, when Yosef said, *"I am Yosef your brother — it is I, whom you sold into Egypt"* (v. 4), this is not a reprimand, but a proof that he did not hate his brothers. Yosef said, "Do you think that I wanted to remain in Egypt, and did not wish to send a message to my father to rescue me? And if you will say that during my tenure as a slave I could not do so, surely since the time I became viceroy, I could have done so. And should you think that I no longer remember the language (of Hebrew — see *Rashi* to v. 12), *Your eyes see . . . that it is my mouth that is speaking to you.*" Thus, Yosef showed the brothers that it was only because he did not want his father to know of their deed, which would cause lasting animosity between them, that he did not notify Yaakov. And if he bore them no grudge after the sale, he certainly acted only with brotherly interest and care before the sale! Citing the Gemara (*Yerushalmi Yoma* 1:1) that states that the Temple was destroyed because of unwarranted hatred, *Ksav Sofer* highlights that Binyamin merited having the Temple built on his portion because he did not participate nor have knowledge of the sale of Yosef; and Yosef, too, had proven that he was innocent of any hatred or malice toward his brothers. But they both saw with Divine vision that this characteristic of *sinas chinam* would ultimately destroy the Temples erected on each other's soil, and so they cried.

MISHNAH OF THE DAY: SHABBOS 11:5

The following Mishnah continues the previous Mishnah's discussion of the status of the sea:

הַזּוֹרֵק מִן הַיָּם לַיַּבָּשָׁה וּמִן הַיַּבָּשָׁה לַיָּם — ***One who throws*** an object ***from the sea to the dry land or from the dry land to the sea,*** **וּמִן הַיָּם לַסְּפִינָה וּמִן הַסְּפִינָה לַיָּם** — ***or from the sea to a ship or from a ship to the sea,*** **וּמִן הַסְּפִינָה לַחֲבֵירְתָּהּ** — ***or from one ship to another,*** **פָּטוּר** — ***is exempt*** from liability to a *chatas.*[1] **סְפִינוֹת קְשׁוּרוֹת זוֹ בָּזוֹ** — In the case of ***ships that are tied together*** without any gap between them,

NOTES

1. As we saw in the previous Mishnah, the sea is a *karmelis.* Thus, even if the land along the shore is a public domain, one who transfers an item from the sea to the shore has transferred only between a *karmelis* and a public domain, for which there is no *chatas* liability. Similarly, although a ship is a private domain (see *Eruvin* 90a,b with *Rashi* and *Tosafos*), one is not liable for transferring between a *karmelis* and a private domain (see *Rav; Rashi; Meiri*). And one is certainly not liable for transferring from one private domain to another (ship to ship).

מְטַלְטְלִין מִזּוֹ לָזוֹ — *we may carry* objects *from this* ship *to that* ship.[2] אִם אֵינָן קְשׁוּרוֹת — But *if they are not tied* together, אַף עַל פִּי שֶׁמּוּקָפוֹת — *even though they are close* together, with no gap between them, אֵין מְטַלְטְלִין מִזּוֹ לָזוֹ — *we may not carry* objects *from this* ship *to that* ship.[3]

NOTES

2. Even if the two ships belong to two different people, they may carry from one to the other by making *eruvei chatzeiros* [a legal procedure that unites the private domains of two or more individuals and permits taking objects from one domain to the other domain on Shabbos, which would otherwise be forbidden by Rabbinic decree]. Although we know from elsewhere that *eruvei chatzeiros* unite separate private domains, the Tanna feels it necessary to teach us that even two private domains such as ships that are not permanently established in one place, also may be united through *eruvei chatzeiros* (*Tosafos* to 101b).

3. *Eruvei chatzeiros* are valid only if the private domains to be united are next to each other with a doorway or window between them, or if they are connected by some passageway which is itself a private domain (*Shulchan Aruch* 372:4). If they are separated by any other domain, they cannot be united for the purposes of passing or throwing from one to another. If the ships are not bound together, they are apt to spread apart, creating a gap of a *karmelis* (i.e., the sea) between them, and thereby invalidating the *eruv*. The Rabbis therefore forbade making an *eruv* between ships that are not tied together (*Rav* from Gemara 10b).

GEMS FROM THE GEMARA

The Mishnah taught that when two ships are tied together, one may carry objects from one ship to the other on the Sabbath. The Gemara (101b) asks: Isn't this obvious? Since the ships are tied, and thus cannot drift apart, why would one not be permitted to carry between them?

Rava answers that this ruling was needed only to permit carrying between the ships by way of a small boat that is wedged between them. The novelty of this ruling lies in the fact that although the boat could conceivably slip from between the ships, and carrying between them would then be prohibited, one is nonetheless permitted to carry between them as long as the boat is there.

However, Rav Safra questioned Rava: The language of the Mishnah indicates that one may carry objects from *this* ship to *that* ship. This wording implies that the Mishnah speaks of a direct transfer between one ship and the other, and *not* one in which the person must first go across a third boat! [Rav Safra holds that Rava's explanation does not fit well with the Mishnah's wording. He therefore explains the Mishnah differently, as we shall see below. However, Rav Safra does not dispute the truth of Rava's ruling, but agrees that one may carry from one ship to another by way of a small boat that is wedged between them, and we would not be concerned that the small boat might become loose (*Rashi*).]

Rav Safra therefore explains the Mishnah's ruling differently, in the manner that we presented in the Mishnah. According to Rav Safra, this ruling was needed only to teach that even in a case of ships that have two different owners, it is permitted to carry from one ship to the other, as long as the owners have joined their domains through the mechanism of *eruvei chatzeiros.* The novelty of the Mishnah's ruling is that even ships are included in the law of *eruvei chatzeiros.*

A MUSSAR THOUGHT FOR THE DAY

In the course of his elaborate exposition on the passage of Yosef's revelation of his identity to his brothers, *Ksav Sofer* quotes the Gemara (*Bava Basra* 10a) that states: גְּדוֹלָה צְדָקָה שֶׁמְּקָרֶבֶת אֶת הַגְּאוּלָּה, *charity is great, because it brings the redemption closer,* and cites as a Scriptural source the verse (*Yeshayah* 56:1): שִׁמְרוּ מִשְׁפָּט וַעֲשׂוּ צְדָקָה כִּי־קְרוֹבָה יְשׁוּעָתִי לָבוֹא וְצִדְקָתִי לְהִגָּלוֹת, *Observe justice and perform righteousness, for My salvation is soon to come and My righteousness to be revealed. Ksav Sofer* ponders why this is so. It is certain that charity is a great mitzvah, and in its merit one is saved from death, as the Gemara (ibid.) states, but what is its relationship to redemption? What element of charity serves to bring the redemption closer?

He answers by citing two Gemaras (one from *Yerushalmi* and the other from *Bavli*) that discuss the reasons for the destruction of the *Beis HaMikdash.* In *Yerushalmi* (*Yoma* 1:1) the Gemara says that the *Churban* (Destruction) was caused by *sinas chinam,* baseless hatred, whereas the Gemara in *Shabbos* (49b) states that it occurred because the people did not admonish one another for the sins that they committed. In explaining this statement, the Gemara likens the people who lived during the time of the Destruction to harts, and says, "Just as the hart walks in a herd with the head of this one next to the tail of that one, so too did the Israelites of that generation bury their faces in the ground, to avoid seeing the wrongdoing around them — and they did not admonish one another."

The fundamental flaw highlighted in both these Gemaras, explains *Ksav Sofer,* is a breakdown in the feeling of *achdus,* unity, that must always exist between the members of society. If each person sees himself as a separate entity rather than as part of a whole, he will adopt a "live and let live" approach to the actions and behavior of others, and can conclude that there is no reason to expend time or effort in their rehabilitation. In the same vein, anyone receiving a reprimand from his fellow will not be interested in heeding it, arguing that his actions are nobody's affair but his own.

If, however, there is a feeling of comradeship and togetherness, every person would be anxious to help his friend to avoid sinning, or to repent from his misdeeds, and the recipient of that aid would be grateful, and more likely to accept reproof.

Charity and acts of benevolence toward others exhibit in a concrete way one's attachment to his fellow. In showing concern and sharing wealth (or knowledge or any other asset) one bridges the gulf of separateness between himself and his fellow. As the underlying reason for the exile was the disunity and disinterest that was exhibited, the feeling of fellowship and togetherness will certainly hasten the redemption.

HALACHAH OF THE DAY

Scooping food from a pot is also a form of stirring. This is because each time a spoon is inserted into the pot for the purpose of removing some of its contents, some of the food is inevitably moved around and stirred. For this reason, one may not scoop out food from a pot on a *blech* that is directly over a flame on Shabbos — even if the contents of the pot are already fully cooked. If one desires to remove food from a pot on a *blech* that is located over a flame, he must first either lift the pot off the flame or relocate it to an area of the *blech* that is not directly over the flame.

To illustrate: If one wishes to serve *cholent* on Friday night, he may not spoon it out of the pot while it is directly over the flame. The proper procedure for serving it depends on the location of the *cholent* pot. If the *cholent* is already fully cooked and is located on the *blech* directly over the flame, the pot must first be relocated to an area of the *blech* that is not directly over the flame. After moving the pot, one may serve out the desired portions of *cholent,* and then return the pot to the area above the flame, provided that the contents of the pot are still warm.

If the *cholent* pot is located in or on a crockpot, the pot must be lifted off the heating source in order to serve the *cholent* from the pot. In these cases, lifting the pot allows one to scoop out *cholent* from the pot. However, returning the pot to the flame is now potentially problematic since this would be subject to the restrictions of חֲזָרָה, *returning [an item to the flame],* which we will discuss below. There are certain cases in which it would not be permissible to return a pot to the flame once it has been removed. In these cases, fully cooked foods may be scooped from the pot while directly above the flame, even though stirring is still prohibited.

For example, if one left his *cholent* pot directly above an open *uncovered* flame before Shabbos, lifting the pot from the flame to serve some *cholent* on Friday night would not be an option, since in keeping with the restrictions of *returning* he would not be permitted to return the pot to the flame. Therefore, in such a case, one may scoop the food from the pot while it remains on the flame, provided that the food is already fully cooked. The same ruling would apply to a pot that is simply too heavy to be lifted. In such cases, one should exercise care not to stir the contents of the pot while removing the food, if at all possible.

It is important to note once again that the above rulings apply only to fully cooked foods. If the food is not yet fully cooked, it is forbidden to remove any of the contents of the pot, since by doing so the cooking of the remaining food will be accelerated.

A CLOSER LOOK AT THE SIDDUR

Tehillim 133:1 is one of the verses that describes how beautiful is the harmony between the various parts of the Jewish nation. It states: הִנֵּה מַה־טּוֹב וּמַה־נָּעִים שֶׁבֶת אַחִים גַּם־יָחַד, *Behold, how good and how pleasant is the dwelling of brothers, especially in unity.*

This is the first verse of the fourteenth psalm in the series of *Shir HaMaalos,* which are recited after the *Minchah* service on Shabbos.

Rashi describes this idyllic scene as occurring when Hashem is residing in the Temple together with Israel. The verse is to be understood as follows: The Jews, who are called אַחִים, *brothers* and comrades, will be in the Temple, and Hashem will *also* (from the word גַּם) be with them. The psalm continues, relating that just as the precious oil used for anointing Aharon, the Kohen Gadol, was a symbol of greatness, so too will the dew of Mt. Hermon flowing onto Mt. Zion be a symbol of honor and majesty for the nation, *for there HASHEM has commanded the blessing.*

Based on the Gemara's interpretation that the "brothers" in the verse refers to Aharon and Moshe, *Radak* explains that the verse is alluding to the two main leaders of national life — the anointed king, who will preside over matters of the realm and justice, and the Kohen Gadol, who will be the primary teacher of Torah and mitzvos. The verse is saying how good it will be when they each rule over their own domain without jealousy.

In a similar vein, *Meiri* describes how the fulfillment of Jewish destiny requires two branches — *Kehunah* (Priesthood) and *Malchus* (Kingship). When the Kohen Gadol will take his rightful place, his spiritual teachings will be *like the precious oil upon the head running down upon the beard . . . running down over his garments* (v. 2), i.e., they will permeate the whole nation. Nevertheless, one will need the steady sustenance of the dew, represented by the king, who will administer a fair and deliberate judicial system. This is signified by the verse (v. 5): *So the dew of Hermon descends upon the mountains of Zion, for there HASHEM has commanded the blessing.*

Malbim interprets the psalm as alluding to the renowned brothers, Yissachar and Zevulun, who forged a partnership of body and soul. By forming a partnership whereby Yissachar studied Torah, while Zevulun engaged in commerce, they each had a share in the true טוֹב, merits for the World to Come, and נְעִימוּת, the pleasantness of this world.

Elaborating on the complementary and symbiotic relationship between Yissachar and Zevulun, *Malbim* explains that the "oil upon the head," referring to the world of intellect, knowledge and everlasting life — which was Yissachar's — flowed down to affect and elevate Zevulun as well. Zevulun's success, however, represented by the bounty brought by the "dew of Hermon," signifies the fleeting needs of this world. This bounty, the verse says, comes to Zevulun because of "the mountains of Zion (Yissachar), for there Hashem has commanded the blessing." Nevertheless, their partnership is equal, and is deemed "good and pleasant."

QUESTION OF THE DAY:

Why did Yosef cry upon the necks of all of his brothers?

For the answer, see page 168.

A TORAH THOUGHT FOR THE DAY

וַיָּפָג לִבּוֹ כִּי לֹא־הֶאֱמִין לָהֶם. וַיְדַבְּרוּ אֵלָיו אֵת כָּל־דִּבְרֵי יוֹסֵף אֲשֶׁר דִּבֶּר אֲלֵהֶם וַיַּרְא אֶת־הָעֲגָלוֹת אֲשֶׁר־שָׁלַח יוֹסֵף לָשֵׂאת אֹתוֹ וַתְּחִי רוּחַ יַעֲקֹב אֲבִיהֶם

And [Yaakov's] heart rejected it, for he could not believe them. However, when they related to him all the words that Joseph had spoken to them, and he saw the wagons (עֲגָלוֹת) *that Joseph had sent to transport him, the spirit of their father Yaakov was revived* (*Bereishis* 45:26,27).

It appears from this passage that the brothers spoke to Yaakov in an attempt to convince him that they were telling the truth about Yosef being alive. Why then does the verse interject the seemingly irrelevant fact that "he saw the *agalos* (wagons)" before telling us that the spirit of their father was revived? *Rashi* explains, based on a Midrash, that the "words of Yosef" refer to a message that Yosef wished to convey to Yaakov — a message that was alluded to by the *agalos.* Yosef reminded Yaakov that the last subject they had studied together was the laws of the *eglah arufah* (a calf whose neck is broken as atonement for an unsolved murder). Since only Yosef could have known this, the mention of *agalos* persuaded Yaakov that the brothers were telling the truth.

Kli Yakar rejects this approach, maintaining that it is too far removed from the simple meaning of the text, which states clearly that Yosef sent *agalos* to transport Yaakov to Egypt. He therefore understands the Midrash to be saying that Yaakov divined the truth by seeing the wagons that *Yosef sent* — that is, he saw that Yosef, and not Pharaoh, had sent them. According to *Kli Yakar,* the Midrash infers from the word שָׁלַח not only that Yosef sent the wagons, but that he escorted them as well. Undoubtedly, says *Kli Yakar,* Yaakov explained to Yosef that the refined characteristic of escorting someone is a lesson taught by the mitzvah of עֶגְלָה עֲרוּפָה, where the elders of the city near which the homicide was discovered must proclaim, "Our hands did not spill this blood." *Rashi* there cites the Gemara which asks incredulously, "Would it occur to anyone that the elders of the court are murderers?" The Gemara answers that they must proclaim that they were not negligent by not feeding the victim nor escorting him on his journey. When the brothers told Yaakov that Yosef had escorted them (and the wagons), he understood that Yosef was alive, for only he, and no Egyptian, would exhibit this refined trait.

Kli Yakar adds another point to this exposition to explain why, immediately after Yaakov sees the wagons, the verse concludes with the dramatic phrase, *the spirit of their father Yaakov was revived.* He says that even a non-Jewish societal norm might require that someone leaving a city be escorted, either to protect him from highwaymen, or at least to instill fear in any lurking bandits. This is true, however, only where there may truly be danger. In Egypt, however, all of the wagons were under the auspices of the king, and therefore nobody would attack or endanger them. It would then be unnecessary to escort the wagons for protection. When Yaakov heard that Yosef did escort the wagons, he understood that not only were the brothers telling the truth, but that Yosef did so because it is a mitzvah and an act of proper behavior. The realization that Yosef, after all his years in Egypt, still behaved out of Torah obligation and not just intelligence, produced the great feelings of joy characterized by the verse as וַתְּחִי רוּחַ יַעֲקֹב, *and the spirit of Yaakov was revived.*

MISHNAH OF THE DAY: SHABBOS 11:6

As we saw in the seventh chapter, one brings a *chatas* only for a שְׁגָגָה, *an inadvertent violation,* of a forbidden labor. The following Mishnah elaborates on the degree of inadvertence necessary to render one liable to a *chatas*:

הַזּוֹרֵק וְנִזְכַּר מֵאַחַר שֶׁיָּצְתָה מִיָּדוֹ — ***One who throws*** an object, intending to transfer it from one domain to another domain,[1] ***but*** then ***recalled*** that it was the Sabbath ***after it left his hand*** but before it landed, קְלָטָהּ אחר — or if ***another*** person ***caught it,***[2] קְלָטָהּ כֶּלֶב — or if ***a dog***

NOTES

1. I.e., a person forgot that it was the Sabbath, and threw something from a private domain to a public domain or vice versa (*Rav; Rashi*). This phrase serves as a preface to all the following cases (*Rav*).

2. This case is unrelated to the previous case (e.g., the person who recalled it was the Sabbath before the completion of the transfer). In this section, the Mishnah lists several possible exemptions for the act of throwing, all based on some unexpected development with respect to how the object came to a rest. In this case, someone else moved to the spot where the object was flying and intercepted it. Since he intercepted the object before it came to rest in the place where the thrower intended it to be, the labor is considered to have been completed by the second person. It is therefore deemed a forbidden labor performed by two people, for which both are exempt (*Tos. Yom Tov; Tiferes Yisrael* from *Rashi;* see above, 10:5, for explanation of this principle).

caught it,[3] אוֹ שֶׁנִּשְׂרְפָה — *or* if *it was burned* up while in midair,[4] פָּטוּר — if any of the above-mentioned possibilities occurred, the thrower ***is exempt*** from a *chatas.* זָרַק לַעֲשׂוֹת חַבּוּרָה — If ***one threw*** an object on the Sabbath in order ***to inflict a wound,*** בֵּין בָּאָדָם וּבֵין בַּבְּהֵמָה — ***upon either a person or an animal,*** וְנִזְכַּר עַד שֶׁלֹּא נַעֲשֵׂית חַבּוּרָה — ***but he*** then ***recalled*** that it was the Sabbath ***when the wound had not yet been inflicted,*** פָּטוּר — he ***is exempt*** from a *chatas.*[5]

זֶה הַכְּלָל — ***This is the general rule:*** כָּל חַיָּיבֵי חַטָּאוֹת אֵינָן חַיָּיבִין עַד שֶׁתְּהֵא תְחִלָּתָן וְסוֹפָן שְׁגָגָה — ***All who are liable to chatas-offerings are not liable unless*** both ***their commencements*** of the misdeeds ***and their completions*** of the misdeeds ***are inadvertent.*** תְּחִלָּתָן שְׁגָגָה וְסוֹפָן זָדוֹן — But if ***their commencements*** of the misdeeds ***were inadvertent, but their completions were deliberate,***[6] תְּחִילָּתָן זָדוֹן וְסוֹפָן שְׁגָגָה — or if ***their commencements*** of the misdeeds ***were deliberate but their completions were inadvertent,*** פְּטוּרִין — ***they are exempt*** from *chatas*-offerings עַד שֶׁתְּהֵא תְחִילָּתָן וְסוֹפָן שְׁגָגָה — ***unless*** both ***their commencements*** of the misdeeds ***and their completions*** of the misdeeds ***are inadvertent.***[7]

NOTES

3. Since a dog's mouth is not an area of 4 square *tefachim,* it does not meet the minimum size for a "place" for the object to be considered to have come to rest. Therefore, the person who threw the object is exempt from a *chatas* (*Tos. Yom Tov; Tiferes Yisrael* from *Rashi;* see Mishnah 1:1 and the first Mishnah in this chapter). Hence, even if the dog stood in its place and the object landed in its mouth, there is no liability (*Tiferes Yisrael*). However, if the one who threw the object *intended* to throw it into the dog's mouth, his intention to have it come to rest there imparts a status equivalent to a 4-square *tefachim* area to the dog's mouth, and he *is* liable (*Tos. Yom Tov* from Gemara 102a; see *Gems from the Gemara*).

4. Here too (as in the previous case), the object has come to "rest" on an area that is less than 4 square *tefachim* — viz., the flames into which the object fell.

5. Although inflicting a wound on the Sabbath is a forbidden labor, in this case the thrower is not liable to a *chatas.* For although the throwing of the object was done inadvertently, by the time the object hit its target, the thrower had become aware of the Sabbath and his violation of it, thus removing himself from the category of inadvertence and exempting himself from a *chatas.*

6. This clause of the general rule comes to add the case of one who carries a distance of 4 *amos* [cubits] in the public domain, who — while still carrying — recalls the Sabbath, yet continues to carry to the end of 4 *amos.* He is exempt from a *chatas* because the completion of the forbidden labor was not inadvertent (*Rav; Tiferes Yisrael*).

7. The repetition of this clause comes to teach that *only* the commencement and the completion of the act need be inadvertent. The recollection of the Sabbath in the *middle* of the act does not exempt one from a *chatas.* For example: One inadvertently threw an object intending that it land 6 *amos* away. However, after the object had traversed the first 2 *amos,* he recalled that it was the Sabbath. Then, after the object

NOTES

had traversed 2 more *amos*, he subsequently forgot that it was the Sabbath again, so that the last 2 *amos* of the flight were again inadvertent! In this case, since both the commencement and the completion of the act occurred during periods in which he was unaware of the Sabbath — and the distances traversed by the object during those periods add up to the 4 *amos* necessary for liability — he is liable to a *chatas* despite his passing recollection in the middle of the act (*Tos. Yom Tov; Shenos Eliyahu; Tiferes Yisrael*).

GEMS FROM THE GEMARA

In our Mishnah, we learned that if one throws an object that lands in a dog's mouth or in a fire, he is exempt. The Gemara explains that this is true only because the thrower did not intend for the object to land in those places. On the other hand, the Gemara (102a) cites Rava, who rules (as we noted in the Mishnah) that in a case in which the thrower *did* intend for the object to land in one of these places, the intended target attains the legal status of a surface that is actually 4 square *tefachim* in area, and the thrower is liable.

Rav Bivi bar Abaye cites a Mishnah in support of this principle. The Mishnah (*Kereisos* 3:4) states: *There is one who performs a single act of eating, and he is liable on account of it to four chatas-offerings and one asham-offering* [the *chatas* and *asham* are two different varieties of sin-offerings]. How so? If a *tamei* person [one who was ritually impure] inadvertently ate *cheilev* [forbidden fat], that was *nossar* [left over beyond the permitted time frame] from consecrated offerings, on Yom Kippur. [Such a person is liable to four *chatas*-offerings: one for eating *cheilev*, one for eating sacrificial meat while *tamei*, one for eating *nossar*, and one for eating on Yom Kippur. In addition, he must bring an *asham* for *me'ilah* — having unlawfully misused *hekdesh* (see *Tiferes Yisrael* to *Kereisos* ibid.).] *R' Meir says: Additionally, if it was the Sabbath and he carried it out [in his mouth] he is liable* to yet another *chatas*.

Rav Bivi analyzes this last ruling to demonstrate his point. Why should one be liable for carrying out a piece of food in his mouth? This is not the normal method of carrying — after all, people do not generally transport objects in their mouths! Rather, we must say that since he intended to eat the food while walking between domains, his intent makes his mouth a normal place for such a transfer to take place. Therefore, here too, since the thrower intends for the object to land in a dog's mouth or in the fire, his intent makes it a legally significant place, equivalent to one of 4 square *tefachim*.

פרשת ויגש

TUESDAY

PARASHAS VAYIGASH

A MUSSAR THOUGHT FOR THE DAY

R' *Shimon Schwab* also examines the significance of the wagons that Yosef sent to Yaakov, and why the verse states that seeing them was instrumental in convincing Yaakov that Yosef was alive (see *A Torah Thought for the Day*). He notes that at first the brothers did not relate to Yaakov the full story of Yosef's sale and their role in it; they merely said to him, "Yosef is still alive!" Thus, initially they did not admit that when they had told him, twenty-two years earlier, "*Identify, if you please: Is this your son's tunic?*" (*Bereishis* 37:33), they had been lying. According to the Tanna R' Shimon (see *Avos D'Rabbi Nassan* Ch. 30), this was the reason Yaakov did not believe the brothers at first. For such is the punishment of a liar; even when he tells the truth, he is not believed!

Seeing their failure in convincing their father that they were telling the truth, the brothers realized that Hashem was preventing them from comforting Yaakov due to their unwillingness to confess. They then understood that their only hope was to reveal the whole episode of Yosef's sale, and to beg for Yaakov's forgiveness. That they indeed admitted the truth to Yaakov is indicated in the continuation of the passage, which states (ibid. v. 27): *they related to him "all" the words that Joseph had spoken to them* — including Yosef's statement, *"I am Yosef . . . whom you sold into Egypt."*

R' Schwab explains further that the message sent by Yosef with his brothers to Yaakov, reminding him that the last subject they had studied together had been the laws of *eglah arufah,* had two purposes. The first was a message to the brothers, encouraging them to confess their terrible behavior to Yaakov and ask for his forgiveness. The second was to his father, imploring him to accept their plea. This dual request is mirrored in the verse that must be spoken by the elders after bringing the *eglah arufah.* They must first declare, "*Our hands have not spilled this blood . . . atone for Your people . . .*" (*Devarim* 20:7), and afterwards, *the blood shall be atoned for them* (ibid. v. 8). When the brothers heeded Yosef's plea and revealed their error to Yaakov, he believed and forgave them, and his spirit was revived.

QUESTION OF THE DAY:

Who actually told Yaakov that Yosef was still alive?

For the answer, see page 168.

HALACHAH OF THE DAY

פרשת ויגש

TUESDAY

PARASHAS VAYIGASH

As we learned earlier, the Sages enacted a prohibition against leaving uncooked food atop an open flame on Shabbos, in order to protect against accidental transgression of the *melachah* of *bishul,* as well as the *melachah* of *mav'ir,* kindling.

We further explained that the origins of the use of the *blech* on Shabbos lies in the fact that the Sages permitted the leaving of food over a flame that has been covered, since the covering indicates a lack of intention to adjust it on Shabbos. In our earlier discussion of the *blech,* we concerned ourselves only with cooking that is taking place over a flame, as is the case with the use of a range top. Now we will discuss the ramifications of this Rabbinic prohibition with regard to other methods of cooking.

Hot plates, hot-water urns, and all similar appliances that operate at a single non-adjustable heat setting, may be used without the addition of any type of *blech.* Since there is no possibility of accidental adjustment of the "flame" or electric heat element, the restrictions of the Rabbinic decree do not apply.

Hot plates that have variable heat settings should be covered with a sheet of aluminum foil prior to the placement of food upon them. As is true of range tops, it is proper to cover the temperature control knobs as well.

When using adjustable crockpots, one should line the entire heating element with foil. The temperature-control knob too should preferably be covered.

If one is keeping uncooked food inside an oven, one must use an oven insert in order to cover the flame. Once again, it is preferable that the oven control knob should also be covered.

All of the above guidelines apply to the maintaining of uncooked food over a flame on Shabbos. Until what point is the food considered uncooked? As we have seen earlier, food that has been cooked to the level of *Ben Derusai* is considered to be cooked to the minimal degree for the purposes of the laws of *bishul.* Since there is a dispute among the *poskim* whether this measurement refers to food that is one-third cooked or food that is one-half cooked, one must use a *blech* to maintain food on a flame unless it is at least one-half cooked prior to the onset of Shabbos. However, in cases of necessity, where there is no *blech* available, one may rely on the less stringent view, and maintain food that is only one-third cooked over an uncovered flame.

It should be noted that these guidelines define the strict obligation of the halachah. It is, however, proper to use a *blech* at *all* times when maintaining food on a flame. One should also preferably make sure that all food is fully cooked prior to the onset of Shabbos. Furthermore, as we shall see further in greater detail, while it is permissible to maintain fully cooked food over an open flame on Shabbos, one will not be able to return the pot to the flame if it is moved off the flame on Shabbos.

A CLOSER LOOK AT THE SIDDUR

Vidui, confession of one's sins, is recited at the end of each silent *Shemoneh Esrei* of Yom Kippur, and it is also repeated along with the *chazzan,* a total of ten times each Yom Kippur. The opening statement of the *Vidui* is: אֲבָל אֲנַחְנוּ חָטָאנוּ, *Truly, we have sinned,* and this statement is followed by an alphabetical recital of sins in the *Ashamnu* prayer, followed by the alphabetical וְעַל חֵטְא prayer.

After the completion of עַל חֵטְא, we recite a prayer preceding the concluding prayer of אֱלֹהַי נְצוֹר, which begins with the words, אֱלֹהַי עַד שֶׁלֹּא נוֹצַרְתִּי אֵינִי כְדַאי, *My God, before I was formed I was unworthy. . .,* which is a heartfelt declaration of one's feelings after having confessed to his sins, and a request for repentance and absolution. In this prayer, preceding our promise not to sin further, and our plea to have our past sins wiped away, we say: הֲרֵי אֲנִי לְפָנֶיךָ כִּכְלִי מָלֵא בוּשָׁה וּכְלִמָּה, *Behold, before You I am like a vessel filled with shame and humiliation . . .,* and continue with a prayer that Hashem give us the strength to withstand our Evil Inclination so that we no longer sin, and that He be merciful in exacting retribution for the sins we have already committed.

The significance of בּוּשָׁה, *shame,* to the process of repentance is emphasized by *Rambam, Rabbeinu Yonah, Orchos Tzaddikim* and many others. [*R' Tzadok HaKohen* points out that the word הַבּוּשֶׁת has the same *gematria* (and the same letters, in reverse) as the word תְּשׁוּבָה (*Machshavos Charutz* §38).] Indeed, the Gemara (*Berachos* 12b) states that "one who sins and is embarrassed by it will be forgiven for all his sins." This Gemara seems to say that *all* of the person's sins are expiated, even if his shame was only induced by a particular sin. *Maharal* explains that shame exhibits one's desire to be completely removed

פרשת ויגש

TUESDAY

PARASHAS VAYIGASH

from the act that causes it; thus, a person truly ashamed of a sin will distance himself from *all* sin. *R' Yerucham Levovitz* cautions, however, that this is true only when one is consumed with shame for having transgressed Hashem's command and Will, not if he is embarrassed as a result of the sin itself, such as if a person is embarrassed because he was caught sinning. It is only when a person's shame stems from having been untrue to Hashem that it will have the result of distancing him from future misdeeds.

Focusing on the phrase בּוּשָׁה וּכְלִמָּה, *Rabbeinu Yonah* explains that בּוּשָׁה is the shame that a sinner feels for having transgressed Hashem's commands. However, there is a more profound shame, כְּלִמָּה, which results from the sinner's realization that Hashem in His mercy postpones the punishment of the sinner, while he, rather than being grateful and penitent, continues in his evil ways! Thus, he is not merely embarrassed by his sinfulness, he is humiliated by his stubborn refusal to relinquish his sinful ways.

פרשת ויגש

WEDNESDAY

PARASHAS VAYIGASH

A TORAH THOUGHT FOR THE DAY

וַיִּסַּע יִשְׂרָאֵל וְכָל־אֲשֶׁר־לוֹ וַיָּבֹא בְּאֵרָה שָּׁבַע
וַיִּזְבַּח זְבָחִים לֵאלֹהֵי אָבִיו יִצְחָק

And Yisrael set out with all that he had; and he came to Beer-sheva, where he slaughtered sacrifices to the God of his father Yitzchak (*Bereishis* 46:1).

The commentaries are puzzled by the fact that Yaakov offered the sacrifices to "*the God of his father Yitzchak.*" Why did Yaakov not slaughter them in honor of his grandfather Avraham as well?

Rashi explains that the reason for this specific focus on Yitzchak is because a person, although bound by the laws of *kibbud av va'eim* (honoring parents) to respect his grandfather as well, is not required to honor him with the same level of respect due to a father. [See *A Taste of Lomdus* for further discussion of this rule.] Thus, even though he prayed in Yitzchak's merit, Yaakov did not feel it necessary to mention Avraham's merits as well in this *tefillah* to Hashem.

Rashbam offers a different reason for Yaakov's particular mention of Yitzchak here, explaining that since these sacrifices were offered on the very altar that Yitzchak had built in Beer-sheva many years earlier, when Hashem had appeared to him after he had left Gerar, Yaakov mentioned Yitzchak when slaughtering sacrifices on this altar.

R' Yaakov Kamenetsky sees a deeper message in *Rashbam's* explanation, pointing out that while it was true that this altar in Beer-sheva had been built and used by Yitzchak, the *Avos'* connection with Beer-sheva in fact began with Avraham, who, as the Midrash (*Bereishis Rabbah* 94:4) relates, planted cedar trees in Beer-sheva that would eventually be used for building the Mishkan after the Jews left Egypt. R' Yaakov explains that these plantings — whose inherent spiritual qualities would one day allow the Jewish people to achieve greatness after a long period of trouble, exile and despair — were the reason why Yitzchak chose Beer-sheva as the place to build an altar and offer sacrifices after his own period of troubles — the disputes with the Pelishtim that led to his being forced to leave Gerar. Yitzchak understood that just as, after the Egyptian exile, Hashem would dwell in the Mishkan that would be built with these cedars, so too, He would become close to Yitzchak after these times of troubles. Furthermore, as *Rashbam* points out, it was at the same time that Yitzchak built an altar in this place, that he, for the first time, merited Divine revelation.

The aim of reaching added closeness with Hashem after times of trouble was also Yaakov's motive for offering these sacrifices before descending to Egypt. However, unlike Yitzchak, Yaakov did not pray for himself; he prayed for his descendants. Understanding that the journey to Egypt was the beginning of what would be a long and bitter exile, Yaakov wished to ensure that the Jewish people would survive these difficulties and, ultimately, flourish spiritually as well. It was for this reason, explains R' Yaakov, that the Torah describes Yaakov's offerings as *sacrifices to the God of his father Yitzchak;* the Torah is telling us that Yaakov prayed to Hashem just as his father Yitzchak had in times of trouble. Thus, Yaakov followed Yitzchak's pattern of traveling to Beer-sheva, and, like Yitzchak, offered sacrifices and prayed there. And indeed, the Torah tells us that Hashem appeared to Yaakov immediately after his prayer, to assure him that his prayers were answered: *Have no fear of descending to Egypt, for I shall establish you as a great nation there. I shall descend with you to Egypt and I shall surely bring you up* (46:3-4).

MISHNAH OF THE DAY: SHABBOS 12:1

Having elaborated in the previous chapters upon the forbidden labor of transferring, the Mishnah proceeds to discuss the laws of other primary labors. Our Mishnah considers the forbidden labor of *building*:[1] הַבּוֹנֶה — ***One who builds,*** כַּמָּה יִבְנֶה וִיהֵא חַיָּב — ***how much must he build to be liable to a chatas?***[2] הַבּוֹנֶה כָּל שֶׁהוּא — ***One who builds any amount*** is liable to a *chatas,*[3] וְהַמְסַתֵּת — ***and*** similarly, ***one who***

NOTES

1. Having dealt (in the previous chapter) with the forbidden labor of transferring, which is the last of the thirty-nine primary labors enumerated in the Mishnah (7:2), it would seem that the Mishnah should proceed in backward order to the forbidden labor immediately preceding it — namely, מַכֶּה בְּפַטִּישׁ, *striking the final hammer blow* (which is 38th on the list). However, since *striking the final hammer blow* is inherently related to the forbidden labor of *building* — and since *building* occurs far more frequently — the Tanna first discusses *building* (*Tos. Yom Tov*).

2. I.e., what is the minimum amount that one must build on the Sabbath to be liable to capital punishment in a case of deliberate transgression, or to a *chatas* in a case of inadvertent transgression?

3. "Building any amount" includes filling up a hole in the wall of a house. The reason one is liable for such a minimal amount of building is because such "micro-building" took place in the construction of the Mishkan — the source for the thirty-nine primary forbidden labors. Specifically, if a wood-worm had bored into the boards of the Mishkan, the hole would be filled with molten lead (*Tos. Yom Tov* from Gemara 102b).

chisels a stone,[4] וְהַמַּכֶּה בְּפַטִּישׁ וּבַמַּעֲצָד — *and one who strikes* the final blow *with a hammer or with a small axe,*[5] הַקּוֹדֵחַ — *and one who drills,*[6] כָּל שֶׁהוּא — in *any amount,* חַיָּיב — *is liable* to a *chatas.*[7] זֶה הַכְּלָל — *This is the general rule:* כֹּל הָעוֹשֶׂה מְלָאכָה וּמְלַאכְתּוֹ מִתְקַיֶּימֶת — *Anyone who performs a forbidden labor, and his labor endures,* בְּשַׁבָּת — if he performed it *on the Sabbath,* חַיָּיב — *he* is *liable.*[8] רַבָּן שִׁמְעוֹן בֶּן גַּמְלִיאֵל אוֹמֵר — *Rabban Shimon ben Gamliel says:* אַף הַמַּכֶּה בְּקוּרְנָס עַל הַסַּדָּן בִּשְׁעַת מְלָאכָה חַיָּיב — *Also, one who strikes with a hammer on the anvil while working is liable,* מִפְּנֵי שֶׁהוּא כִּמְתַקֵּן מְלָאכָה — *because he is like one who improves the work.*[9]

NOTES

4. I.e., he cut the stone into a square, or smoothed it, or in any other way put the finishing touches on it in preparation for use in construction. This is a derivative of the forbidden labor of *striking the final hammer blow* (*Rav; Rashi; Rambam Commentary*).

5. This is the final step performed in the process of quarrying. After the stone has been hewn on all sides and has been almost entirely separated from the mountain, the person quarrying the stone deals it one final blow with a hammer, thus separating it completely from the mountain. Similarly, anyone who puts the finishing touches on any article, thus completing a process, is guilty of a derivative of *striking the final hammer blow* (*Rav; Rashi*).

6. I.e., he bored a hole in the wood or stone of a wall (*Rav; Rashi*).

7. This applies to all the aforementioned labors, viz., chiseling a stone, striking with a hammer or an adz, and drilling. A person is liable to a *chatas* for performing any amount of these forbidden labors (*Rav; Rash*).

8. I.e., anyone who works on the Sabbath and whose work endures is liable (*Rashi; Ran;* see *Gems from the Gemara*).

9. I.e., even in striking the anvil itself, and not the utensil upon which he is working, the smith becomes liable to a *chatas.* This is because it was the custom of metalworkers (including those involved in the construction of the Mishkan) to beat upon the anvil once for every three blows struck upon the metal they were beating into a utensil. This was intended to flatten any unevenness that may have deformed the hammer-head when it hit the metal plate. Thus, although this blow is not dealt to the metal upon which he is working, he is nevertheless liable for *striking the final hammer blow* (*Rav; Rashi*).

GEMS FROM THE GEMARA

The Mishnah taught a general principle: Anyone who works on the Sabbath and whose work endures is liable. The Gemara (103a) explains that in regard to the laws of the Sabbath, any state of completion in which *some* people would retain the object for use in its present form (i.e., without further enhancement) is considered to be enduring.

Moreover, once work can be considered enduring by some people, even one who intended to further enhance the work is liable for the part he has already performed. For example, a person who carves a hole the size of three quarts in a block of wood which is large enough to accommodate a hole the size of six quarts is liable for finishing the vessel. Since some people use the carved-out block in this smaller size, even one who intends to enlarge the hole is liable for what he has already done (*Rashi; Ran; Tos. Yom Tov* from Gemara 103a).

According to this understanding of the Mishnah, the intent of the ruling is: *anyone who works on the Sabbath and whose work endures.* Others, however, understand the sentence exactly as it is written in the Mishnah: *anyone who works, and his work endures on the Sabbath.* According to this understanding, one is liable only if the work he performs has reached its permanent status *on the Sabbath,* and he does *not* intend to add to it. Thus, if one carved a three-quart hole in a block large enough to accommodate a six-quart hole, and he intends to enlarge the hole later, he would *not* be liable (*Pri Chadash*). [For yet another interpretation of the Mishnah's ruling, see *Shenos Eliyahu.*]

A MUSSAR THOUGHT FOR THE DAY

As we discussed in *A Torah Thought for the Day,* Yaakov emulated the pattern established by his father Yitzchak when he offered sacrifices and prayed to Hashem as he neared Egypt. *R' Yitzchak Blazer* points out that a person's need to look to his forefathers as a model upon which to base his life is even more clearly illustrated in *Sforno's* explanation of why Yaakov prayed to Hashem as *"the God of his father Yitzchak";* since Hashem had instructed Yitzchak (see above, 26:2) that he was not to leave Eretz Yisrael to travel to Egypt, Yaakov understood that this restriction naturally applied to him as well. Thus, although the famine apparently called for Yaakov's family to travel to Egypt to Yosef, Yaakov thought that he was forbidden to do so; the tradition regarding the proper way to serve Hashem that he had received from his father did not include such action. Unable to leave Eretz Yisrael, Yaakov prayed to Hashem, *"the God of his father Yitzchak"* — i.e., He who had given Yitzchak direction — for guidance as to what would be the proper course of action under these circumstances. In reply, Hashem appeared to him in a dream and told him that only Yitzchak was forbidden to leave Eretz Yisrael (as a result of having been brought upon the altar at the *Akeidah*); Yaakov, however, should *have no fear of descending to Egypt.*

Explaining the reason why a person must always turn to the example shown by his forefathers and teachers, *R' Yerucham Levovitz* offers an example of a hiker walking in a forest. When this person reaches a route that he has never traveled before, he need not despair, for he may easily reach his destination by following the trails and signposts that have been marked by the forest rangers familiar with the territory. These people are intimately acquainted with the terrain, and the directions they leave for future hikers can safely be followed. However, points out R' Yerucham, even when clear signs and directions are available, not everyone is able to find his way around a forest, for maps and signposts only help those who are able to read them. A child, a person unfamiliar with the local language, or someone who is unable to read a map will still get lost. The only way that such a person can reach his destination and not get lost in the maze of the forest is to follow another person who, since he can read the directions, knows where he is going. As long as one follows in this person's path, he will make it to safety.

The same is true, continues R' Yerucham, of a person journeying through life, who is searching for the proper way to serve Hashem. He, no different than any traveler, does not have to find the right road on his own; Hashem gave clear guidelines in His Torah that, properly followed, will allow a person to easily travel the proper path. However, these guidelines will only help a person who understands how the Torah's message is to be applied to every aspect of his daily life. A person unsure of the proper way to serve Hashem in a particular circumstance, however, need not despair. Like the child in the forest, he has only to follow the example of others who knew where they were going; namely, spiritually greater previous generations who understood how the Torah's "signposts for life" provide guidance in all situations. By acting as these people did when they were faced with a similar challenge, every person can be sure that he will properly serve Hashem.

QUESTION OF THE DAY:

When had Yaakov previously been in Be'er-sheva?

For the answer, see page 168.

HALACHAH OF THE DAY

With respect to liquids, a *blech* must be used unless the liquids are above the temperature of *yad soledes bo* at the onset of Shabbos. As we noted earlier, the exact temperature of *yad soledes bo* is a matter of dispute. For this reason, only liquid that stands at a temperature of 160 degrees or higher can be considered definitely *yad soledes bo*. Any liquids cooler than this at the onset of Shabbos require a *blech* in order for them to be maintained on a flame during Shabbos.

Just as we noted in regard to solid foods, it is still proper to always use a *blech,* even if the liquid was *yad soledes bo* at the onset of Shabbos. Furthermore, it is proper to make sure that all liquids were boiled prior to the onset of Shabbos, and that they are still warm at the beginning of Shabbos.

If one wishes to use a kettle, or any other pot that will be removed from and replaced upon the *blech* during Shabbos, it is imperative to use a *blech,* since it is never permissible to replace a pot onto an open flame on Shabbos.

The *poskim* speak of one exception to the requirement of covering the flame. One may place a pot containing raw meat on an open flame immediately before the onset of Shabbos. The reasoning for this exception is that the Rabbinic prohibition against the maintaining of food over an open flame is based on the fear that one may adjust the flame in order to speed the cooking process. The Sages therefore reasoned that since a pot of raw meat placed on the flame right before Shabbos will obviously not be cooked in time for the Shabbos night meal, the owner of such a pot would not wish to accelerate the cooking process, since he is not expecting that food to be available to him in any case.

Nowadays this leniency is generally not relied upon, since with modern cooking apparatus almost any type of food can be prepared in very short order. However, it is possible to apply this ruling to the use of a crockpot which is designed to cook slowly. It is therefore permissible to place raw meat in a crockpot without any *blech* immediately before Shabbos, if one is certain that it will not be ready in time for the evening meal. Moreover, one may simply add one piece of raw meat to such a pot immediately before Shabbos, and thereby exempt the entire pot from the requirement of a *blech.* [Once again, it is important to note that this pot will not be able to be replaced on the heat source after being removed, since there is no *blech,* as we shall discuss further.]

A CLOSER LOOK AT THE SIDDUR

We explained in *A Torah Thought for the Day* that Yaakov offered sacrifices to *the God of his father Yitzchak.* Although many answers are offered by the commentaries as to why Yaakov referred to Hashem as *the God of his father Yitzchak* and not also as the God of his grandfather Avraham, most of these explanations are based on one idea: it was obvious to Yaakov that one's service to Hashem should be based on the messages and spiritual values that were received from previous generations.

We find this idea mentioned in *Az Yashir,* which we recite every morning in *Pesukei D'Zimrah.* We say: זֶה אֵלִי וְאַנְוֵהוּ אֱלֹהֵי אָבִי וַאֲרֹמְמֶנְהוּ, *This is my God and I will glorify Him, the God of my father and I will exalt Him* (*Shemos* 15:2). *Rashi* explains that the Jewish people's desire to become closer to Hashem after experiencing His great *chesed* is expressed in the commitment to *glorify Him* by building a *Beis HaMikdash* to show His glory to the world. However, the Jewish people understand that such a lofty relationship with Hashem cannot be created without a firm foundation; only when He is *the God of my father,* i.e., by declaring that His Godliness and glory has been inherent in my family for many generations, will He be truly *exalted* by my efforts.

Mechilta explains why this is so, likening the desired relationship between Hashem and the Bnei Yisrael to that sought by a man attempting to find a mate. Although several women were proposed to him, he found a fault in each one. He was uncomfortable with one woman's behavior; another, although personally acceptable, came from a disreputable family; and a third had an unsavory past. The man was at a loss what to do until one woman stood and exclaimed, "You may marry me; I have none of these problems!" Similarly, when the Jewish nation declares its intent to glorify Hashem, it can proudly announce that the Jews are able to do so completely, for, unlike other nations whose devotion to Hashem is only superficial, the Jewish nation is, in the words of the *Mechilta*: *a princess, the daughter of princesses; beloved, the daughter of beloved ones; holy, the daughter of holiness; and pure, the daughter of purity.* Since the single-minded goal of sanctifying Hashem, received from Avraham, Yitzchak and Yaakov, has been part of Jewish identity for generations, the Jewish people are fully worthy of exalting Hashem.

R' Yerucham Levovitz points out another, related, reason as to why praise of Hashem is more complete when "inherited" from one's fathers. Since a person is unable to praise Hashem beyond his own limited perception, any awareness of Hashem's *chesed* — and the resulting desire to offer thanksgiving to Hashem that a person may feel — is restricted to the narrowness of his experience, making praise for this salvation, however sincere, somewhat limited. A person who comes from a long line of ancestors who have always praised Hashem when saved from their own troubles, however, does not have this problem. Having absorbed the perspectives of thanks offered in response to many years of challenges, he is able to unite them with his own feelings of gratitude and thus better understand Hashem's multifaceted goodness. This leads to a higher level of praise that may be offered — that of exalting Hashem. Thus, the Jews when singing *Az Yashir,* and Yaakov, upon offering sacrifices to Hashem before descending to Egypt, included the relationship that their fathers had enjoyed with Hashem in their praise to Him.

A TASTE OF LOMDUS

R*ama* (*Yoreh Deah* 240:24) teaches that in addition to the obligation to respect one's parents, a person is obligated to honor his grandfather as well. As *Gra* and *Sefer Chareidim* (12:3-10) explain: *bnei banim harei heim k'banim,* "grandchildren are viewed as children," implying that they too must relate to a grandparent in the manner that a child relates to his parent, i.e., in a reverential manner. However, continues *Rama,* the level of this obligation does not require a child to respect a grandparent to the same extent as an actual parent. As the source for this rule *Rama* cites the Midrash quoted in *Rashi's* explanation of why Yaakov referred to Hashem only as *the God of his father Yitzchak* and did not also mention Avraham; a grandfather is simply not due the same amount of respect as a father.

Ramban disputes *Rashi,* pointing out that we find other occasions, such as in *Parashas Vayishlach* where Yaakov prayed to Hashem as: אֱלֹהֵי אָבִי אַבְרָהָם וֵאלֹהֵי אָבִי יִצְחָק, *the God of my father Avraham and the God of my father Yitzchak* (*Bereishis* 32:10), mentioning both of his forefathers. In fact, he even placed Avraham ahead of Yitzchak, in effect affording him greater honor. Therefore, concludes *Ramban,* Yaakov's decision to refer to Hashem as *the God of his father Yitzchak* here was based on other reasons unconnected to the laws of *kibbud av va'eim* [as we discussed in *A Torah Thought for the Day* and *A Mussar Thought for the Day*].

Livyas Chein defends *Rashi's* explanation against *Ramban's* question.

פרשת ויגש

WEDNESDAY

PARASHAS VAYIGASH

He notes that in *Parashas Vayishlach,* when Yaakov mentioned both of his forefathers in his prayer to be saved from Eisav, Yitzchak was still alive. Thus, although it is true, as *Rashi* states, that a person's father is intrinsically due more respect than a grandfather, there was another reason, explains *Livyas Chein,* why Yaakov mentioned Avraham first at that time — the rule of שְׁנֵיהֶם חַיָּיבִים בִּכְבוֹדוֹ, *they* (i.e., the son and grandson) *are both required to honor him* (the grandfather). Since Yitzchak was also commanded to respect Avraham, who was *his* father, this obligation rendered it appropriate for Yaakov, his son and Avraham's grandson, to mention Avraham in addition to, and even before, mentioning Yitzchak.

However, when Yaakov was traveling to Egypt, Yitzchak was no longer alive, and thus he had no mitzvah to honor his father in this manner. Since this was the case, Yaakov was able to sacrifice offerings to *the God of his father Yitzchak* without needing to respectfully mention Avraham as well.

R' Akiva Eiger (*Teshuvos* 1:68) applies *Livyas Chein's* explanation of Yaakov's actions to a different case. He discusses the case of a child, orphaned of both parents, who realizes that the instructions in his mother's will were entirely against those in his father's. Although the Gemara (*Kiddushin* 31a) states that a person whose father's instructions contradict his mother's is to obey his father, for both he and his mother are obligated to honor the father, the Gemara states that this is true only when the parents are still married. If they are divorced, so that the mother is no longer obligated to respect the father, the child is free to decide which directive he wishes to follow. Using the *Livyas Chein's* explanation that the reason why Yaakov did not mention Avraham in his offerings was because a person (i.e., Yitzchak) is [unable and therefore] not enjoined to honor his parents after he himself dies — and this subsequently absolved Yaakov from offering a higher level of honor to his grandparent — R' Akiva Eiger argues that the same would be true in a marriage relationship. The wife no longer has to honor the husband after her death. Thus, the child's obligation to honor his father more than his mother would change as well; accordingly, the child would be free to follow the dictates of whichever testament he wishes.

R' Yaakov Moshe Kulefsky asks a question on *Livyas Chein's* assumption that the father's need to honor *his* father — the child's grandfather — overrides the need for the child to show greater honor to the father than to the grandfather. He notes that *Shulchan Aruch* (*Yoreh Deah* 240:17) rules that a married woman is not obligated to honor her father in a situation where it will detract from the honor that she must show to her husband. Now, the halachah (ibid. 240:24) also states that a married man is required to honor his father-in-law. Why, then, he asks, must a married woman disregard her father's wishes and listen to her husband instead? The husband also has to listen to her father, who is his father-in-law! If *Livyas Chein's* approach is indeed correct, the husband's requirement to respect his father-in-law should mean that his wife, who is commanded to respect him, should in fact obey the one whom *he* also has to respect — her father!

To answer his own question, Rav Kulefsky clarified that *Livyas Chein* did not mean that the principle of *they are both required to honor him* ***creates*** the obligation to honor one's grandfather, for, as was stated above, *Vilna Gaon* and *Sefer Chareidim* explain that this obligation is learned from the general Talmudic principle of *b'nei banim harei heim k'banim,* "grandchildren are viewed as children." Rather, the rule of *they are both required to honor him* is used only to decide which of two already established obligations should be carried out when in conflict; the answer is that the one whom the two other people must honor is afforded the greater respect. In the case of a married woman's apparent contradictory obligations to her husband and father, however, there is in truth no conflict; the Torah's directive that the husband be followed in this situation means that she, in this area, is not obligated to listen to her father *at all.* Since there no longer a conflict, the rule of שְׁנֵיהֶם חַיָּבִים בִּכְבוֹדוֹ, *they are both required to honor him,* does not apply.

פרשת ויגש

THURSDAY

PARASHAS VAYIGASH

A TORAH THOUGHT FOR THE DAY

כָּל־הַנֶּפֶשׁ הַבָּאָה לְיַעֲקֹב מִצְרַיְמָה יֹצְאֵי יְרֵכוֹ . . . כָּל־נֶפֶשׁ שִׁשִּׁים וָשֵׁשׁ . . . כָּל הַנֶּפֶשׁ לְבֵית־יַעֲקֹב הַבָּאָה מִצְרַיְמָה שִׁבְעִים

All the persons coming with Yaakov to Egypt, his own descendants . . . sixty-six persons in all . . . All the people of Yaakov's household who came to Egypt — seventy (*Bereishis* 46:26,27).

To reconcile the obvious contradiction between v. 26, which states that sixty-six people arrived in Egypt, and v. 27, which states that there were seventy, *Rashi* explains that there were sixty-six people who *left* Canaan, and seventy who were together in Egypt. The figure of seventy is arrived at by adding Yosef and his two children (Ephraim and Menasheh), and Yocheved the daughter of Levi, who was conceived during the journey to Egypt. This is also the interpretation of *Targum Yonasan,* and is based on the Gemara (*Bava Basra* 123b) that states that Yocheved was conceived after Yaakov's family had already left Canaan, which is why she is not enumerated among the sixty-six that set out. *Rashbam* (ibid.) explains that she is not mentioned explicitly because at the time of their arrival in Egypt, she had not yet been born. Somewhat difficult, however, is that though she is not considered part of the sixty-six people who left Canaan, she *is* counted as one of the thirty-three children of Leah, and the Torah does *not* exclude her from the count by saying she was born in Egypt, as it does regarding Yosef and his sons. [*Rashi* (to 46:15) addresses this, and notes that although the Torah states that the children of Leah were thirty-three, only thirty-two are listed; Yocheved is not mentioned. He explains that she is not mentioned for this very reason; she was not yet born.]

Ibn Ezra, Rashbam, and *Abarbanel* all have an alternative approach to explain the count of seventy people. They explain that Leah indeed had only thirty-two children, but Yaakov himself was counted with her family (perhaps because it was the biggest), as indicated in the introductory verse to the census (v. 8): *These are the names of the Children of Israel who were coming to Egypt — Yaakov and his children.* Thus, the verse states that Leah had thirty-three. Although this should yield a total of *sixty-seven* people going down to Egypt (Leah's thirty-three, Zilpah's sixteen, eleven of Rachel's fourteen [three were already in Egypt], and seven of Bilhah's), the Torah states that only sixty-six left because the verse specifically states, *All the persons coming* ***with*** *Yaakov to Egypt —* ***his own descendants*** (v. 26), thereby excluding Yaakov from the count.

The entire family in Egypt, however, consisted of the sixty-six children and Yaakov, in addition to Yosef, Ephraim and Menasheh, equaling seventy.

R' Zalman Sorotzkin (*Oznaim LaTorah*) suggests a novel approach to resolve the identity of the seventieth person. In his calculation, the thirty-three members of Leah's family do not include Yaakov (who was not offspring), nor Yocheved (who was not yet born), but Osnas, who was Dinah's daughter (fathered out of wedlock by Shechem). She was Yosef's wife, and thus was already living in Egypt (see *Targum Yonasan* 46:20), but the Torah does not mention her by name, so as not to recall the distasteful episode of Dinah. Thus, the count of sixty-six people journeying to Egypt is precise (32 + 16 + 11 + 7 = 66), and, when the four members already in Egypt (Yosef, Menasheh, Ephraim and Osnas) are added, we arrive at a total of seventy.

Through this exposition, R' Zalman answers another difficulty addressed by the commentators, regarding the phrase בָּנָיו וּבְנוֹתָיו שְׁלֹשִׁים וְשָׁלֹשׁ, *his sons and daughters numbered thirty-three* (v. 15). Seemingly, the use of the plural בְּנוֹתָיו is difficult, as only Dinah is mentioned! (see *Ramban* and *Ibn Ezra*). According to R' Zalman, it refers to Dinah and her daughter Osnas, in line with the Talmudic dictum that children of daughters are considered one's children (*Yevamos* 62b).

MISHNAH OF THE DAY: SHABBOS 12:2

The following Mishnah discusses the forbidden labor of *plowing*:[1] הַחוֹרֵשׁ כָּל שֶׁהוּא — ***One who plows any amount,***[2] הַמְנַכֵּשׁ — as

NOTES

1. The following Mishnah, which discusses plowing, follows the previous Mishnah, which discussed building, because in a certain sense plowing is the reverse of building: Building generally consists of filling up holes or augmenting a structure, whereas plowing consists of digging holes or diminishing that which is already there. Furthermore, both these forbidden labors share the characteristic that one who does them in any amount is liable (*Tos. Yom Tov;* see *Tiferes Yisrael*).

2. One is liable for plowing any amount, since even the smallest area plowed is fit for planting a single seed. This measure of significance is derived from the Mishkan, where even the smallest area was fit for planting one stalk of a dye-producing herb (*Tos. Yom Tov* from Gemara 103a). [Although with regard to transferring from one domain to another we learned (9:7) that one is not liable for carrying fewer than *two* seeds, that is because one would not ordinarily take the trouble to carry out just one seed to plant. With regard to plowing, however, each hole must be dug individually in any case, and the digging of each hole is therefore regarded as a significant activity (*Tos. Yom Tov* from *Rashi* ibid.).]

well as *one who weeds,*[3] וְהַמְקַרְסֵם — *and one who prunes dry branches,*[4] וְהַמְזָרֵד — *and one who prunes young shoots,*[5] כָּל שֶׁהוּא — *in any amount* חַיָּב — *is liable* to a chatas.

הַמְלַקֵּט עֵצִים — Regarding ***one who gathers wood*** by cutting branches off a live tree, אִם לְתַקֵּן — *if* his intent is ***to effect an improvement*** in the tree or the fertility of the surrounding soil, כָּל שֶׁהֵן — he is liable for ***any amount;***[6] אִם לְהֶיסֵק — but *if* his intent is to obtain wood ***for kindling,*** כְּדֵי לְבַשֵּׁל בֵּיצָה קַלָּה — he is liable only if he gathers ***the measure*** of wood ***required to cook an easily cooked egg.***[7]

הַמְלַקֵּט עֲשָׂבִים — ***One who gathers grasses,***[8] אִם לְתַקֵּן — *if* his intent is ***to effect an improvement*** in the soil, כָּל שֶׁהוּא — he is liable for ***any amount;***[9] אִם לִבְהֵמָה — but *if* his intent is to use the grass ***for animal*** fodder, כִּמְלֹא פִּי הַגְּדִי — he is liable only if he gathers ***the measure of a kid goat's mouthful.***[10]

NOTES

3. I.e., he pulls out weeds from between the plants (*Rav*). Since this will cause the remaining plants to grow better, he is liable for performing a derivative of the forbidden labor of *planting* (*Kesef Mishneh, Hil. Shabbos* 8:2; see *Moed Katan* 2b).

4. Dead branches are pruned from a tree in order to stimulate the tree's growth (*Rav; Rashi; Tiferes Yisrael*). This is, in effect, "planting" the extra growth of the tree. He is therefore liable for planting (*Tos. Yom Tov*).

5. Pruning excess young shoots that, due to their abundance, diminish the strength of the tree, is also a derivative of planting (*Rav; Rashi*).

6. A person can gather wood — i.e., cut branches off a tree (*Rav; Rashi; Meiri;* cf. *Rambam Commentary; Tiferes Yisrael*) — for various reasons. If his intent is to improve the soil, he is liable for performing a derivative of the forbidden labor of plowing; if his intent is to improve the tree, he is liable for a derivative of planting. In either case, the liability is for any amount (*Rav; Meiri*).

7. On the other hand, if his intent is to obtain firewood, he is liable for performing a derivative of harvesting, and he is liable to a *chatas* as he would be for cutting down any growing plant.

Accordingly, he is liable only if he harvests a significant amount — viz., the measure necessary to cook an amount of egg equal in volume to a dried fig (see Mishnah 8:5). For this measurement we use a chicken egg, which is the most easily cooked of all eggs [i.e., it requires the least amount of heat] (*Rav; Rashi* from Gemara 80b).

8. I.e., he uproots growing grass (*Meiri;* cf. *Rambam Commentary; Tiferes Yisrael*).

9. The ruling here is the same as in the previous case. Here too the liability is for a derivative of plowing.

10. As in the case of the firewood above, here too the liability is for harvesting. The measure is set at a kid goat's mouthful, because a kid is the smallest animal to which one regularly feeds grass, and therefore, a kid's mouthful is the smallest amount that is considered significant (see Mishnah 7:4).

GEMS FROM THE GEMARA

As we saw in the Mishnah, the determination as to whether an act is the derivative (*toladah*) of one forbidden labor (*melachah*) or of another often depends upon the intent of the one who performs the act. The same act may at times be considered a derivative of one forbidden labor, and at other times be considered a derivative of another forbidden labor. This occurs whenever an act achieves two ends. For example, pruning branches from a tree both strengthens the tree's growth — a derivative of planting — and results in the gathering of useful wood — a derivative of harvesting. The determination as to which specific forbidden labor the person pruning the tree has violated is based on his intent. If his intent is to strengthen the tree, his act is categorized as a derivative of planting. But if his intent is to gather wood, his act is categorized as a derivative of harvesting. If his intent is for both purposes, his act is categorized as a derivative of both primary forbidden labors (Gemara 73b).

[However, even if his intent is to gather wood, he may also be liable for having strengthened the tree, due to the well-known rule of פְּסִיק רֵישֵׁיה — the principle that renders a person liable for the unintended but inevitable performance of a forbidden labor as a consequence of another act. As long as the person who performs the act benefits from that consequence, he is liable for the consequence as well. Accordingly, if by cutting wood for kindling from his own tree a person also benefits from the consequential strengthening of the tree, he is liable for a derivative of planting in addition to the forbidden labor of harvesting.

This, however, cannot be the case of our Mishnah, since it would then follow that he would be liable for *any* amount of pruning (liability for planting is incurred for any amount, as opposed to the larger amount necessary to be liable for harvesting). Therefore, we must conclude that our Mishnah is referring to a case of cutting the branches from *someone else's* tree. Since he is not the owner, he derives no benefit from the strengthening of the tree, and therefore he is not liable for planting (see Gemara 103a; see also *Tos. R' Akiva Eiger*).]

On the other hand, if his intent is only to strengthen the tree and *not* to gather its wood, he is liable only for planting and not for harvesting — even though he is inevitably harvesting the wood. This is because wood is not usually a harvested crop. Therefore, the forbidden labor of harvesting is not automatically violated by the activity of cutting wood, and one is liable only when he specifically intended to collect the pruned branches (*Tosafos* to *Shabbos* 73b).

פרשת ויגש

THURSDAY

PARASHAS VAYIGASH

A MUSSAR THOUGHT FOR THE DAY

Ibn Ezra, commenting on the interpretation of *Rashi* that Yocheved, Levi's daughter, is included in the count of seventy members of Yaakov's family arriving in Egypt, notes that according to this calculation, Yocheved gave birth to Moshe when she was 130 years old (for the Jews remained in Egypt for 210 years, and Moses was 80 years old when they left Egypt). [Indeed, the Gemara states this explicitly in *Bava Basra* (120a).] Why, asks *Ibn Ezra,* does the Torah not highlight this miraculous event, just as it does concerning Sarah, who gave birth to Yitzchak when she was 90 years old?

Ramban responds that the Torah only relates miracles that were predicted by a *navi* or by an angel as an emissary of Hashem. Miracles that are performed to aid the righteous or punish the wicked, which were not previously announced, are not recorded. We find this to be a recurring theme of *Ramban;* rewards and punishments in this world are administered as hidden miracles, and are arranged so that they may appear to be merely part of the natural order of the world (see *Ramban, Shemos* 6:3, *Vayikra* 26:11).

R' Yerucham Levovitz (*Daas Torah* 1:261) elaborates on this concept. One could understand, he argues, that "random" occurrences might be construed by the non-discerning mind to be part of the natural order, since they do not defy or overrule natural laws. Thus, winning a lottery or inheriting a huge fortune might be viewed as luck or happenstance, just as being struck by a tidal wave or a disease might be deemed to be a random misfortune. A person of faith, principled in the knowledge of הַשְׁגָּחָה (*hashgachah*), *Divine design,* though, will understand that Providence has specially visited the good or bad upon him, and merely cloaked them as natural phenomena.

However, R' Yerucham points out, *Ramban* is referring here to the birth of a child to a woman who was 130 years old — a truly miraculous event! What person would attribute this occurrence to anything other than a miracle from Hashem?

One must deduce, then, that *Ramban,* when speaking of a hidden miracle versus a revealed miracle, is not contrasting an unusual occurrence masked as an admittedly improbable but conceivable happening with a supernatural one, which would be attributed to Hashem. Rather, he is stating that *even* such a supernatural occurrence would not be recorded in the Torah, because, although there is no explanation for it, it was not foretold, and thus could not be conclusively classified as a miracle performed by Hashem.

Implausible as it may seem, continues R' Yerucham, Avraham Avinu's exit from Nimrod's fiery furnace unscathed was not recorded in the Torah, for it was deemed a "hidden miracle," since it was not foretold. It would indeed be considered "wondrous," but not a miracle of Hashem. So too, says R' Yerucham, if not for the public pronouncements of each impending plague in Egypt and the parting of the Sea, these would be thought of as נִסִּים נִסְתָּרִים, *hidden miracles.* The essential purpose of the predictions and actions of Hashem surrounding the Exodus from Egypt was to conclusively show that Hashem is the Master of miraculous events, from which one must learn that He is master of *all* events, and that nature is Hashem's servant and not His master, as is stated: כִּי אֲנִי ה׳ בְּקֶרֶב הָאָרֶץ, *I am HASHEM in the midst of the land* (*Shemos* 8:18).

HALACHAH OF THE DAY

It is sometimes necessary to remove a pot from the *blech* on Shabbos in order to take out food, and subsequently it is necessary to return that pot to the *blech.* It may also be necessary, on occasion, to transfer hot food from one *blech* to another (e.g., by taking the food to a different house within an *eruv*). These actions, known as חֲזָרָה, *returning,* resemble cooking, and are permitted only when certain specific conditions are met.

As we learned earlier, *initially placing* food on a flame or *blech* is prohibited on Shabbos. *Returning* food that was removed from a *blech* on Shabbos is, within the restraints of certain guidelines, permitted. Transferring food from one *blech* to another is considered a form of *returning,* and is at times also permitted. However, in order for the replacing of a pot onto a *blech* to qualify as *returning* as opposed to *initially placing,* the following five conditions must be met.

First, the flame to which the food is being returned must be covered with a *blech.* Second, the food must be completely cooked. The third condition is that the food must still be warm when the pot is returned to the *blech.* The fourth requirement is that the pot must be *still in his hand,* i.e., one must not let go of the pot during the entire time it is off the *blech.* The fifth stipulation is that one's original intention, when removing the pot, must be to return it to the *blech.*

We will now elaborate on each of these conditions in greater detail.

The first condition that must be met in order to allow returning food to a flame on Shabbos is that the flame must be covered by a *blech.* Returning a pot to an open flame is never permitted. Even fully cooked foods, which may be *maintained* on Shabbos on an open flame, may not be *returned* to the open flame once removed from the fire. It is thus advisable to always use a *blech,* in order to allow for lifting and returning pots, as needed.

All appliances whose normal use is for cooking require a *blech* in order to permit *returning.* For example, if one wishes to return food to an oven, there must be an insert in the oven; if one wishes to return food to a crockpot or adjustable hot plate, the appliance in question must be lined with aluminum foil.

A CLOSER LOOK AT THE SIDDUR

Rabbeinu Bachya, commenting on the makeup of the seventy people who established the community of Israel in Egypt, adopts the position of *Rashi* (and the Gemara in *Bava Basra*) that Yocheved was the 70th person. He asks, however, why Yaakov is not also included, which would bring the count to seventy-one. He explains that when counting a group that has a recognized or authorized leader, the leader is not enumerated, and it is understood that he is counted apart from the group. For example, we find that the Torah relates that there were seventy elders, though Moshe, as chief elder, brought the count to seventy-one. Similarly, the Great Sanhedrin is described as having seventy members, excluding the head of the Sanhedrin; and the nations of the world total seventy, without the nation of Israel.

Rabbeinu Bachya then highlights the extraordinary quality of Yaakov who, through his influence as patriarch of this small group of "seventy souls," successfully began the nurturing of what would become a nation of millions, who were then able to receive the Torah and become the chosen nation of Hashem. Furthermore, from that time onward, the *Shechinah* rested firmly upon the nation, until the destruction of the first *Beis HaMikdash.*

The historical importance of the "seventy souls" is recounted during the recital mandated as part of the mitzvah of *Bikkurim,* the bringing of the "First Fruits" to Yerushalayim and giving them to a Kohen. As part of the mitzvah, one must read from *Parashas Ki Savo* (*Devarim* 26:5-10), to offer thanks to Hashem for having taken us from our (Yaakov's) trying life with Lavan, and to recall our humble beginnings, when Yaakov went to Egypt בִּמְתֵי מְעָט, *few in number* (only seventy people). Initially, we endured the bondage and persecution of Egypt, until we were redeemed by Hashem and brought to Eretz Yisrael.

This entire theme is recited by Jews every year at the Pesach Seder in the *Maggid* section of the Haggadah, immediately after וְהִיא שֶׁעָמְדָה, and serves as a preamble to our relating the miracles and greatness of Hashem in our salvation from the hand of Pharaoh and the establishment of the nation.

Maasei Nissim (*Otzar HaTefillos*) poses the following question on the Haggadah. When seeking a source for the statement that the Jews descended to Egypt בִּמְתֵי מְעָט, *few in number,* the Haggadah cites the verse (*Devarim* 10:22): *With seventy souls did your ancestors descend to Egypt and now, HASHEM, your God, has made you like the stars of heaven for abundance.* Why, he asks, does the Haggadah cite a secondary text from *Devarim,* when it could have cited the primary text, *All the people of Jacob's household who came to Egypt — were seventy*? (*Bereishis* 46:27).

He explains that there is an important lesson that can be learned only from the verse in *Devarim* 10:22. In the passage detailing the *Bikkurim* recital, the verse (ibid. 26:5) states: וַיָּגָר שָׁם בִּמְתֵי מְעָט, *he resided there few in number,* which might imply that they remained few in number for a long period of their exile, which is incorrect. Therefore, the Haggadah cites the verse (ibid. 10:22) that clearly states that they were seventy souls only when "your ancestors descended to Egypt," implying that their numbers increased soon after.

Rabbeinu Bachya concludes his remarks to the verse in *Vayigash* by assuring us that although the *Shechinah* left the nation after the destruction of the First Temple, It did not do so completely, and still hovers around us, though It is devoid of its full majesty and beauty. Nevertheless, in the future *the number of the Children of Israel will be like the sand of the sea, which can neither be measured nor counted* (*Hosea* 2:1) and Hashem's glory and honor will be restored.

QUESTION OF THE DAY:

Which Jews who went down to Egypt were not counted in the count of seventy souls?

For the answer, see page 169.

פרשת ויגש

FRIDAY

PARASHAS VAYIGASH

A TORAH THOUGHT FOR THE DAY

וַיֶּאְסֹר יוֹסֵף מֶרְכַּבְתּוֹ וַיַּעַל לִקְרַאת־יִשְׂרָאֵל אָבִיו גֹּשְׁנָה וַיֵּרָא אֵלָיו וַיִּפֹּל עַל־צַוָּארָיו וַיֵּבְךְּ עַל־צַוָּארָיו עוֹד

Yosef harnessed his chariot and went up to meet Yisrael his father in Goshen. He appeared before him, fell on his neck and he wept on his neck excessively (*Bereishis* 46:29).

R*ashi* explains that it was Yosef who fell upon his father's neck and cried excessively, maintaining that the word עוֹד connotes "a great quantity." *Ramban*, however, disagrees on both points, arguing that it would be unseemly for Yosef to fall upon his father's neck at their first encounter, rather than bowing before him as a sign of respect. Second, עוֹד implies "in addition to" (or "a second time"), rather than "a great quantity." Therefore, *Ramban* interprets the phrase as alluding to *Yaakov* falling upon *Yosef's* neck, as one would expect from an aging father who had been reunited with a long-lost son, and *weeping* again, as he had so many times in the past in his grief.

Rashi addresses another point. Why is there no mention of Yaakov reciprocating Yosef's emotional embrace? [Obviously, this difficulty does not exist according to *Ramban's* approach.] *Rashi* answers by citing a Midrash stating that Yaakov was reciting *Krias Shema* at that moment. The obvious difficulty with this Midrash — if Yaakov was required to recite *Krias Shema* at this juncture, then Yosef should have been as well. And if there was time to do so later, why did Yaakov not wait?

Many commentators address this difficulty. Perhaps the most famous of the answers is that of *Sifsei Chachamim,* who says that it was, indeed, the time for *Krias Shema* to be recited. However, Yosef was exempt from the mitzvah, for he was engaged in the mitzvah of *kibbud av,* honoring his father, and one need not abandon one mitzvah to perform another. The *Steipler Gaon* (in *Bircas Peretz*) questions this explanation, based on the Gemara (*Kiddushin* 32a) that states that if one's father requests something of him when he is about to perform a mitzvah, he should perform the mitzvah first, and then attend to his father's needs. It would appear then, that the mitzvah of *kibbud av* does not supersede another mitzvah! To resolve this difficulty, the Steipler cites *Ran,* who makes the following distinction. The Gemara's ruling that one should do the mitzvah rather than fulfill his father's request is applicable only when one had not yet begun to perform the mitzvah of *kibbud av*. If, however, he had already begun to perform the mitzvah of *kibbud av,* he is exempt from the second mitzvah. Based on this *Ran,* says the Steipler, we might suggest that Yosef's journey to greet his father was deemed to be the beginning of the mitzvah.

A second solution, suggests the Steipler, is that Yaakov recited *Krias Shema* at the earliest possible time, in accordance with the dictum that the zealous hurry to do mitzvos early. Yosef, however, who was performing the mitzvah of *kibbud av,* was obligated to postpone his recital of *Krias Shema,* since he could do so afterwards.

R' Chaim of Brisk offers a novel solution. The underlying assumption of the difficulty is that this moment was the first possible time that one could recite the *Shema,* and neither Yaakov nor Yosef had yet done so. However, says R' Chaim, this is a faulty assumption, for Yaakov during his entire journey was fulfilling Hashem's command to go down to Egypt, and was therefore exempt from other mitzvos. It was only upon his arrival in Egypt that he became obligated in *Krias Shema,* and it was now some time after the earliest halachically acceptable time for reciting the *Shema.* Thus, Yosef had already recited *Krias Shema,* and only Yaakov recited it at the moment of their meeting.

MISHNAH OF THE DAY: SHABBOS 12:3

The following Mishnah considers the forbidden labor of writing: **הַכּוֹתֵב שְׁתֵּי אוֹתִיּוֹת** — ***One who writes two letters,*** **בֵּין בִּימִינוֹ בֵּין בִּשְׂמֹאלוֹ** — ***whether with his right*** hand ***or with his left*** hand,[1] **בֵּין מִשֵּׁם אֶחָד בֵּין מִשְּׁתֵּי שֵׁמוֹת** — ***whether of one "name" or of two "names,"***[2] **בֵּין מִשְּׁתֵּי סַמָּנִיּוֹת** — ***whether with*** one or ***two*** different ***inks,***[3] **בְּכָל לָשׁוֹן** — ***in any language,***[4] **חַיָּב** — ***is liable*** to a *chatas.*

NOTES

1. In fact, this ruling applies only to a person who is ambidextrous. A right-handed person, however, is liable to a *chatas* only if he writes with his right hand. For him, writing with his left hand is not a normal mode of writing, and therefore incurs no liability — although it is still Rabbinically prohibited (see below, Mishnah 5). Similarly, a left-handed person is liable only for writing with his left hand (*Rav* from Gemara 103a).

2. I.e., whether one wrote the same letter twice, e.g., *aleph aleph* [אא], or he wrote two different letters, e.g., *aleph beis* [אב] (*Rav; Rashi*).

3. E.g., he wrote one letter with ink and one with vermilion [bright red mercuric sulfide that was used as an ink] (*Rashi;* cf. *Rambam Commentary* and *Rashba*).

4. I.e., in the script used by any nation (*Rav; Rashi; Rambam Commentary*).

לא חִייבוּ שְׁתֵּי אוֹתִיּוֹת אֶלָּא — **R' Yose said:** אָמַר רַבִּי יוֹסֵי — *They only held* one who writes *two letters liable* מִשּׁוּם רוֹשֵׁם *on account of marking,* שֶׁכָּךְ כּוֹתְבִין עַל קַרְשֵׁי הַמִּשְׁכָּן — *for thus would they write on the boards of the Mishkan* לֵידַע אֵיזוֹ בֶּן זוּגוֹ — *to know which one was its mate.*[5]

אָמַר רַבִּי — *Rebbi said:* מָצִינוּ שֵׁם קָטָן מִשֵּׁם גָּדוֹל — *We find a short word* that is part *of a long word.*[6] שֵׁם מִשִּׁמְעוֹן וּמִשְּׁמוּאֵל — For example: *Shem from Shimon or Shmuel,* נֹחַ מִנָּחוֹר — *Noach from Nachor,* דָּן מִדָּנִיֵּאל — *Dan from Daniel* גָּד מִגַּדִּיאֵל —and *Gad from Gadiel.*[7]

NOTES

5. R' Yose maintains that the liability for writing two letters is on account of the letters serving as markers or symbols — i.e., the essence of the forbidden labor of writing is the making of symbols, whether or not they are representative of any formal language. This is because the letters written in the Mishkan served this purpose, in that they were not written on the boards of the Mishkan to spell words, but rather so that when the boards were reassembled after traveling, the identifying letters would enable the builders to reassemble the boards in their original order. Consequently, one who writes any two symbols is just as liable as one who writes two letters (*Rav; Rashi; Rambam Commentary*). [R' Yose differs from the Tanna Kamma (first opinion) in the following respect: The Tanna Kamma considers one liable only for using written characters which are part of a conventionally accepted symbol system of some language or nation (e.g., alphabet, hieroglyphic, or mathematical symbol) but not for making arbitrary signs which hold no generally accepted meaning (e.g., scratches or chalk marks made by workmen to mark various points on their work). R' Yose, however, considers one liable even for such marks and symbols (*Rav; Tiferes Yisrael*).]

6. The Mishnah here considers a person who intended to write a long word, but after writing two letters of it reminded himself that it was the Sabbath and stopped writing. If the letters he wrote comprise a short name by themselves, he is liable to a *chatas* even though he did not complete the word he intended to write (*Rav; Rashi*).

7. In all these cases, the first two letters of the long name form a complete name themselves. Hence, once one writes them he is liable to a *chatas,* even if he had intended to write the longer name. [In addition, he is liable for writing the name *Shem* of the word *Shmuel,* even if the *mem* was written in the form usually used in the *middle* of a word.]

QUESTION OF THE DAY:

Who was the first member of Yaakov's party to reach Egypt?

For the answer, see page 169.

GEMS FROM THE GEMARA

We saw in the Mishnah that the law that one who writes two letters is liable is based on the practice of writing symbols on the boards of the Mishkan, to enable the assemblers to match each board to its mate. In this way, they would be able to use the same order of boards each time they erected the Mishkan.

Why was it necessary for the boards to be assembled in the same order each time? Some explain that this was because of their varying degrees of sanctity: The closer the proximity of the boards to the holy utensils of the Mishkan, the greater their sanctity. Moreover, the holy utensils themselves represented different degrees of sanctity. Thus, the boards that stood on the north side (where the *Shulchan* — the Table for the twelve *lechem hapanim* — was placed) were not as holy as the boards that stood on the south side (where the Menorah was placed). Similarly, the boards nearer the east (the entrance to the Sanctuary) were not as holy as those nearer the west (the Holy of Holies, where the Ark was located) (*Tiferes Yisrael; Ran* from *Yerushalmi* 12:3).

As a commemoration of this practice, many Jews mark the boards of their *succos*, to assure that they will be placed in the same position every year (*Maharil*). [Of course, there are no holier or less holy boards in the *succah*, so the actual reason for marking the boards does not apply — the custom is intended only to commemorate the marking of the Mishkan's boards.]

Another place where we find the idea of marking an item so it will always be used in the same position is with respect to a *tallis*. It is customary to sew a strip of silk or other fabric onto the top of the *tallis*, so that the *tallis* will always be worn the same way. This will ensure that the front fringes retain their honored position (*Magen Avraham, Orach Chaim* 8:6).

A MUSSAR THOUGHT FOR THE DAY

Maharal, in his *Gur Aryeh,* offers a completely different explanation of the Midrash that states that Yaakov did not cry upon Yosef's neck at their first meeting, because he was reciting *Krias Shema* (see *A Torah Thought for the Day*).

During the time of the encounter, says *Maharal,* it was not yet the time for the daily recital of *Krias Shema*, and indeed, Yaakov had no intention of performing this mitzvah. However, exceptionally righteous people are keenly aware of Hashem's mastery of the world, and express their cognizance of His control at any opportune moment. Upon experiencing the extraordinary joy of seeing Yosef again, Yaakov was immediately overcome with desire to be close to his Creator, to praise and thank Him for this favor. For this reason, he recited the *Shema*, to express his joy and love of Hashem.

The Steipler Gaon explains that Yosef may very well have also had such feelings, and possibly also had the inclination to say *Krias Shema* in gratitude to Hashem. However, he was engaged in the obligatory fulfillment of the mitzvah of *kibbud av,* and it is not proper for one to exercise the quality of חֲסִידוּת, *exceptional piety*, at the expense of one's obligations.

This concept is found in *Chovos HaLevavos* (*Shaar Yichud HaMaaseh* Ch. 5), which states that if one wishes to undertake additional stringencies upon himself out of a genuine desire to elevate his spiritual standing, he may do so. Nevertheless, concludes *Chovos HaLevavos,* Hashem will not accept this pious behavior as beneficial unless the person first fulfills all of his obligations.

Mesillas Yesharim devotes the entire Chapter 20 to assessing the validity or appropriateness of pious behavior, which he describes as an extraordinarily fundamental subject filled with fine distinctions that are difficult to discern. He explains that although, at first glance, such behavior would seem to be unquestionably good and beneficial, one must approach it delicately, and keep three criteria in mind: (1) His motives must be pure, wishing *only* to create joy for Hashem. (2) He must examine and investigate carefully the precise nature of the deed, to determine if and how it will help him reach his elevated goal. (3) He must rely on Hashem to guide him properly to his desired end. If one's pious behavior is lacking in any of these conditions, he says, his efforts will almost certainly result in failure, and the חֲסִידוּת, *exceptional piety,* will be transformed to רְשָׁעוּת, *evil.*

As a historical example of *chassidus* which led to disaster, *Mesillas Yesharim* cites the episode of Gedalyah ben Achikam, whose refusal to accept *lashon hara* about Yishmael's intention to kill him resulted in Gedalyah's assassination, and marked the end of a Jewish presence in Eretz Yisrael. The Gemara (*Niddah* 61a) states that although Gedalyah need not have believed the *lashon hara*, it should have made him suspicious, and all of the deaths caused by this episode were thus his fault.

Similarly, the destruction of the Second Temple was instigated by Bar

Kamtza, who conspired to slander the Jews as rebellious, since they refused to accept the Caesar's offering on the altar (because it had a blemish). The Sages wished to kill him, but R' Zechariah refused because he felt that someone might derive an incorrect halachah from this action. Commenting on this decision and the subsequent destruction of the Temple, R' Yochanan said, "The tolerance displayed by R' Zechariah destroyed our Temple, burned down our Sanctuary, and exiled us from our Land" (*Gittin* 56a).

Thus, says *Mesillas Yesharim,* while one must perform all obligatory actions and avoid all transgressions, even if doing so incites jeering or embarrassment, the results that emanate from *chassidus*, rather than halachah, must be viewed carefully to assess whether they are indeed helpful or detrimental, whether they are better done in private than in public, and whether Hashem's will would be better served if the behavior were discontinued.

HALACHAH OF THE DAY

The second condition that must be met in order to allow one to return food to a *blech* on Shabbos is that the food must be completely cooked. As we have learned previously, "completely cooked" means that the food has been cooked to an extent that most people would eat it without further cooking. Partially cooked food, even if it is edible (like the food of *Ben Derusai*), may not be returned to a *blech* once it has been removed. Doing so violates the Torah prohibition of *bishul*.

The third condition mentioned above is that the food must still be warm when returned to the *blech.* This means that the food could still be enjoyed as a warm food or drink. Once it has cooled, it may not be returned to the *blech*, as replacing it at this point is considered a new warming process, not *returning*.

The fourth requirement is that the pot must still be "in his hand." While it is not necessary to keep the pot suspended in midair in order to be able to return it to the *blech*, one must not release his grip on the pot if it is put down on the table or counter. If one puts the pot down and releases his grip on the pot, he is not permitted to return it to the *blech*.

Some *poskim* differentiate between placing the pot on a counter or table, and placing the pot on the floor. According to these *poskim,* once the pot was set down completely onto the floor, even if one held onto the pot handle the entire time, the pot may not be returned to the *blech.*

As described earlier, the fifth stipulation is that one's original intention when removing the pot must have been to ultimately return it to the *blech.* If, when removing the pot, one intended to remove it permanently, one is no longer permitted to return it to the *blech.* If, however, one had no particular intention when removing the pot, he is permitted to return it.

The first three conditions mentioned above are definite requirements, without which it is absolutely forbidden to return food to a *blech* on Shabbos. If the flame does not have a *blech,* or the food is not completely cooked, or the food is no longer warm, *returning* is out of the question. The last two requirements, that the food be "still in his hand" and that one has the intention to return it to the *blech*, must be adhered to *lechatchilah*, whenever possible. However, some leniencies do apply if one *inadvertently* neglected to abide by these last two conditions, as we shall see below.

A CLOSER LOOK AT THE SIDDUR

Although the word חָסִיד (*chassid*) is generally translated to mean exceedingly pious or devout, conjuring up visions of fasting, prayer and religious zeal, its origin is in the concept of חֶסֶד (*chesed*), giving freely of oneself for the benefit of others. It is a quality practiced by Hashem, as described in many verses, and which we are encouraged to emulate as part of the obligation to follow in Hashem's ways.

The relationship between חֶסֶד and חָסִיד can be seen clearly in a verse from *Ashrei*, which we recite three times daily: during *Pesukei D'Zimrah,* before *U'Va LeTzion,* and before the *Shemoneh Esrei* of *Minchah.* As we have mentioned earlier, the praises of *Ashrei* follow an alphabetical format. This is an allusion to the Torah which was given with the twenty-two letters of the *aleph-beis* (*Maharsha*).

The verse beginning with the letter *tzadi* states: צַדִּיק ה׳ בְּכָל דְּרָכָיו וְחָסִיד בְּכָל מַעֲשָׂיו, *HASHEM is righteous in all His ways, and a chassid in all His deeds. Ibn Ezra* explains that this verse represents a retort to anyone doubting the "fairness" of his lot in life. First, Hashem is a *tzaddik,* perfectly righteous in His judgment, and is meticulous in prescribing the correct dosage of well-being and circumstances that all of His creations require. Second, He is a *chassid,* in that everything which He gives is out of a desire to benefit His creations, and not out of obligation. [See *Siach Yitzchak* in *Siddur HaGra* for elaboration on this theme.]

The *Vilna Gaon* explains that the beginning of the verse is describing Hashem's quality of scrupulously judging people according to their deeds. Nevertheless, the verse continues by saying that Hashem is a *chassid,* magnanimous in punishment, meting it out mercifully.

According to either exposition, the term *chassid* as used here signifies a genuinely altruistic desire to cast a benevolent eye upon others.

It is this concept which underlies the definition of *middas chassidus* as לִפְנִים מִשּׁוּרַת הַדִּין, behavior *above and beyond the requirements of the law.* Thus, as it pertains to matters between man and Hashem, *chassid* refers to those who are constantly examining the wonders of Hashem, seeking an evermore enhanced appreciation and recognition of their Creator. In relations between man and his fellow man, it represents one's willingness to overlook his own needs and be concerned for those of his fellow.

פרשת ויגש

SHABBOS

PARASHAS VAYIGASH

A TORAH THOUGHT FOR THE DAY

וַיֹּאמְרוּ אֶל־פַּרְעֹה לָגוּר בָּאָרֶץ בָּאנוּ . . .
And they said to Pharaoh, "We have come to sojourn in the land . . ." (*Bereishis* 47:4).

In the Haggadah Shel Pesach, the Sages adduce from this verse that Yaakov went to Egypt to reside there temporarily, and not to settle there permanently. This is derived from the word לָגוּר, *to sojourn,* whose root is גר, meaning *foreigner* or *sojourner.* Nevertheless, we find that the Jews in fact stayed in Egypt willingly for many years, even before their bondage as slaves began. One must ask what factors caused this change of heart.

R' Yaakov Kamenetsky addresses this question, first pointing out the seemingly strange progression of events described in this chapter. After narrating that Yosef settled his family in Ramses and sustained them with food (vs. 11,12), the Torah shifts to a description of the measures that Yosef implemented as the minister of the granaries during the famine. The chapter enumerates three actions which Yosef took: (1) He nationalized all the land of Egypt, whereupon it became the property of Pharaoh. (2) He resettled the populations of all cities to other cities. (3) He established a 20-percent tax on all the produce that was harvested, but exempted the priestly class. It is only after telling us of these steps that the chapter returns to state that *Israel settled in the land of Egypt . . . they acquired property in it* (v. 27). Why, asks R' Yaakov, does the Torah interrupt the settlement of the Jews with the legislative actions of Yosef, and why does the Torah deem it necessary to tell us of them?

R' Yaakov explains that Yaakov stopped in Be'er-sheva on his way to Egypt to request permission from Hashem to go to Egypt, fearing that the deleterious influences of the Egyptian people would preclude such a move, and did not continue on his journey until Hashem guaranteed his safety by proclaiming, *"Have no fear of descending to Egypt"* (46:3). However, when Pharaoh told Yosef, *"The land of Egypt is before you — in the best part of the land settle your father and brothers,"* an invitation implying permanent settlement and full participation in Egyptian society, Yosef became fearful of the effect that this would have on the family. In response to this fear, says R' Yaakov, and not only because of agricultural concerns, Yaakov enacted the laws that the Torah mentions. Yosef reasoned that by disenfranchising all Egyptians from their property, nobody would be considered "owners" of the land, or standard-setters of national norms. Both Jews and Egyptians could be considered

פרשת ויגש

SHABBOS

PARASHAS VAYIGASH

equal guests in Pharaoh's land. To strengthen this feeling of equality, Yosef transferred all the Egyptians from their cities to new locations, in effect making the Jews' status as exiles no more so than that of the Egyptians. Finally, by exempting priests from the tax that he established, he ensured that there would always be an independent group among the Jews, free to practice and maintain their traditions. The Leviim, the clerical tribe, were thus never subject to the servitude of the other tribes and were able to engage in Torah study, enabling them to withstand the temptations and pitfalls that would plague the Jews later on, including the episodes of the Golden Calf and the rebellion engendered by the Spies.

R' Yaakov adds that undoubtedly, the wisdom exhibited by Yosef emanated from the teachings of Yaakov, whose Torah was singularly adaptive to the travails of exile. Yaakov learned these lessons during the fourteen years he spent at the yeshivah of Shem and Ever, in preparation for the twenty years of exile that he would suffer with Lavan in Charan.

The narrative of the chapter can now be understood. The original intention of Yaakov was indeed to settle the Jews in Egypt, but only as foreigners, with his family remaining a separate and distinct entity. Fearing, however, that eventually this safeguard would break down and they would assimilate into Egyptian culture and society, Yosef enacted laws that would prevent this assimilation and provide at least one avenue of safety, the Leviim. Only then could the concluding verse be written: *Thus Israel settled in the land of Egypt, in the region of Goshen; they acquired property in it and they were fruitful and multiplied greatly* (v. 27).

MISHNAH OF THE DAY: SHABBOS 12:4

The following Mishnah continues to consider the forbidden labor of writing:

הַכּוֹתֵב שְׁתֵּי אוֹתִיּוֹת בְּהֶעְלֵם אֶחָד חַיָּיב — ***One who writes two letters in one lapse of awareness is liable*** to a *chatas.*[1]

NOTES

1. I.e., if one forgot that it was the Sabbath, or that it is forbidden to write on the Sabbath, and did not remind himself until after he had written two letters, he is liable to a *chatas.* This ruling is superfluous, since the Mishnah already stated (11:6) that a minimum of two letters must be written to incur liability, and it also stated (12:3) that one is not liable to a *chatas* unless both the beginning and the end of the forbidden labor were performed inadvertently. The ruling is repeated here merely by way of introduction to a related dispute below, in Mishnah 6 (*Tos. Yom Tov;* cf. *Sfas Emes*).

The Mishnah considers the types of ink for which one incurs liability:

כָּתַב בִּדְיוֹ בְּסַם בְּסִיקְרָא בְּקוֹמוֹס וּבְקַנְקַנְתּוֹם — Whether ***he wrote with ink,***[2] ***with yellow arsenic, with vermillion, with gum arabic, with ferrous sulphate,*** וּבְכָל דָּבָר שֶׁהוּא רוֹשֵׁם — ***or with anything*** else ***that marks;***[3] עַל שְׁנֵי כוֹתְלֵי זָוִיּוֹת — ***on two walls forming a corner,*** וְעַל שְׁנֵי לְוָחֵי פִּינְקָס — ***or on two*** facing ***tablets of a ledger,***[4] וְהֵן נֶהְגִּין זֶה עִם זֶה — ***provided that they can be read together,*** חַיָּיב — ***he is liable*** to a *chatas.*[5]

The Mishnah now discusses the writing surface:

הַכּוֹתֵב עַל בְּשָׂרוֹ חַיָּיב — ***One who writes on his flesh*** with ink ***is liable*** to a *chatas.*[6] הַמְסָרֵט עַל בְּשָׂרוֹ — ***One who etches*** letters ***on his flesh*** using a stylus or with lime, רַבִּי אֱלִיעֶזֶר מְחַיֵּיב חַטָּאת — ***R' Eliezer holds him liable to a chatas,*** וְרַבִּי יְהוֹשֻׁעַ פּוֹטֵר — ***but R' Yehoshua exempts*** him.[7]

NOTES

2. I.e., with black ink, that maintains its color on parchment (*Tiferes Yisrael* to *Megillah* 2:2).

3. This clause comes to indicate that a person who writes with water in which gallnuts have been soaked is also liable (*Rav* from Gemara 104b).

4. This refers to a ledger that consisted of tablets coated with wax, upon which merchants would write with a stylus (*Rashi*).

5. I.e., one who writes two letters on two adjacent walls or on two facing pages of a ledger, in such a manner that they are near enough to one another to be read together, is liable to a *chatas* (*Rav; Rashi; Tiferes Yisrael*).

6. Human flesh is considered a viable writing surface, upon which the script endures. Hence, although the body's heat will cause the script to disappear after a while, the writer is still liable. This is analogous to one who writes something inherently durable that will later be erased (*Rambam, Hil. Shabbos* 11:16).

7. The two Tannaim disagree as to whether etching letters on human flesh is a "normal" manner of writing [R' Eliezer] or not [R' Yehoshua] (*Rambam Commentary; Ran*).

GEMS FROM THE GEMARA

After it discusses various rules concerning the letters of Torah script, the Gemara (104a) digresses to demonstrate that the very names and shapes of the letters of the *aleph-beis* may be expounded upon to teach numerous lessons. [The letters of the Torah contain much sanctity and esoteric meaning, and as such deserve detailed study as to their form and sound (*Maharsha*).]

The first two letters, *aleph* and *beis,* stand for *"a'leph binah"* (learn insight) — i.e., study the Torah. The next two letters, *gimmel* and *dalet,* stand for *"gemol dalim"* (aid the needy). And why is the leg of the *gimmel* extended toward the *dalet*? Because it is the manner of one who bestows kindness to run after the needy, to help them. And why is the leg of the *dalet* extended toward the *gimmel* (i.e., why is it bent backward at an angle?). It is to indicate that the pauper should make himself available to his benefactor, so as not to trouble the benefactor to chase after him. And why is the face [e.g., the open part] of the *dalet* turned away from the *gimmel*? It is to indicate that the benefactor should give the charity to the pauper discreetly, in order that the pauper should not be embarrassed of him.

The next two letters are *hei* and *vav*: This combination represents the name of Hashem, in which these letters are found. These letters are followed by *zayin* and *ches, tes* and *yud, chaf* and *lamed.* The allusion contained in these letters together with the earlier six letters of the *aleph-beis* is that if you do these things (e.g., study Torah and aid the needy), Hashem will *"zan"* (sustain) you; show you *"chein"* (favor); *"meitiv"* (benefit) you [*tes* represents the word טוב, *goodness*]; give you a *"yerushah"* (inheritance); and bind upon you a *"keser"* (crown) *l'Olam Haba* (for the World to Come).

The open *mem* and closed *mem,* which come next, allude to an open *"maamar"* (statement) and a closed *"maamar,"* meaning that some Torah matters should be revealed and some should be concealed.

The curved *nun* and the straight *nun,* which follow, allude to a bent *"ne'eman"* (faithful person) and an erect *"ne'eman."* This teaches that a faithful person who is humble (i.e., "bent over") in this world will stand tall in the World to Come.

The next two letters, *samech* and *ayin,* stand for *"semoch aniyim"* (support the poor). Another version of exposition for *samech* and *ayin* is *"simanim asei"* (make mnemonics) for the Torah, so that it will be remembered.

The curved (i.e., "closed") *pei* and straight (i.e., "open") *pei* allude to an open *"peh"* (mouth) and a closed *"peh."* A person should sometimes speak out publicly, and at other times hold his silence. The curved *tzadi* and the straight *tzadi* allude to a bent *"tzaddik"* (righteous person) and an erect *"tzaddik."*

The Gemara asks: Isn't that the same allusion as the one concerning a bent *"ne'eman"* and an erect *"ne'eman"*? The Gemara answers that Scripture added an extra degree of bending to the righteous person's bent state, and from here we derive that the Torah was given with trembling of the head — i.e., it is through trembling and extraordinary humility that a person merits the acquisition of Torah knowledge.

The letter *kuf* stands for *"Kadosh"* (the holy One) — i.e., Hashem; and the *reish* stands for *"rasha"* (an evil person). And why is the face of the *kuf* turned away from the *reish*? It is because Hashem says, "I am unable to look at the face of an evil person." And why is the crown [a small *zayin*-shaped crown on the roof of the *kuf* that is situated at the edge of the roof near the *reish* (*Rashi*)] of the *kuf* turned toward the *reish*? It is because Hashem says, "If he repents, I will bind upon him a crown like my own." And why is the leg of the *kuf* suspended, instead of being attached to the top? So that if the evil person repents, he can enter the *kuf* through the opening above the leg.

The Gemara asks: Why can't he enter through the opening on the bottom of the *kuf*? The Gemara answers that this is in accordance with Reish Lakish's comment on the verse (*Mishlei* 3:34): *If to cynics he will act cynically, but to the humble He will grant favor* — viz., that if one comes to defile himself, they provide an opening for him; but if one comes to purify himself, they actually help him — even opening up a new door for him.

Finally, *shin* stands for *"sheker"* (falsehood) and *tav* stands for *"emes"* (אֱמֶת, *truth*) whose last letter is *tav*. And why are the letters of *sheker* juxtaposed and the letters of *emes* spread out? [The letters *shin, kuf* and *reish* of שֶׁקֶר appear together near the end of the alphabet, whereas the *aleph* of אֱמֶת begins the alphabet, the *mem* is in the middle, and the *tav* is at the very end (*Rashi*).] It is because falsehood is common, whereas truth is not common. And why do the letters that spell "falsehood" stand on one leg, while the letters spelling "truth" are set like bricks? [The three letters of שֶׁקֶר each have only one point reaching the bottom of the letter (*Rashi*). By contrast, the three letters of אֱמֶת are each firmly ensconced on a sturdy base: The *aleph* has two legs, one of which is wide; the *mem* has a broad base; and the *tav* has two legs like the *aleph* (*Rashi*).] Because truth stands, whereas falsehood cannot stand. [I.e., the truth is enduring whereas falsehood is eventually exposed and toppled. As *Tikkunei Zohar* (475) states succinctly: *Falsehood has no legs* (to stand upon).]

QUESTION OF THE DAY:

In what year after Creation did Yaakov and his family descend to Egypt?

For the answer, see page 169.

A MUSSAR THOUGHT FOR THE DAY

The problem of Jews assimilating with the nations while in exile is an existential danger that is discussed by many commentators throughout *Tanach. Meshech Chochmah,* commenting on the verse: *God spoke to Yisrael in night visions . . . and said . . . have no fear of descending to Egypt, for I shall establish you as a great nation there* (*Bereishis* 46:2,3), notes that only with respect to Yaakov do we find the description of a prophecy as a "night vision." He explains that Yaakov was about to enter a prolonged exile in Egypt, where the nation would be plunged into an abyss of darkness, losing hope of freedom and a return to Canaan. Hashem therefore assured Yaakov that the *Shechinah* would accompany them, and that their destiny of greatness would eventually arrive. For this reason, the prayer of *Maariv,* recited at night, which is symbolic of exile, is attributed to Yaakov, for he is the patriarch whose lessons must overcome the darkness and usher in a new day and future.

Nevertheless, says *Meshech Chochmah,* the guarantee of the *Shechinah* traveling with Israel in exile is conditional on their maintaining their traditions and behaving in the proper ways of their ancestors.

He deduces this from the fact that all prayers symbolize (or take the place of) particular offerings that were brought in the *Beis HaMikdash.* At night, no offerings are brought, yet we have Yaakov's prayer of *Maariv,* because the various flesh and fats of the offerings, which were slaughtered and whose blood was sprinkled (the essence of atonement) during the day, may be burned on the Altar at night. Thus, the night has a Divine aspect only when it is in conjunction with the day. He explains that this is the underlying reason for the fact that Yechezkel was able to continue prophesying during the "night" of the exile in Bavel, for he had already been empowered as a prophet with the *Shechinah* upon him in Eretz Yisrael (see *Moed Katan* 28a; *Rashi, Yechezkel* 1:3).

In an extraordinarily poignant exposition in *Parashas Bechukosai, Meshech Chochmah* describes the incredible cycle of persecution, exile, survival and serenity that the Jewish people have experienced in the Diaspora for not heeding this lesson. After residing in a host country for one or two hundred years, a storm of persecution will rise up against them and mercilessly inundate them with afflictions and mistreatment until they are forced to flee. Settling together in new places, they reestablish their Torah institutions and take their place in the economic life of the new country. Eventually, however, they cease to think of themselves as foreigners in an alien land, who aspire to their redemption in the appointed time. The next generation particularly, raised in this new culture, adopts a "modern" approach and a rejection of the "outdated" ways. In order to ensure the continuity of the nation, Hashem induces a new wave of persecution, in which the Jew is invariably (and to his shock) singled out for his individuality and forced to flee again. Realizing that it must mend its ways, the nation will again reestablish its own institutions and reinvigorate its faith in Hashem and the Torah. But, unfortunately, once again the people become comfortable in their new homes, and the cycle begins anew.

HALACHAH OF THE DAY

Let us now discuss some examples of the laws that apply if one of the final two conditions for returning food to a *blech* was not satisfied:

If, while arranging the food on the *blech* before Shabbos, one removed a pot and forgot to return it, the law is as follows: If the food is completely cooked and still warm, one may return the food to the *blech* on Shabbos, as long as his original intention was to place the pot on the *blech.*

Also, if one removed a pot from the *blech* on Shabbos with the intent to return it, and inadvertently put it down, one is permitted after the fact to return it to the *blech.* Similarly, if one lifted the pot off the *blech,* intending *not* to return it to the *blech,* but has not yet released his grip on the pot, he is permitted to return the pot to the *blech.* Thus, we see that in cases of necessity, even if one of the last two conditions was not fulfilled, one can be lenient, and return food to a *blech.*

Furthermore, in a case of genuine need, *returning* is permitted even if *neither* of these final two conditions was satisfied. For example, if a pot of essential Shabbos food was removed from the *blech* with the intent not to return it, *and* it was put down, one is nonetheless allowed to return it to the *blech,* provided that the first three conditions were met. Namely, there must be a *blech,* the food must be completely cooked, and still warm.

If fully cooked food was left on a *blech,* and the flame was accidentally extinguished, the food may be transferred to another *blech,* as long as it is still warm. This is true even if the flame went out before Shabbos and one did not notice it until Shabbos.

If one mistakenly took the wrong pot off of the *blech,* one is permitted to return it, even if it was put down and one did not intend to return it.

For example, one accidentally removed the *cholent* pot from the *blech* on Friday night instead of the soup pot, and it was set down with the intent not to return it to the *blech*, since he thought it was the soup. Nonetheless, if the *cholent* is fully cooked and still warm, it may be put back on the *blech*.

In cases where *returning* is permitted, one is also permitted to pour the food from one pot to another, and *return* the new pot to the *blech*.

This halachah has some very practical applications:

One may pour boiling water from a kettle that is on the *blech* into a pot of *cholent* (or other food) that is in danger of drying out. One may also pour the boiled water into a cup, and pour from the cup into the *cholent* pot. In both these cases, hot water from the kettle is being returned to the *blech* in a different pot (i.e., the *cholent* pot). However, since it is forbidden to stir food while it is on the fire, and adding water to a pot will cause the contents to be stirred about, one should lift the pot off the *blech* before adding the water, or move it to an area where it is not directly above the fire. If this is not possible, one should pour the water into the *cholent* very slowly.

A CLOSER LOOK AT THE SIDDUR

The centerpiece of the middle blessing of the Friday night *Shemoneh Esrei* is the recital of the *Vayechulu* prayer, which is also recited as part of the Friday night *Kiddush*. The prayer, which consists of the verses of *Bereishis* 2:1-3, is cited as a Scriptural source for the statement that we recite in *Shemoneh Esrei* (which we discussed last week), that Hashem blessed and sanctified the Sabbath day.

The Gemara attaches great importance to the recital of *Vayechulu*. Indeed, in Tractate *Shabbos* (119b), we find a surprising statement: One who recites the *Vayechulu* prayer on the eve of the Sabbath is reckoned as if he partnered with Hashem in Creation! How are we to understand this enigmatic Gemara?

The commentators offer several interpretations. *Maharsha* and others note that the Gemara refers specifically to one who recites the *Vayechulu* prayer on *the eve of Sabbath*. They therefore relate this Gemara to the halachah that a person is supposed to accept the Sabbath upon himself several minutes before it actually begins (to ensure that he will not accidentally violate any of its laws). Now, when Hashem created

the Sabbath, He obviously did not need to begin it any earlier than the exact time it was to begin, as He was able to pinpoint the exact moment of its onset. Thus, when a person begins the Sabbath early, the holiness of Sabbath that descends upon those extra minutes are solely *his* creation; in a sense, then, he has become a partner in Creation. This, says *Maharsha,* is the Gemara's meaning: One who recites *Vayechulu* and begins the Sabbath, has created a bit of the Sabbath all by himself.

Anaf Yosef understands the Gemara to be referring not simply to the *recital* of *Vayechulu,* but the observance of the Sabbath that it implies. He states that while the world came into being solely through the Word of Hashem, the power for the world to endure is drawn from the observance of the Sabbath; each Sabbath in turn that is observed by the Jews provides the world with the spiritual sustenance it requires to exist for the next six days. Thus, although the initial Creation was of course accomplished by Hashem alone, the subsequent provision of the world's continuing need for spiritual sustenance is indeed furnished, at least in part, by those who keep the Sabbath. Accordingly, those who keep the Sabbath are partners in helping Creation endure.

ANSWERS TO QUESTIONS OF THE DAY

Sunday:

To indicate that although they had sold him, his brotherly love for them remained intact (*Ohr HaChaim*).

Monday:

Ralbag states that he did so to reassure the brothers that he was not harboring any thoughts of revenge against them; *Zohar* states it was because Yosef foresaw that in the future the Ten Tribes would be exiled.

Tuesday:

Sefer HaYashar relates that it was Serach, the daughter of Asher, who told the news to Yaakov in song. As a reward, he blessed her that she would never die; she was one of the righteous individuals who entered the World to Come without first dying (see *Pirkei D'Rabbi Eliezer*).

Wednesday:

Yaakov had gone to Be'er-sheva before leaving for Lavan's house (see above, 28:10). The Midrash says that he went there to seek permission from Hashem to leave Eretz Yisrael.

Thursday:

The verse states (*Bereishis* 46:26) that the wives of Yaakov's children were not counted.

Friday:

Yehudah. The verse (46:28) relates that Yaakov sent him ahead; *Rashi* cites a Midrash stating that Yaakov instructed Yehudah to prepare a house of study for them.

Shabbos:

In the year 2238, 190 years after Yitzchak's birth.

פרשת ויחי

Parashas Vayechi

פרשת ויחי

A TORAH THOUGHT FOR THE DAY

SUNDAY

PARASHAS VAYECHI

וַיְהִי אַחֲרֵי הַדְּבָרִים הָאֵלֶּה וַיֹּאמֶר לְיוֹסֵף הִנֵּה אָבִיךָ חֹלֶה וַיִּקַּח אֶת־שְׁנֵי בָנָיו עִמּוֹ אֶת־מְנַשֶּׁה וְאֶת־אֶפְרָיִם. וַיַּגֵּד לְיַעֲקֹב וַיֹּאמֶר הִנֵּה בִּנְךָ יוֹסֵף בָּא אֵלֶיךָ וַיִּתְחַזֵּק יִשְׂרָאֵל וַיֵּשֶׁב עַל־הַמִּטָּה

And it came to pass after these things that someone said to Yosef, "Behold! — your father is ill." So he took his two sons Menasheh and Ephraim with him. Yaakov was told, "Behold — your son Yosef has come to you." So Yaakov exerted himself and sat up on the bed (*Bereishis* 48:1-2).

Rashi (based on *Mechilta*) comments that we learn an important lesson from the fact that Yaakov exerted himself and sat up on the bed — a person is obligated to show respect to a king. Although Yosef was Yaakov's son, and a father normally does not display honor to his child, Yaakov sat up when Yosef entered the room. The reason for this, explains *Rashi,* is because Yosef was a king; Yaakov understood that it was inappropriate to be lying down when Yosef came in. *Rashi* concludes by noting that Yaakov's display of respect for Yosef is not the only place in the Torah where this lesson is taught. The need to respect a monarch is seen also from the fact that Moshe and Aharon spoke respectfully to Pharaoh even when warning him of the plague of *Makkas Bechoros* that would destroy Egypt (*Shemos* 11:8), and from Eliyahu's respect when prophesying to the wicked king Achav.

The commentaries point out that although the Torah already stated (*Bereishis* 47:31) that Yaakov had bowed to Yosef during Yosef's previous visit [וַיִּשְׁתַּחוּ יִשְׂרָאֵל עַל־רֹאשׁ הַמִּטָּה, *and Yisrael bowed toward the head of the bed*], *Rashi* there explained Yaakov's bowing with the aphorism: תַּעֲלָא בְּעִידָּנֵיהּ סְגִיד לֵיהּ, *[when] a fox [is] at his time [of greatness], bow to him.* I.e., Yaakov reasoned that since his son Yosef was the only one with the power to fulfill his wish to be buried in Eretz Yisrael, he had to show him respect, although as a father he was not bound to do so. On the occasion of Yosef's second visit, when *Yaakov exerted himself and sat up on the bed, Rashi* explains that the Torah is teaching us about the honor that must be shown to a king.

The commentators offer several explanations of why *Rashi* does not explain that Yaakov bowed to Yosef during the first visit also because of the honor due him as royalty. *Levush HaOrah* writes that *Rashi* noted the fact that during the second visit, the verse states that Yaakov sat up *before* Yosef entered, while during the first visit, he bowed *after* their conversation. Thus, *Levush HaOrah* explains that the first bowing was a *result* of their conversation. The sitting up before the second visit, however, was done without Yosef's knowledge, and therefore was not performed so that Yosef would see it; rather, Yaakov sat up only because of the honor due Yosef as king.

The Brisker Rav offers a different explanation. He states that the fact that Yaakov bowed during the first visit would not prove that there is a necessity to do so, for perhaps Yaakov bowed only as required by proper etiquette. Before the second visit, however, Yaakov had already taken ill, and was weak. The fact that he nevertheless strengthened himself to sit up before Yosef entered proves that there must be an *obligation* to do so, because of the homage due to a king.

Additionally, the Brisker Rav points out that the need to honor a king, even in situations when etiquette does not apply, is also seen in the example of Moshe and Aharon that *Rashi* cites. The Midrash states that Pharaoh treated Moshe and Aharon in a very insulting manner, even going so far as slapping their faces! Certainly, they would have been excused for not treating him with proper etiquette! Nevertheless, they were respectful, for the requirement to honor a king has nothing to do with how he acts or what he does.

For further explanation of *why* the Torah commanded that a monarch be respected, see *A Mussar Thought for the Day*.

MISHNAH OF THE DAY: SHABBOS 12:5

The following Mishnah lists those inks whose use in writing does not render a person liable to a *chatas*:

כָּתַב בְּמַשְׁקִין — If ***one wrote with liquids,***[1] **בְּמֵי פֵירוֹת** — ***with fruit juices,***[2] **בַּאֲבַק דְּרָכִים** — ***with dust of the roads,***[3] **בַּאֲבַק הַסּוֹפְרִים** — ***with scribes' dust,***[4] **וּבְכָל דָּבָר שֶׁאֵינוֹ מִתְקַיֵּם** — ***or with anything*** else ***that is not lasting,*** **פָּטוּר** — ***he is exempt*** from a *chatas.*[5]

NOTES

1. I.e., he wrote with mulberry juice or some other liquid that produces a black coloring (*Rav; Rashi*).

2. I.e., he wrote with juices of any other fruits (*Rav; Rashi*).

3. I.e., he formed letters in the dust of the road (*Rav; Rashi*), or on some other surface upon which the dust had settled (*Tiferes Yisrael*).

4. I.e., he wrote with the residue found at the bottom of the inkwell (*Rav; Rashi*).

5. That is, he is exempt from a *chatas.* Nevertheless, it is Rabbinically prohibited to write with any of these substances (*Ritva*).

The Mishnah lists other cases in which a person who writes is exempt:
לְאַחַר יָדוֹ — If one wrote ***with the back of his hand,***[6] בְּרַגְלוֹ בְּפִיו וּבְמַרְפֵּיקוֹ — ***with his foot, with his mouth or with his elbow;***[7] כָּתַב אוֹת אַחַת סָמוּךְ לַכְּתָב — or if ***he wrote one letter alongside*** previous ***writing,***[8] וְכָתַב עַל גַּבֵּי כְּתָב — ***or*** if ***he wrote over*** existing ***writing;***[9] נִתְכַּוֵּין לִכְתּוֹב חי״ת וְכָתַב שְׁתֵּי זייני״ן — or if ***one intended to write a ches but wrote two zayins;***[10] אַחַת בָּאָרֶץ וְאַחַת בַּקּוֹרָה — or if he wrote ***one*** letter ***on the ground and one*** letter ***on a beam,***[11] כָּתַב עַל שְׁנֵי כוֹתְלֵי הַבַּיִת — or if ***he wrote*** two letters ***on two*** non-adjacent ***walls of the house,*** עַל שְׁנֵי דַפֵּי פִנְקָס וְאֵין נֶהְגִּין זֶה עִם זֶה — or ***on two columns of a ledger, and they cannot be read together,***[12]

NOTES

6. I.e., he held the pen with the point toward him, and then turned his hand around and wrote (*Rav; Rashi; Tiferes Yisrael*).

7. I.e., he held the pen with his toes, in his mouth, or with his elbow, and wrote. In both the previous case (of writing back-handed) and in this case, the writer performs the forbidden labor in an unusual manner, and the Mishnah therefore exempts him from a *chatas*.

8. I.e., a letter had been written [even by this same person] before the Sabbath, and he wrote a second letter alongside it on the Sabbath, thereby completing a two-letter unit (*Rashi; Tiferes Yisrael*). Despite the fact that his writing resulted in a complete word, the Mishnah exempts him from a *chatas* because he did not perform the minimum amount of writing required for liability on the Sabbath itself.

9. I.e., he rewrote two letters over the same two letters that were already written there, thereby reinforcing them (*Rav; Rashi*). Here, despite the fact that he wrote the minimum two-letter measure, the Mishnah exempts him from a *chatas,* because he did not create new letters.

10. In the script used to write a Torah scroll, the letter *ches* (ח) is composed of two *zayins* (ז) that are joined together on top. In this case, he intended to write a *ches* — i.e., to write two *zayins* and connect them — but his pen skipped and he failed to complete the roof of the *ches* (*Rav; Rashi; Tiferes Yisrael*). Since his writing of two letters was unintentional, he is exempt from a *chatas.*

11. I.e., he wrote one letter on the floor and one letter on a beam of the ceiling, making it impossible to read them together (*Tiferes Yisrael*). In this case, and in the next two cases as well, he is exempt from a *chatas* because the two letters that he wrote cannot be combined.

12. The ledger referred to here [unlike the one mentioned above] is one in which information is entered in columns, so that a letter written in one column cannot be read together with a letter written in another column unless the intervening parchment is cut away. Therefore, the letters that the person wrote are not considered a two-letter unit for which he would be liable.

[The Mishnah first stated the ruling concerning the case of two different walls, where it is obvious that the letters cannot be read together, and then proceeded to the

פָּטוּר — *he is exempt.*[13]

The Mishnah concludes:

כָּתַב אוֹת אַחַת נוֹטָרִיקוֹן — *One who wrote one letter as an abbreviation:*[14] רַבִּי יְהוֹשֻׁעַ בֶּן בְּתֵירָא מְחַיֵּיב — *R' Yehoshua ben Beseira holds* him *liable;* וַחֲכָמִים פּוֹטְרִין — *but the Sages exempt* him.[15]

NOTES

case of two columns that are side by side, where the ruling is more novel. The same ruling would apply to someone who writes two letters on a single wall of a house, but far enough apart from one another so that they cannot be read together. That case is analogous to that of writing letters in different columns of the same scroll (*Rav; Rashi*).]

13. In all the preceding cases, he is exempt, in each case for its own particular reason.

14. I.e., he wrote one letter followed by a period or an apostrophe to indicate that it stands for an entire word (*Rav; Rashi*).

15. R' Yehoshua ben Beseira holds that since a complete word is understood from the initial, it is as though he wrote the complete word. The Sages, however, disagree and exempt the person, since, after all, he actually wrote only one letter (*Rav; Rambam Commentary; Tiferes Yisrael*).

GEMS FROM THE GEMARA

Our Mishnah presents several cases in which a person is exempt from a *chatas* because he is not considered to have written the minimum amount for liability, since the two letters that he wrote cannot be combined. On the other hand, the Gemara (104b) explains that in cases in which the two letters *can* be brought together (and therefore read together) he is liable, even if they are never actually brought together.

According to *Rashi,* this is so only when the two can be brought together (and therefore read together) without altering the surface upon which they are written; for example, in a case in which the two letters are written on two separate pieces of paper. Since it is possible to set the pieces of paper next to each other and read them together, they can combine to form the minimum measure for liability, even though they were not together at the time they were written, and even if they are never brought together. However, if it would be necessary to alter the surface in order to bring the two letters together — for example, in a case in which the two letters are written at some distance from each other on the same piece of paper, where they cannot be brought together without either cutting away the intervening paper or folding the page — one is not liable to a *chatas.*

SUNDAY

PARASHAS VAYECHI

On the other hand, *Rambam* (*Hil. Shabbos* 11:12, as understood by *Maggid Mishneh*) holds the person liable even in a case where the two letters can be brought together by folding the paper, since there is no need to actually alter the writing surface in doing so. But even *Rambam* concedes that in a case in which folding the surface will not suffice, and the letters can be brought together only if they are cut from the paper upon which they are written (for example, where the letters are written on opposite sides of the same sheet, so that they cannot be seen together even if the paper is folded), they do not combine to form the minimum measure, and one who writes them in this manner is not liable to a *chatas* (see *Shaar HaTziyun* 340:42).

A MUSSAR THOUGHT FOR THE DAY

We explained in *A Torah Thought for the Day* that the reason why Yaakov exerted himself even in his illness to sit up on his bed when his son Yosef entered the room was because Yosef was a king, and a monarch must always be treated with respect and awe. The guidelines for the appropriate honor due to a king are derived from the instruction: שׂוֹם תָּשִׂים עָלֶיךָ מֶלֶךְ, *You shall surely set over yourself a king* (*Devarim* 17:15), which, as the Gemara (*Sanhedrin* 19b) explains, implies *so his awe will be upon you. Rashi* (*Kesubos* 17a ד״ה שום תשים; see also *Shitah Mekubetzes* there) explains that this implication is understood from the Torah's usage of the double verb שׂוֹם תָּשִׂים (literally, *Set, you shall set*); the Torah is saying that the Jewish people are commanded to maintain a constant awareness of the ruling monarch.

In his *Alei Shur* (vol. II p. 425), *R' Shlomo Wolbe* explains one of the Torah's goals in commanding a person to constantly feel the awe of the king; the awe that is felt when a king is seen will help a person to feel the awe of Hashem. This tool is needed because Hashem cannot be tangibly appreciated. Since there is nothing that a person will naturally sense about Hashem and His omnificence that will inspire him to live his life with the ongoing perspective of total *yiras Shamayim,* awe of Heaven, the only way to begin to attain this sense of reverence is to develop it in other ways, such as by being filled with awe of a human king. The many commandments designed to engender this feeling toward a monarch, R' Wolbe explains, habituate a person in living a life that includes uncompromising reverence for someone greater than himself. The feeling of awe that is naturally felt when the monarch is mentioned provides one with a perspective that may then be channeled toward the service of Hashem. [See *A Taste of Lomdus* for further discussion of this concept.]

R' Wolbe explains that reaching the end result of feeling awe for Hashem by respecting a king is the purpose that the Torah intended for monarchy in general, and it is also why Hashem has historically placed monarchs in the world. It may be true that a successfully functioning democracy is better than a corrupt sovereign. Nevertheless, a proper, just monarch, who understands that his job is to lead the people and not abuse his absolute powers, serves, in a small but meaningful way, as a symbol of total omnipotence that can be used to comprehend Hashem's rule.

Nowadays, continues R' Wolbe, most of the world is not privileged to live under a proper monarchy, for the simple reason that Hashem understands that the institution of monarchy would no longer help us. Once the generations' spiritual decline over the years reached the point where people did not properly use the feeling of awe of a ruler to better relate to Hashem, there was no longer any reason for Hashem to maintain the institution of monarchy. [Although other historical reasons for the move away from monarchies obviously existed, R' Wolbe is explaining why Hashem arranged for these reasons to arise.]

For a way in which we, in our times when we are not ruled by a king, can nevertheless use the idea of a human king to better relate to Hashem, see *A Closer Look at the Siddur.*

HALACHAH OF THE DAY

As additional protection against the accidental transgression of the *melachah* of *bishul,* as well as the *melachah* of *havarah* (kindling), the Sages enacted a prohibition against הַטְמָנָה, *insulating.*

It is forbidden by Rabbinic decree to insulate a pot of hot food on Shabbos by enclosing it in any material which retains heat, such as a towel. In some instances, it is even forbidden to insulate a pot on Erev Shabbos.

Insulation refers to a supplementary covering, which is wrapped around a container of food for the purpose of causing the pot to retain its heat. A primary wrapping is not considered insulation. For instance, aluminum foil covering food would be considered a primary wrapping, which serves the purpose of preserving the food, i.e., making sure it

does not dry out. Additional layers of foil that are unnecessary for the purpose of keeping the food fresh, however, may be considered insulation if their only purpose is to keep the food warm, not to preserve it.

In order for a covering to be seen as insulation, it must enclose the container of food completely. In other words, it must cover the container on top as well as around all the sides. If a substantial part of the container is not covered by the wrapping, it is not considered to be insulated. For this reason, a pot that was partially insulated prior to the onset of Shabbos may not be fully enclosed on Shabbos.

The prohibition against *insulating* applies to both completely cooked and partially cooked foods.

In the context of the laws of *bishul,* insulating materials are grouped into two different categories. First, there is the majority of materials — those that simply retain heat; and second, there are those materials that intensify the heat of the foods they enclose.

We will now discuss the restrictions that apply to the first category, materials that simply *retain* heat.

Most materials, when wrapped around a container of hot food, simply assist in the retention of the heat. These *heat-retaining substances* include cloth, aluminum foil, paper, wool and cotton. It is permissible to wrap a pot of hot food in a heat-retaining substance *before* Shabbos, in order to insulate it and keep it warm for later use. For instance, a hot pot of soup may be wrapped in a towel on Erev Shabbos in order to keep it warm for the evening meal. It is forbidden, however, to wrap a pot in any such substance on Shabbos itself.

A CLOSER LOOK AT THE SIDDUR

In *A Mussar Thought for the Day* we cited R' Wolbe, who explains that nowadays, since living under the rule of a king would not serve to assist man in reaching awe of Hashem, the institution of monarchy has largely passed from the world. *R' Wolbe* states, however, that even in recent times, there was still one type of kingship that a person could use as a tangible inspiration to become closer to Hashem — that of a government-in-exile, such as what the rulers of many European nations maintained in free England during the Second World War, after their countries had been overrun by the Germans. The people who had not managed to escape their respective countries, although ostensibly living under German rule, nevertheless felt a connection to their king who was living in a distant land, and, although they did not feel his rule on a daily basis, they yearned for the day when he would be able to return and actively lead his people. Moreover, many people did all that they could, through acts of resistance against the Germans, to restore the king's rule. For his part, the ruler would do his best to communicate with his people by giving them messages of inspiration and hope, as well as offering direction to the resistance fighters in their struggle against the occupying forces.

Looking at even this limited relationship between these people and their king, explains R' Wolbe, allows us to better understand a *tefillah* that we repeat many times on Rosh Hashanah: מְלוֹךְ עַל כָּל הָעוֹלָם כֻּלּוֹ בִּכְבוֹדֶךָ וְהִנָּשֵׂא עַל כָּל הָאָרֶץ בִּיקָרֶךָ וְהוֹפַע בַּהֲדַר גְּאוֹן עֻזֶּךָ עַל כָּל יוֹשְׁבֵי תֵבֵל אַרְצֶךָ, *Reign over the entire universe in Your glory; be exalted over all the world in Your splendor; reveal Yourself in the majestic grandeur of Your strength over all the dwellers of Your inhabited world.* We ask Hashem to quickly reveal Himself, so that the entire world will appreciate our King. The conquered peoples during the war years, although their king was distant from them and they were unable to feel his might on a daily basis, nevertheless understood that they still had a king. They maintained whatever relationship with him was possible under the circumstances, and yearned for his quick return. We too, although presently unable to comprehend the awe of Hashem's actual Kingship, are able to do the same; we must understand that although He is hidden from us, Hashem is our King, Who will soon return and reveal Himself to the world. We yearn for the day when His Kingship will be revealed; and we ask Hashem in our prayers to quickly reveal Himself and reign over the entire world openly. Our constant prayers to this end (this concept is found throughout our prayers — for example, in the second chapter of *Aleinu,* which we say three times daily) demonstrate that even though it is difficult for us to see His workings clearly, Hashem is still very much our King.

QUESTION OF THE DAY:

The Gemara states that certain visitors to the sick can remove one-sixtieth of their illness. Where is this alluded to in our verse?

For the answer, see page 221.

פרשת ויחי

SUNDAY

PARASHAS VAYECHI

A TASTE OF LOMDUS

We explained in *A Mussar Thought for the Day* that the obligation to honor a king requires that everyone approach him with deference and awe. The Gemara (*Kiddushin* 32b) comments that unlike a parent or Torah scholar, who may excuse others from paying them the proper respect, the need for royal awe is absolute, and the king is therefore not allowed to excuse any form of homage due to him.

In addition to requiring forms of respect such as bowing when approaching the king and the prohibition to sit in his throne or use his personal horse or chariot, the need for royal awe even precludes the king from performing mitzvos that will lessen his prestige in the eyes of the people. One example of an action that a king may not perform is showing honor to a bride or groom; since all must defer to the monarch, any special homage that he shows to others in effect diminishes his office, making such displays of honor inappropriate (*Kesubos* 17a).

A king's permission to perform other mitzvos is the subject of dispute in the Mishnah, with R' Yehudah ruling that a king may marry his childless brother's wife through *yibum,* levirate marriage, or perform the *chalitzah* ceremony (which involves allowing her to spit toward him), if he does not wish to marry her. Even though *chalitzah* is not a dignified process, and it could have the result of lessening the king's respect in the eyes of the people (and in regard to *yibum,* it is unbefitting that a king be required to marry a commoner's former wife), the Gemara (*Sanhedrin* 19b) explains that according to R' Yehudah, *a mitzvah is different;* a mitzvah that must be performed, even if it involves a less than dignified act, does not decrease royal honor, for it is obvious to all that the king is only following the rule of the Torah, to which both king and commoner must be subservient.

Other opinions in the Mishnah argue with R' Yehudah, ruling that a king is not allowed to perform the undignified actions of *yibum* and *chalitzah.* However, even these opinions agree that King Agrippas acted admirably when he stood to read from the Torah, even though royal protocol mandates that a king sit when in public (see *Sotah* 41b). The commentaries struggle to explain the rationale of this opinion; what is the difference between this display of respect for the Torah at the expense of his personal prestige (that all opinions agree was correct), and R' Yehudah's broad permission of *"a mitzvah is different,"* that allows a king to perform any mitzvah when it is clear that he is only following the Torah's directions (that these opinions reject)?

Rabbeinu David (cited in *Chidushei HaRan* to *Sanhedrin* 19b) explains that the reason R' Yehudah's disputants do not feel that *a mitzvah is different* in regard to allowing a king to perform *yibum* and *chalitzah* is because, unlike a king's standing up to read from the Torah, these mitzvos involve other people as well. While no one disputes the basic premise that following the Torah's higher standard of conduct does not diminish the king's honor even when coming at the expense of his own royal pageantry, a monarch may not allow *other people* to interact with him in any way that is less than appropriate. As the Gemara teaches: מֶלֶךְ שֶׁמָּחַל עַל כְּבוֹדוֹ אֵין כְּבוֹדוֹ מָחוּל, *if a king forgives the honor due him, his honor is not forgiven,* and he still must be honored. It is only when performing a mitzvah that does not involve anybody else, such as standing to read from a Torah scroll, that a king is permitted to decrease his personal prestige in order to increase the honor of Hashem.

Perhaps *Rabbeinu David's* distinction between interpersonal mitzvos and mitzvos that do not involve anyone else may be better understood in light of the explanation of *Ayeles HaShachar* (*Kiddushin* 32b) as to the reason why one must honor a king. Unlike the need to honor a parent or Torah scholar, where the person's elevated status effectively determines that he be treated differently, the commandment to respect a king is understood from שׂוֹם תָּשִׂים עָלֶיךָ מֶלֶךְ, *You shall surely set over yourself a king,* which, as explained above, the Gemara understands to be instructing — honor him, *so his awe will be upon you. Ayeles HaShachar* points out that the need to honor a king is not for *the king's* benefit; rather, the Gemara is in effect stating that the purpose of respecting a king is to engender awe among the people. Thus, while a person who is being respected for his own accomplishments or status can excuse dimensions of honor that are being shown toward him, a king cannot; the people, commanded to have awe, must respect him nonetheless. With this in mind, *Rabbeinu David's* application of the Gemara's rule — מֶלֶךְ שֶׁמָּחַל עַל כְּבוֹדוֹ אֵין כְּבוֹדוֹ מָחוּל, *if a king forgives the honor due him, his honor is not forgiven* — to the opinions in the Mishnah that do not allow a king to perform *yibum* and *chalitzah* makes sense; the directive to honor a king has nothing to do with the monarch's own actions and desires, but is a Torah commandment that must be fulfilled under all circumstances.

Rav Yosef Shalom Elyashiv (*He'aros B'Maseches Sotah* 41b) points out that based on the intrinsic difference between the mitzvah to honor a king and the mitzvah to honor a sage, an apparent paradox is resolved; namely, that a king must stand while testifying in court, while a Torah scholar is permitted to remain seated, due to the mitzvah to show him great honor. Similar to the distinction drawn above, Rav Elyashiv explains that even though a king is afforded a greater level of respect than a Torah scholar — who must defer to the monarch like everybody else — the Torah scholar's right to honor is a reflection of his intrinsic greatness, while a king is respected only because the Torah requires that other people treat him deferentially. Since standing in court is a procedural part of testifying, unrelated to encouraging other people to interact with him in an unfitting manner, there is no reason why a king should not have to stand; no one is actively showing him disrespect when he does so. A Torah scholar, on the other hand, is included in the commandment to honor a person who exemplifies greatness in Torah — even if that person happens to be himself — and must sit in court, so he does not show disrespect to the Torah.

וַאֲנִי בְּבֹאִי מִפַּדָּן מֵתָה עָלַי רָחֵל בְּאֶרֶץ כְּנַעַן
בַּדֶּרֶךְ בְּעוֹד כִּבְרַת־אֶרֶץ לָבֹא אֶפְרָתָה וָאֶקְבְּרֶהָ
שָּׁם בְּדֶרֶךְ אֶפְרָת הִוא בֵּית לָחֶם

But as for me — when I came from Paddan,
Rachel died on me in the land of Canaan on the road,
while there was still a stretch of land to go to Ephras,
and I buried her there on the road to Ephras,
which is Bethlehem (*Bereishis* 48:7).

Rashi explains that Yaakov was excusing himself to Yosef for not burying his mother in the Cave of Machpelah where Yaakov himself desired to be buried. Yaakov told Yosef: It was not weather or distance that prevented me. On the contrary, it was a dry season, and I did not even bring her into Bethlehem to be buried. I know that you have hard feelings in your heart against me, but you should know that I buried her there in accordance with the word of Hashem, so that at a later date she would pray for the Jews going into exile, and her prayers would guarantee that they will indeed return to Eretz Yisrael.

Ramban's explanation is more in line with the simple meaning of the verse. In his opinion, Yaakov was explaining to Yosef that since Rachel died in Eretz Yisrael, wherever she was buried, the site was a holy place. And because she died "on the road," it was not possible to leave all the children and all their belongings and to take her to the Cave of Machpelah. There were also no doctors to embalm and preserve her body until burial. This is the meaning of the word עָלַי, *on me;* Yaakov explained that Rachel had died at a time when the burden of caring for the children and livestock was entirely upon him.

Ramban offers another explanation of why Yaakov did not bury Rachel in the Cave of Machpelah. Yaakov did not wish to bury both Leah and Rachel in the same place, for this would be testament that he had married two sisters (something later forbidden by the Torah), and he would be ashamed before his forefathers who were buried there. As *Ramban* states elsewhere (26:5), the *Avos* kept the entire Torah even prior to being commanded to do so. However, their observance occurred only when they lived in Eretz Yisrael. That is why in Aram — where Lavan lived — Yaakov agreed to marry two sisters, although it would one day be Biblically forbidden. Rachel died upon their entrance to the Holy Land, but he did not bury her in the Cave, lest it appear that even in Eretz Yisrael he had been married to two sisters.

Leah was entitled to burial in the Cave, because she was the one married to him first, permissibly. Rachel was taken second because of his promise to take her; that is why she was buried in Bethlehem.

The Brisker Rav is unwilling to accept the possibility that Yaakov did not keep a Biblical law even outside of Eretz Yisrael. He explains that for the prohibition of marrying two sisters to exist, there must first be an institution of Jewish marriage, which could not occur until the Torah was given. This means that any marriage that took place before the Torah was given was entirely different from a marriage that occurred afterward. Thus, although Yaakov kept all the laws of the Torah, this refers only to mitzvos that were by nature possible to keep. Since there was no Jewish marriage, the prohibition against marrying two sisters did not apply.

MISHNAH OF THE DAY: SHABBOS 12:6

This Mishnah concludes the discussion about liability for writing: הַכּוֹתֵב שְׁתֵּי אוֹתִיּוֹת בִּשְׁתֵּי הַעֲלָמוֹת — ***One who writes two letters in two lapses of awareness,***[1] אַחַת שַׁחֲרִית וְאַחַת בֵּין הָעַרְבַּיִם — or ***one in the morning and one in the afternoon,***[2] רַבָּן גַּמְלִיאֵל מְחַיֵּיב — ***Rabban Gamliel holds*** him ***liable*** to a *chatas,*[3] וַחֲכָמִים פּוֹטְרִין — ***but the Sages exempt*** him.[4]

NOTES

1. I.e., unaware that he was violating the Sabbath, a person wrote one letter. He then became aware of his violation, but then once more lapsed into unawareness and wrote a second letter alongside the first one (*Rav*).

2. That is, even if he does not become aware of his violation between the writing of the first and second letters, but an interval of time long enough for him to have learned of his mistake elapses before he writes the second letter (*Rav; Rashi*).

3. Rabban Gamliel holds that becoming aware that one has committed less than the minimum amount of work required for a *chatas* is not considered true awareness of a violation, and does not, therefore, prevent the two half-measures from combining to create one liability (*Rav*).

4. The Sages maintain that his awareness between the two half measures separates them, and does not allow them to be counted as one forbidden act in order to create liability to a *chatas* (*Rav*).

GEMS FROM THE GEMARA

According to *Rav* and *Rashi,* the first case of our Mishnah is one in which, unaware that he was violating the Sabbath, a person wrote one letter. He then became aware of his violation, but once more lapsed into unawareness, and wrote a second letter alongside the first one. The second case of the Mishnah is one in which he did not become aware of his violation between the writing of the first and second letters, but an interval of time long enough for him to have learned of his mistake elapsed before he wrote the second letter.

Tosafos question this explanation, on the grounds that the Mishnah should have specified the minimum time required for this presumption of realization (of one's mistake) to take effect, since this is the entire point of this case of the Mishnah. Furthermore, *Tosafos* quote the Gemara (104b) as saying that a person may be liable even for writing one letter in each of two cities. Presumably, this would necessitate a lapse of several hours. Since, according to *Rashi,* the Sages consider him exempt where there has been a substantial lapse between the time he wrote the first letter and the time he wrote the second letter, and since the halachah follows the view of the Sages, how can the Gemara rule that he is liable in such a case!?

Maginei Shlomo answers on behalf of *Rashi* that we do not consider the inadvertent transgressor as having become aware unless so much time has elapsed that he must surely have become aware of his transgression. This presumption can safely be made only if he wrote one letter in the morning and one letter in the afternoon. Thus, the Mishnah is actually giving the time limit necessary for this presumption to be made.

Tos. Yom Tov also takes issue with *Rav's* and *Rashi's* understanding of the Mishnah. He questions whether the Mishnah deals with one who was aware that it was the Sabbath but forgot that writing is proscribed, or with one who was aware that writing is proscribed on the Sabbath, but forgot that it was the Sabbath. If it is the latter case, then how are we sure that he reminded himself during the interval between morning and afternoon? The Mishnah above (7:1) implies that we can only be sure that he became aware of it by the following Sabbath! After the short lapse of time from morning to evening, there is no assurance that he discovered that it was the Sabbath.

Maginei Shlomo responds that the Mishnah deals with one who knew that it was the Sabbath, but forgot that writing is proscribed. Since he once knew of this prohibition, we are certain that he will remind himself during the lapse of time from morning to afternoon. The above Mishnah (7:1), however, deals with one who *never knew* that writing is forbidden on the Sabbath. We have, therefore, no assurance that he will become cognizant of this restriction unless he studies the laws of the Sabbath.

A MUSSAR THOUGHT FOR THE DAY

There is an interesting lesson to be learned from the fact that Yaakov Avinu excused himself to Yosef for not burying Rachel in the Cave of Machpelah only when he asked Yosef to bury him there. As *Rashi* states (see *A Torah Thought for the Day*), Yaakov said, "I know that you have hard feelings toward me for the way I buried your mother, but you should know that it was done in accordance with the word of Hashem." An obvious question may be asked: If Yaakov had known all along that Yosef had questions and complaints as to why Yaakov buried Rachel where he did, why did he wait over forty years to set the record straight? Why didn't he explain to Yosef at the earliest opportunity that he had acted as he had because Hashem had told him to do so?

Rav Berel Soloveitchik would say that we can learn from here that when someone is following the exact word of Hashem, he is not obligated to explain his actions to everyone, unless a *chillul Hashem* is involved, or there will be some other suspicion that he is transgressing a law of the Torah with his actions. Otherwise, a person must simply follow the word and will of Hashem as accurately as he can. There is an important reason for this. When someone adopts the attitude that he will keep the mitzvos only when his actions receive the approval of others, there is a danger that he will eventually start changing and altering his mitzvah performance to gain that approval. This can lead to situations where one does not fulfill the mitzvos as he should, and eventually cause a serious decline in the level of his *avodas Hashem.*

In the first chapter of *Orach Chaim,* the *Shulchan Aruch* teaches us that when one performs mitzvos, he must not be intimidated by those who scorn the true servants of Hashem. He must be strong and stubborn, and hold his head high with pride as he performs the service of Hashem.

Yaakov had no reason to excuse himself, for he knew that he was acting in accordance with Hashem's will. Yosef might have been unhappy with his actions, but Yaakov did not seek his approval. However, when Yaakov wanted to be sure that Yosef would carry out his wishes and bury him in Eretz Yisrael, he did not want any misconception to hinder Yosef's resolve to do so, so he explained the reason behind his actions.

HALACHAH OF THE DAY

The following cases are exceptions to the restriction against insulating, in which a container may be insulated with a heat-retaining material on Shabbos:

If a pot of fully cooked food was wrapped in a *heat-retaining substance* before Shabbos, and was subsequently uncovered on Shabbos, it may be re-wrapped. Moreover, it is permissible for one to unwrap the container on Shabbos in order to remove some food, and then re-insulate the container in order to keep the remaining contents warm. One may also add an additional layer of insulation, such as a towel, to a pot which was already insulated before Shabbos (provided that it was completely covered before Shabbos, as mentioned above).

The prohibition against insulating with heat-retaining substances applies only to a *kli rishon* (i.e., the original pot that was heated on the flame). If the food is transferred to a *kli sheni* (i.e., a second vessel), it is permissible to insulate the vessel with a heat-retaining material. Thus, if the need arises to insulate hot food on Shabbos, one may transfer the food to a *kli sheni* in order to insulate it.

An additional exception applies only in cases of necessity. If the food necessary for the Shabbos meal has cooled to the extent that it is no longer at or above the temperature of *yad soledes bo,* it is permissible to insulate the pot with a heat-retaining material even if the food is still located in a *kli rishon.* In such a case (if there is no container available to which the food can be transferred), the *kli rishon* can be used to preserve hot food essential to the Shabbos meal.

Hot liquids may be poured into a thermos on Shabbos.

We will now discuss the restrictions that apply to materials in the second category: materials that *intensify* the heat of the food they enclose.

There are some materials that have the ability to increase and intensify the heat of the items they enclose. These items include salt, peat, lime, sand, wet cotton, grass and straw. These materials are known as *heat-intensifying substances.* It is forbidden, without exception, to insulate any container — even a *kli sheni* — in a *heat-intensifying substance,* even on Erev Shabbos.

Although it is unusual nowadays to store food in any of the aforementioned items, there are some practical applications to this halachah, which we will discuss tomorrow.

A CLOSER LOOK AT THE SIDDUR

When Yaakov blessed Ephraim and Menasheh, he told Yosef that he had given him Shechem as an extra inheritance, the land that he (Yaakov) had taken from the hands of the Amorites בְּחַרְבִּי וּבְקַשְׁתִּי, *with my sword and with my bow* (48:22). *Targum Onkelos* defines these two words as follows: בִּצְלוֹתִי וּבְבָעוּתִי, *with my prayer and my supplications.* [We find these words in our recital of the full *Kaddish*: תִּתְקַבֵּל צְלוֹתְהוֹן וּבָעוּתְהוֹן, *May the prayers and supplications (of Israel) be accepted.*] According to *Targum,* Yaakov alluded to the fact that he had been able to conquer Shechem through the power of prayer.

We may ask, however: If Yaakov meant to say that he had received Shechem because of his prayers, why did he describe them as "his sword and his bow"? What is the meaning behind these two descriptions of prayer?

The Brisker Rav explains that there are two types of prayer: (1) the standard text of *tefillah,* which the 120 Sages of the *Anshei Knesses HaGedolah* (the Sages of the Great Assembly) instituted as a set daily prayer and as seasonal prayers for festivals; (2) prayers that one can insert privately, everyone according to his needs and wishes.

There is a major difference between these two types of prayers. A private prayer does not always get answered. It depends on how much concentration and dedication the person puts into his prayer. Such a prayer is compared to a קֶשֶׁת, *a bow,* where the distance that the arrow will fly depends on how much force is put into the drawing of the bow.

On the other hand, the set standard prayers are compared to a sword, which does not need extra force to give it the strength to do its job. Its power is set in place. These are the prayers which were prepared with all the power necessary to reach their intended destination. As the *Nefesh HaChaim* says, if a person just has the simple meaning of the words in mind, the daily prayers ascend to Heaven armed with all the deep and mystical intentions that were programmed into their words by those great Sages. [Of course, the greater the concentration one can muster even for these prayers, the more powerful they will be.]

Meshech Chochmah also explains that there are two types of *tefillah,* but he makes a distinction between a *tefillas chovah* (the three obligatory daily prayers), which always gets answered, even with only basic concentration, and a *tefillas nedavah,* a voluntary prayer, which must be said with added *kavannah,* intent, and requires full concentration. [Indeed, *Mishnah Berurah* states that additional prayers said either during the *berachah* of *Shomei'a Tefillah* or at the conclusion of the *Shemoneh Esrei* should be recited in the language one best understands, to facilitate full concentration.]

QUESTION OF THE DAY:

When Yaakov spoke to Yosef of Rachel's death, why did he say, "Rachel died . . .," and not, "your mother died . . ."?

For the answer, see page 221.

פרשת ויחי

TUESDAY

PARASHAS VAYECHI

A TORAH THOUGHT FOR THE DAY

פַּחַז כַּמַּיִם אַל־תּוֹתַר כִּי עָלִיתָ מִשְׁכְּבֵי אָבִיךָ

[Because of your] water-like impetuosity, you cannot be foremost; because you went up upon your father's bed (*Bereishis* 49:4).

In this verse, Yaakov tells his firstborn son Reuven that his sin of switching the place of his father's bed after Rachel had died (see above, 35:22 with *Rashi*) had cost him the privilege of receiving all the rights of the firstborn. As a result, the double portion of Eretz Yisrael that would have been his birthright was given to Yosef's sons instead, and Ephraim and Menasheh received two portions instead of one. [For a discussion of why Yosef's children were chosen to receive the extra portion, see *Bava Basra* 123a.]

Nevertheless, *Yalkut Shimoni* to this verse states that Reuven did *teshuvah* and repented of his sin — indeed, the *Yalkut* states that Reuven was the first to do *teshuvah.* This statement, however, seemingly contradicts the statement found in the Midrash that it was Yehudah's confession about fathering Tamar's child that spurred Reuven to repent. According to that Midrash, Yehudah seemingly repented *before* Reuven!

The *sefer Taam VeDaas* (to 33:7) notes that this second Midrash is problematic for another reason as well. How can it be that Reuven repented only after Yehudah confessed? The verse immediately following the sale of Yosef (*Bereishis* 37:29) states that *Reuven returned to the pit,* and *Rashi* there writes (in his second interpretation) that Reuven had been occupied with fasting and wearing sackcloth in penitence for his sin. This occurred well before Yehudah's confession — so how can the Midrash say that Yehudah caused Reuven to repent?

The *Taam VeDaas* answers that although Reuven had begun to repent his sin before Yehudah confessed, he had never performed *Vidui,* verbal confession of his sin. He had clothed himself in sackcloth and fasted, but had never acknowledged his sin by saying, "I have sinned!" It was only when Yehudah publicly confessed in the matter of Tamar that Reuven did the same. Thus, while Reuven was the first to do *teshuvah,* Yehudah was the first to perform *Vidui.* [*Mizrachi* explains similarly, stating that Reuven's earlier *teshuvah* was performed in private, while Yehudah was the first to repent of his sin *in public,* an example that Reuven followed.]

MISHNAH OF THE DAY: SHABBOS 13:1

פרשת ויחי

TUESDAY

PARASHAS VAYECHI

The following Mishnah continues the tractate's ongoing elaboration of the various forbidden labors, and begins a discussion of acts forbidden as *weaving*: רַבִּי אֱלִיעֶזֶר אוֹמֵר — ***R' Eliezer says:*** הָאוֹרֵג שְׁלֹשָׁה חוּטִין בַּתְּחִילָּה — ***One who weaves three threads at the beginning,***[1] וְאַחַת עַל הָאָרִיג ***or one*** who adds thread ***to fabric that is*** already partially ***woven,***[2] חַיָּב — ***is liable*** to a *chatas.* וַחֲכָמִים אוֹמְרִים — ***But the Sages say:*** בֵּין בַּתְּחִילָּה בֵּין בַּסּוֹף — ***Whether at the beginning or at the end,*** שִׁיעוּרוֹ שְׁנֵי חוּטִין — ***its*** minimum ***measure*** for *chatas* liability ***is two threads.***[3]

NOTES

1. I.e., a person who commences to weave a new fabric on the Sabbath is liable for the forbidden labor of *weaving* once he has woven three threads (*Rav; Rashi*).

2. I.e., one who adds even one thread to a previously woven material is liable (*Rav; Rambam Commentary; Rashi*). Since this thread is combined with already woven material, it is of greater significance, and the one who wove it is therefore liable to a *chatas* (*Rashi*).

3. I.e., whether one starts to weave a new fabric or whether he adds to an already woven fabric, he is not liable unless he weaves two threads. [The expression "at the end" is not meant to denote the completion of the garment, for if he completes the garment he is liable for weaving even one thread. This is similar to completing a book by writing one letter, for which one is liable, as explained above (12:5) (*Tos. R' Akiva Eiger* from *Tos.* 105a).]

GEMS FROM THE GEMARA

Elucidating the view of R' Eliezer, R' Yitzchak cites a Baraisa that states that according to R' Eliezer, a person is liable to a *chatas* for weaving *two* threads in the beginning of a new fabric.

The Gemara (105a) asks: Did we not learn in our Mishnah that R' Eliezer renders one liable only for weaving *three* threads? The Gemara answers that both versions are correct, but they deal with different cases. One version of R' Eliezer deals with thick threads, while the other version deals with thin threads.

The Gemara offers two explanations as to which ruling deals with thick threads and which deals with thin threads. In the first version, the Gemara assumes that the Mishnah, which holds one liable only for weaving three threads, deals with *thick* threads. The rationale for this is as follows: Thick threads do not make a tight weave — therefore, two woven threads will unravel, and are not considered woven. Three woven thick threads, however, will not unravel, and one is therefore not liable unless he weaves three thick threads. However, if thin threads are used, even two woven threads will not unravel. Therefore, R' Eliezer rules in the Baraisa cited by R' Yitzchak that a person is liable for weaving even two thin threads.

According to the second approach of the Gemara, the distinction between two threads and three threads is that thick threads are considered significant even if there are only two of them, while two thin threads are considered insignificant. According to this view, one is liable for weaving thin threads only if he weaves three of them. This is the explanation of R' Eliezer's ruling in the Mishnah (which refers to *thin* threads according to this approach). Thick threads, however, are significant even if only two of them are woven. Thus, R' Eliezer, as cited in the Baraisa, ruled that one is liable even for weaving two thick threads.

A MUSSAR THOUGHT FOR THE DAY

Chovos HaLevavos states that the essence of *teshuvah* is a person's return to the service of Hashem, attaining the status he lost when he strayed. How is this to be accomplished? *Chovos HaLevavos* explains that the nature of the *teshuvah* necessary is dependent upon the nature of the sinful behavior. He illustrates with an analogy: Two people are ill, both because they were not eating properly. However, while one simply was not eating enough, the other was consuming unhealthy foods that were affecting his health in a negative way. For the first, the remedy is straightforward; he must simply begin to eat the right foods and receive proper nutrition. There is nothing that he must now cease to eat. The remedy for the second person, however, involves two stages. First, he must stop eating the foods that are injurious to him, and then he must replace them with an equal amount of healthy foods. If he persists in his unhealthy eating, eating healthy foods in addition will not cure him.

So too, says *Chovos HaLevavos,* it is with sinners. Someone who has become lax in his mitzvah observance and is not doing what he should, need only concentrate upon performing his mitzvos with greater zeal; this is his *teshuvah.* But if one has done *aveiros* as well, then it does not suffice for him to perform virtuous acts; he must desist from his evil ways as well.

Chovos HaLevavos lists seven things of which a sinner must be cognizant if he is to attain true *teshuvah.* (1) He must be regretful and ashamed of his evil behavior. (2) He must know that the deed was wrong, and recognize the wickedness of his act. (3) He must know that Hashem is aware of his misdeed, and that punishment (without forgiveness) is inevitable. (4) He must understand that *teshuvah* is the cure that he requires. (5) He should make an accounting of all the good that Hashem has done for him. (6) He must contrast this with his own disobedience, and use it as a spur to his resolve not to sin further. (7) He must take concrete steps to avoid sinning again. One who undertakes to satisfy these requirements can attain true *teshuvah.*

HALACHAH OF THE DAY

As we learned yesterday, it is forbidden to insulate a pot with material that increases the heat of the pot's contents. This prohibition extends even to Erev Shabbos.

A pot that is wrapped in a towel and then placed onto a *blech* or hot plate is considered to be insulated in a *heat-intensifying substance,* since the towel combines with the heat from below to raise the temperature of the pot. In this case, the wrapping does not only help the pot retain its heat; rather, it creates a situation where the flame is able to increase the temperature of the food. Thus, it is forbidden to enwrap a pot and place it on a *blech* or hot plate, even if this was done before Shabbos. [If one wishes to do this, he must take care to leave a portion of the pot uncovered. As we learned above, a pot is not considered to be insulated unless it is completely enwrapped.]

Using the same logic, insulating a hot water urn by covering it with a padded cover or the like would also be considered insulating with a *heat-intensifying* substance, since, as in the case of the pot on the *blech,* the wrapping, combined with the heating element of the urn, helps raise the temperature of the water. Thus, an urn may not be completely covered with any type of wrapping, *even on Erev Shabbos.*

A container that is completely submerged in hot food is considered to be insulated in a *heat-intensifying substance,* since the hot food will help raise the temperature of the container. Thus, it is forbidden to submerge a small pot in a larger pot of hot food or water, even on Erev Shabbos. For the same reason, food that is completely wrapped in aluminum foil also may not be totally submerged in a pot of hot food, even on Erev Shabbos. However, there is an important exception to this rule: If one's intention in submerging the food is to have the submerged food absorb the flavor of the food in which it is being placed — not just to be insulated and warmed — it is then permissible to submerge wrapped food in a pot of hot food. An example of this would be a foil-wrapped *kishke* or *kugel* that is submerged in a pot of *cholent.* Since the intention is for the *kishke* or *kugel* to absorb the flavor of the *cholent,* it is permissible to place the wrapped *kishke* or *kugel* into the *cholent.* [If the intent is simply to keep the food hot, it may be placed on top of the *cholent,* but not completely within it.]

There are methods of wrapping that do not fall under the prohibition of *insulating.* If a substantial part of the wrapping is not touching the surface of the pot that it is wrapped around, so that it is only a loose covering, it is not considered to be *insulation* according to halachah, and is thus permitted. For this reason, one may drape a towel over a pot or urn, allowing it to hang loosely, even though the entire pot is covered. Likewise, if the top of the pot is covered with a plate that is wider than the pot itself, the pot may then be wrapped in a towel, since the towel will not touch the entire pot; it will rather slope inward from the wide plate on top to the more narrow base of the pot. This method satisfies the criteria of being a loose-fitting covering, and is not considered to be *insulation.*

This concludes our discussion of the *melachah* of *bishul.*

A CLOSER LOOK AT THE SIDDUR

The fifth *berachah* of the *Shemoneh Esrei,* in which we ask Hashem to assist us in attaining repentance, opens with the words: הֲשִׁיבֵנוּ אָבִינוּ לְתוֹרָתֶךָ וְקָרְבֵנוּ מַלְכֵּנוּ לַעֲבוֹדָתֶךָ וְהַחֲזִירֵנוּ בִּתְשׁוּבָה שְׁלֵמָה לְפָנֶיךָ, *Return us, our Father, to Your Torah; and bring us close, our King, to Your service; and bring us back, in complete repentance, before You.* It concludes with the blessing: בָּרוּךְ אַתָּה ה׳ הָרוֹצֶה בִּתְשׁוּבָה, *Blessed are You,* HASHEM, *Who desires repentance.*

Baal HaTurim notes that this blessing begins and ends with the letter *hei* (ה). He explains that this is because the *hei* has an extra opening on its side (as opposed to the similar letter *ches* (ח), which does not); this opening alludes to *teshuvah,* as it symbolizes Hashem's willingness to allow sinners back into His good graces if they repent. He also notes that the numerical value of *hei* is five, and when the opening *hei* and the closing *hei* are added together, they total ten, which symbolizes the Ten Days of Repentance, during which Hashem brings Himself close to each Jew to encourage his prayer and repentance.

In our Yom Kippur prayers, we say: עַד יוֹם מוֹתוֹ תְּחַכֶּה לוֹ אִם יָשׁוּב מִיָּד תְּקַבְּלוֹ, *until the day of [a person's] death, He waits for him; if he repents, He will accept him immediately.* This prayers reveals the tremendous mercy that Hashem shows toward his creations. A person may have been a sinner his entire life, doing evil constantly without regard for Hashem or His Torah. As his life is coming to an end, when he does not even have strength left to sin, he contemplates his future, and repents of his past. Surely this is a less than perfect *teshuvah*! Yet Hashem not only will accept it, He does so *immediately,* without reservation. As we say elsewhere in the Yom Kippur prayers: אָנוּ מְלֵאֵי עָוֹן וְאַתָּה מָלֵא רַחֲמִים, *we are filled with iniquity, but You are filled with mercy.*

As we pray each day, the knowledge that Hashem is not wrathful or vengeful, but is rather a merciful God Who desires our sincere repentance, should act as a powerful stimulant, giving us the fortitude to mend our ways and live our lives as servants of Hashem.

QUESTION OF THE DAY:

Where in the Torah do we find that Reuven retained the status of firstborn?

For the answer, see page 221.

A TORAH THOUGHT FOR THE DAY

בְּסֹדָם אַל־תָּבֹא נַפְשִׁי בִּקְהָלָם אַל־תֵּחַד כְּבֹדִי
Into their conspiracy may my soul not enter; within their congregation may my honor not join (*Bereishis* 49:6).

R*amban* explains that Yaakov was stating here that the actions of Shimon and Levi in the matter of Shechem were planned and executed without his knowledge or consent — they were a conspiracy to which he had not been privy. *Rashi,* however, cites a Midrashic interpretation, according to which Yaakov was voicing a prayer that his name not be associated with events that would occur in the future involving the descendants of Shimon and Levi. His prayer with regard to Shimon was that he not be mentioned as an ancestor of Zimri, who sinned publicly with a Midianite woman and was slain by Pinchas (see *Bamidbar* 25:6 ff.). The prayer was accepted, for when the Torah traces the lineage of Zimri, Shimon is mentioned, but Yaakov is not. With respect to Levi, Yaakov prayed that he not be mentioned as the ancestor of Korach, who rebelled against Moshe. This prayer was also accepted, for when the Torah writes the lineage of Korach, he is described only as *the son of Yitzhar, son of Kehas, son of Levi* (ibid. 16:1); Yaakov is not mentioned.

Why were these sins especially disturbing to Yaakov, so that he would pray to have his name removed from any association with them? *R' Yitzchak Kirzner* explains that Yaakov personified the *middah* of *emes,* truth, and the study of Torah. His service of Hashem was based simply on following the exact commands issued by Hashem, without attempting to use logic or reasoning to modify his obligations. Both Zimri and Korach attempted to warp the laws of the Torah through logic. Zimri asked Moshe, "If Midianite women are forbidden, who permitted you to marry the daughter of Yisro?," ignoring the fact that he was committing a clearly forbidden act. Korach, too, came with a fallacious argument: "If one string of *techeiles* (specially dyed blue wool) is enough for a whole *tallis,* should a *tallis* made entirely of *techeiles* not be exempt from the one thread?" They, in their arrogance, convinced themselves that they were smarter than the Torah — and Yaakov prayed that his name not be associated with such a grievous sin.

[R' Kirzner notes further that the idea that one must obey Hashem without attempting to rationalize is indeed seen from the *tzitzis* themselves. It is true that *tzitzis* must contain *techeiles,* which logically lead a person to recall Hashem, for, as the Gemara explains, blue is reminiscent of the sea, which in turn is reminiscent of the sky, which leads one eventually to think of Hashem's Throne. However, it is also important to have *white* strings, for white symbolizes that which we *cannot* see. White contains all the colors of the spectrum, but they are not visible. This reminds us that even if we do not understand Hashem's directives, we must always fulfill them.]

MISHNAH OF THE DAY: SHABBOS 13:2

The following Mishnah considers the forbidden *melachah* of setting two heddles while setting up a loom for weaving:

הָעוֹשֶׂה שְׁתֵּי בָתֵּי נִירִין בַּנִּירִין — ***One who makes two heddles in heddles,*** [1] בַּקֵּירוֹס — ***or*** inserts two weft threads ***in a cloth made of palm fiber,*** [2] בַּנָּפָה בַּכְּבָרָה וּבַסַּל — in ***a fine sieve, a coarse sieve or a basket,*** [3] חַיָּיב — ***is liable*** to a *chatas.*

The Mishnah concludes with the minimums for two more related forbidden labors:

NOTES

1. I.e., one who passed two warp threads through the eyes of the heddles. As we learned above (7:2), between the two horizontal rollers of a loom and perpendicular to them are two frames (called harnesses) through which the warp threads must pass. Each of these harnesses has numerous vertical threads or wires mounted upon it. Each set of adjacent threads on the harness is knotted in two places to form a loop (or eye) at the center. This arrangement of threads and a loop is called a heddle. [Heddles may also be made by tying a ring between two lengths of thread. Modern hand looms often use a metal strip pierced at its center.] Every other warp thread (for example, each odd-numbered thread) passes through the eye of a heddle of the front harness and between two heddles on the second harness. The even-numbered warp threads each pass between two heddles on the first harness and through the eye of a heddle in the second harness. Placing two threads through the heddle eyes constitutes the *av* of setting two heddles (*Rav* here and 7:2; *Rashi* to 105a and above, 73a; cf. *Tiferes Yisrael*).

2. Fabric of palm fiber was used for sifting. It was woven in the manner in which sieves and baskets are woven (*Rav; Rambam Commentary;* cf. *Rashi, Tiferes Yisrael*).

3. The manner in which these three utensils were woven is similar. After the warp reeds of the sieve or basket are laid out side by side, they are fastened in place by looping one reed in the weft direction around the top of each of the warp reeds in order, and then doing the same at the bottom of each warp reed. This holds the reeds in place so that the weaving can be performed efficiently. Since the function of this looping is to hold the warp reeds in place for weaving, twisting the loops serves a purpose similar to setting warp threads into the heddles. One is therefore liable with this act for performing the forbidden labor of setting two heddles (*Rashi; Tos. Yom Tov*).

וְהַתּוֹפֵר שְׁתֵּי תְפִירוֹת — *One who sews two stitches*[4] וְהַקּוֹרֵעַ עַל מְנַת לִתְפּוֹר שְׁתֵּי תְפִירוֹת — *and one who tears in order to sew two stitches* is liable to a *chatas.*

NOTES

4. The Mishnah here teaches that a minimum of two passes of the needle [one in and one out] are required for one to be liable for sewing. [This in-and-out motion actually results in only a single stitch. We have nevertheless translated שְׁתֵּי תְפִירוֹת loosely as two "stitches" because there is no equivalent word in English for a single pass of the needle.] Although we have already learned of these forbidden labors (above, 7:2), they are repeated here in order to introduce the following Mishnah, which discusses instances in which one is exempt for tearing (*Tos. Yom Tov* from Gemara 105a).

GEMS FROM THE GEMARA

Our Mishnah taught that one who tears in order to sew two stitches is liable to a *chatas.* Tearing is one of several *melachos* that are inherently destructive. Now, as a rule, destructive labors are not Biblically forbidden, for the Torah prohibited only מְלֶאכֶת מַחֲשֶׁבֶת, *calculated labor;* thus, the Mishnah emphasizes that the tearing being done was performed for a constructive purpose — in order to resew the garment.

The Gemara (105a-b) inquires as to the exact circumstances under which it would be necessary to first tear a garment in order to sew it. [Seemingly, a garment that is not torn need not be sewn; and if it is already torn, it should suffice to simply sew the tear up without any further tearing!] The Gemara answers that it is necessary to tear the garment before resewing it in a case in which the surface of the garment was lumpy like a pocket. That is, we are not dealing with the case of a torn garment, but rather with a garment in which the seams were initially sewn inexpertly, leaving lumpy folds — "pockets" — in the fabric. The seams of such a garment must be torn open, and a new set of stitches sewn, so that the fabric will lay neatly and evenly *(Rashi).* When a person tears a section of such a garment in order to resew two stitches, he is performing constructive labor, and is therefore liable to a *chatas* on account of the forbidden labor of *tearing.*

Another instance where one would tear fabric in order to resew it is described in an earlier Gemara (75a). The Gemara states that if small moth holes were found in the curtains of the Mishkan, threads adjacent to the hole would be torn to broaden and square the hole, so that the craftsmen could make a neat repair of the damaged area. Such tearing is also considered constructive, and renders the tearer liable to a *chatas.*

A MUSSAR THOUGHT FOR THE DAY

In *A Torah Thought for the Day* we discussed the concept of following the commandments of Hashem even when we do not understand them, and the fact that one should not apply logic to decide how to fulfill mitzvos. This concept sheds light upon one of the more perplexing requirements of halachah — the obligation to become intoxicated on Purim until one cannot distinguish between "Cursed is Haman" and "Blessed is Mordechai" (see *Orach Chaim* 695:2). We also can use it to understand the famous, enigmatic comment of the *Shelah HaKadosh* that Yom Kippur is a "Yom K'Purim" — a day like Purim. In what way is Yom Kippur, a holy day of fasting and prayer, like Purim?

R' Chaim Shmulevitz explains that to understand the essence of Purim, one must first understand what it means to be a true servant of Hashem. The true servant does not ask why; he merely says, "I will do and I will listen," as the Jewish people did at Mt. Sinai. A true servant does not need to rationalize and understand what he is being told to do — he just does whatever he is told.

Throughout the year, we arrive at our *emunah* using logic and reasoning. But there is a higher level to be reached — removing our intellect from the equation, and simply serving Hashem as He wills, because He tells us to. That is the task of Purim — to reach a level where we will not try to reason, and we will simply obey. Hence, the requirement to render ourselves unable to reason intelligently.

In this way, Purim is indeed greater than Yom Kippur; for while on Yom Kippur we may reach great heights, our own reasoning is still involved. It is only on Purim that we reach for the rarefied level of total, instant, unthinking obedience.

We find several places in *Tanach* where allowing logic to cloud knowledge of Hashem's commands resulted in grave punishments. Moshe was not allowed to enter Eretz Yisrael because he reasoned that hitting the rock so it would release water would cause a great *kiddush Hashem.* But he did not follow Hashem's command as it was stated, and for this he was punished. Similarly, Chizkiyahu, king of Yehudah, decided not to have children because he foresaw that they would be wicked (see *Berachos* 10a). He was rebuked by the prophet Yeshayah, who told him that he was deserving of death. When Chizkiyahu revealed his reasoning, Yeshayah told him: "Of what concern to you are the secrets of the Merciful One? Do as you are commanded, and Hashem will do as He wills!"

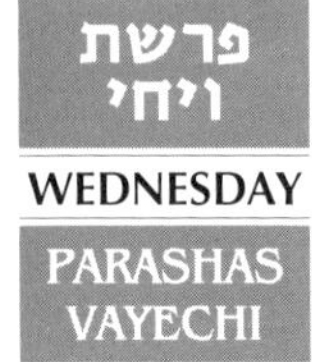

Mitzvos must always be performed with the attitude that we are servants of a master. Trying to reason or use intellectual arguments to sidestep our obligations is a serious violation of the proper relationship that a person should have with his Creator.

HALACHAH OF THE DAY

Now that we have completed our study of the first eleven forbidden *melachos* of Shabbos, we turn our attention to the next thirteen of the thirty-nine *melachos,* all of which are labors performed in the manufacture of textiles. The first of these is the *melachah* of גּוֹזֵז, *shearing.* Shearing was a necessary part of the construction of the Mishkan, because it was necessary to shear sheep in order to obtain wool for the curtains and the ceremonial garments of the Kohanim.

The definition of *shearing* is to remove from a person or other creature something that grows on the body, such as hair or nails. Cutting off a part of the body itself, such as a limb or flesh, is not considered *shearing.*

There is a dispute among the *poskim* as to when the Biblical prohibition of shearing applies. Some *poskim* maintain that it applies only when the item being sheared is needed for its own intrinsic value, as it was in the time of the Mishkan, when wool was sheared for its use in making curtains and clothing. Others maintain that the accomplishment of any beneficial purpose renders the shearing a Biblical prohibition. This would apply, for instance, if one cuts one's hair for aesthetic purposes. Although the hair itself is not being used, the benefit would be one's improved appearance; thus, the shearing would be Biblically prohibited. The halachah follows this latter view.

Under Biblical law, it is forbidden to shear something only in the usual manner, using the implement commonly used to remove this item from the body. This includes cutting hair with a scissors, cutting nails with a scissors or nail clipper, and plucking eyebrows with a tweezer. It can also include using a depilatory cream or powder to remove hair. The Sages extended the prohibition to include even shearing in an unusual manner, such as biting or tearing off nails.

The prohibition against *shearing* includes cutting hair, shearing an animal's hair, cutting nails, removing dead or loose skin, plucking fur — even from a finished garment — and plucking feathers from a bird.

We will now discuss each of the forbidden activities mentioned above in greater detail.

It is Biblically forbidden to cut even a single hair off any part of the human body, or off an animal's hide. This applies regardless of whether one cuts the hair at its root, or merely shortens it. Thus, it is forbidden on Shabbos to take a haircut, trim one's beard or mustache, shave one's legs or arms, pluck out unwanted facial hairs, tweeze eyebrows, or apply a depilatory agent to any hairy part of the body.

A CLOSER LOOK AT THE SIDDUR

This week, we will discuss the ninth of the Thirteen Fundamental Principles (י״ג עיקרים) enumerated by *Rambam.*

The Ninth Principle states:

> אֲנִי מַאֲמִין בֶּאֱמוּנָה שְׁלֵמָה שֶׁזֹּאת הַתּוֹרָה לֹא תְהֵא מֻחְלֶפֶת וְלֹא תְהֵא תּוֹרָה אַחֶרֶת מֵאֵת הַבּוֹרֵא יִתְבָּרַךְ שְׁמוֹ.
>
> *I believe with complete faith that this Torah will not be exchanged, nor will there be another Torah [received] from the Creator, blessed be His Name.*

This principle is closely connected to the eighth principle, which speaks of our faith that the Torah now in our hands is the original, God-given Torah from Sinai. Here we state that not only do we believe that the Torah has not been changed by man during the passage of time, we also believe that it will never be changed by God.

This principle stands as a rebuttal to those faiths that believe that Hashem "retracted" His Torah and appeared to certain individuals with new directives and laws, superseding the "old" Torah. We believe that the Revelation at Sinai was a singular event never to be duplicated or canceled. The Torah was given to us then, and it will always remain the cornerstone of our faith and our lives.

This principle also dismisses those who claim that the Torah is "old-fashioned," "out of touch," and simply "not meant for the contemporary Jew." Not so! The Torah is as fresh and relevant today as it was on the day it was given to the Jews. Every issue, from the most ancient to the most modern, can be viewed through the lens of the Torah, and there is no such thing as a subject upon which there is no Torah perspective. Those seeking to "modernize" the Torah deny the truth of the Mishnah in *Avos* (5:26): *Delve into [the Torah] and delve into it, for everything is in it.*

The fact that the Torah, which was given to us so many centuries ago (and which, according to the Gemara, existed even before the Creation of the world), can be utilized and expounded to address even the most modern and contemporary subjects is just further proof of its Divine origin. Moreover, by saying that we believe that the Torah view can be applied to all situations, we are affirming our acceptance of the Sages and Torah leaders of every generation, who, with their great wisdom and fear of Heaven, reveal to us how to understand Hashem's will in every given situation. It is this combination — the timeless, Divine Word of Hashem and our *emunas chachamim* — that provides us with an anchor in life, and the knowledge that we can discern the correct path.

QUESTION OF THE DAY:

How did Levi's descendants redeem themselves from Yaakov's censure?

For the answer, see page 221.

A TORAH THOUGHT FOR THE DAY

פרשת ויחי

THURSDAY

PARASHAS VAYECHI

אָרוּר אַפָּם כִּי עָז . . .

Cursed is their anger, for it was fierce . . . (*Bereishis* 49:7).

Although a simple reading of the verse would possibly lead one to conclude that Shimon and Levi were hotheaded, easily angered zealots, the commentators tell us that this was not the case. Indeed, one Midrash states that Shimon and Levi became truly angry only once in their lives — when Shechem defiled their sister Dinah. If this is so, the question must be addressed: Why was Yaakov so harsh in his criticism, if their wrath was a one-time occurrence?

Chasam Sofer explains that indeed, what Yaakov really meant to say was that he understood that Shimon and Levi had acted as they did, killing the entire populace of Shechem, *only* because they had been seized by their anger. The other *shevatim,* he explains, were content to avenge Dinah by killing Shechem and his father Chamor, and then taking Dinah and leaving. Yaakov thus testified that he knew that Shimon and Levi had not originally intended to kill everyone — they too, would have been satisfied to exact justice from Shechem and Chamor alone. However, when they actually went to do so, their anger was kindled, and in their rage, they slew all of the city's inhabitants. [This fits well with the fact that Yaakov cursed not them but *their anger,* as *Rashi* notes.]

Ramban explains that by calling Shimon and Levi "brothers," Yaakov was actually *defending* their behavior in the matter of Dinah, by saying that they, alone among all of the *shevatim,* had acted with true brotherly zeal when it came to defending the honor of their sister. While certainly not condoning their actions — indeed, Yaakov cursed their anger precisely because of the fact that *in their anger they murdered people* — he noted that their culpability was somewhat mitigated by the motive that had led them to be so angry. [In this, *Ramban* follows his approach above (34:14), that the citizens of Shechem were *not* legally deserving of death. This is actually the subject of a major debate among the authorities; see *Rambam, Hil. Melachim* Ch. 9, *Responsa* of *Chasam Sofer* 2:14, and *Gur Aryeh* for further discussion.]

QUESTION OF THE DAY:

Why is anger described by using the word אַף (which literally means "nose")?

For the answer, see page 221.

MISHNAH OF THE DAY: SHABBOS 13:3

The following Mishnah continues to consider the forbidden labor of *tearing*:

וְעַל הַקּוֹרֵעַ בַּחֲמָתוֹ — ***One who tears in his anger,*** [1] וְעַל מֵתוֹ — ***or*** as a sign of mourning ***for his dead,*** [2] וְכָל הַמְקַלְקְלִין — ***and all who act destructively*** and merely destroy an object without any constructive purpose whatsoever, פְּטוּרִין — ***are exempt*** from a *chatas.* [3] וְהַמְקַלְקֵל עַל מְנָת לְתַקֵּן — ***But one who destroys in order to repair*** is liable to a *chatas,* שִׁעוּרוֹ כִּמְתַקֵּן — and ***his*** minimum ***measure*** to incur liability ***is the same as for one who repairs.*** [4]

NOTES

1. I.e., a person tore a garment in order to vent and dissipate his anger (*Rav;* see *Rambam Commentary;* cf. *Rashi, Tosafos*).

2. Although the language of the Mishnah is "*his* dead," since the Mishnah's ruling in this case exempts the person tearing the garment from a *chatas* because his act is destructive, the case must be one in which he tore his garment in mourning for a relative *other* than those close relatives mentioned in *Vayikra* 21:23 (viz., wife, father, mother, son, daughter, brother, and sister). [For the relatives mentioned in *Vayikra,* the rending of garments is obligatory (see *Moed Katan* 3:7). Hence, doing so is regarded as a constructive act, and would render one liable to a *chatas* (*Rav* from Gemara).]

3. Labor that is destructive is not forbidden by Scripture (although it is Rabbinically prohibited). This is based on the principle of: מְלֶאכֶת מַחֲשֶׁבֶת אָסְרָה תוֹרָה, *the Torah prohibited only calculated labor* (*Rashi* above, 31b). Hence, one is exempt from a *chatas* for the destructive act of tearing his garment where there is no obligation to do so. Even if (as in the cases of our Mishnah) the tearing of the garment is indirectly "constructive" in that it dissipates his anger or expresses his sorrow, the act still falls into the category of מְלָאכָה שֶׁאֵינָהּ צְרִיכָה לְגוּפָהּ, *labor not needed for its defined purpose.* Now, we saw above (2:5) that R' Yehudah considers one liable for such an act. Accordingly, he would rule that the cases of our Mishnah *do* render a person liable. Hence, our Mishnah must be understood as a ruling of R' Shimon, who exempts a person who performs *labor not needed for its defined purpose* from a *chatas* (*Rav; Rambam Commentary* from Gemara 105b).

4. For example, if one tears a garment so that it can be properly resewn, he is liable for making a tear long enough to require two stitches (see *Tiferes Yisrael*).

GEMS FROM THE GEMARA

The Gemara (105b) cites a Baraisa that contradicts our Mishnah. One of the contradictions concerns the case of a person who tears a garment in his anger. In this case, the Baraisa rules that he is liable to a *chatas,* contradicting our Mishnah, which exempted him in such a case.

The Gemara resolves the contradiction by clarifying that the Baraisa follows the view of R' Yehudah — who maintains that one is liable for performing a *labor not needed for its defined purpose* — while the Mishnah follows the view of R' Shimon (see our commentary to the Mishnah).

However, the Gemara then raises a difficulty: Even R' Yehudah exempts a person who acts *destructively*! Therefore, even according to R' Yehudah, the person should not be liable for tearing his garment.

R' Avin answers that in this case, the person who tore his garment in anger did perform a constructive act, for in doing so, he satisfied his evil inclination by cooling off his anger.

But, objects the Gemara, is this type of behavior permitted? Did we not learn in a Baraisa that R' Shimon ben Elazar said in the name of Chilfa bar Agra, who in turn said in the name of R' Yochanan ben Nuri: "One who tears his garments in his anger, breaks his utensils in his anger, or scatters his money in his anger, should be in your eyes as one who is performing idolatry! For thus is the craft of the evil inclination: Today it tells him, 'Do this'; and the next day it tells him, 'Do this'; until it tells him, 'Perform idolatry'; and he goes and performs it."

After elaborating upon the Baraisa, the Gemara answers that a case in which tearing a garment in conjunction with "anger" is constructive is one in which the person only *feigns* anger, in order to impress upon the members of his household the gravity of some issue. Moreover, he tears the garment on a seam, so that it can be easily mended. For example, Rav Yehudah pulled off the border of a garment to demonstrate his displeasure. This case (as are other, similar cases that the Gemara subsequently cites) is one in which the person who tore the garment was not truly angry. He is allowed to *act* angry to insure that the members of his household will behave properly (*Rambam, Hil. Dei'os* 2:3). [Nevertheless, *Meiri* writes that one should not become accustomed to act this way, because others, who do not realize that he is not truly angry, may learn from him to act in an inappropriate manner.] Since in such a case the tearing is a constructive act, he is liable according to R' Yehudah (even though the labor was not performed for its defined purpose of preparation for re-sewing).

A MUSSAR THOUGHT FOR THE DAY

Mesillas Yesharim describes several types of people who possess the dangerous trait of כַּעַס (*kaas*), *anger.* Worst of all is a person who is literally filled with anger. The Sages compare such a person to one who worships idols (*Shabbos* 105b), because once he is gripped by his anger, he cannot be controlled, and acts without fear of Hashem. A person of this type becomes enraged by any resistance to his will; he loses mastery over his emotions, and cannot think clearly when he is seized by rage. A person of this nature would destroy the entire world in his anger, were he given the chance. He is literally like an animal when he is angry, completely lacking in reason, and is capable of transgressing the most severe prohibitions in the throes of his wrath, as he is ruled completely by his anger.

Another type of person is one who is not easily angered, but, once his anger is aroused, is exceedingly harsh. This person, although not as dangerous as the first person, is still capable of severe harm, since during the time when he is angry, he can often do great damage that cannot later be undone.

A third type of person does not anger quickly, and, even when angry, does not lose control of himself completely. However, when his anger cools, it does not leave him completely, and he still nurses resentment in his heart. Although this person will not cause the type of harm that the previous two types are capable of inflicting, since the hurt remains in his heart, he is considered to possess the *middah* of *kaas.*

The fourth type of person is even less inclined to get angry, and when he is stirred to anger, the effect is negligible. He remains angry only for a moment, until his powers of intellect reassert themselves and subdue the anger. This person is considered to have mastered his anger, and is praiseworthy. It is to such a person that the Sages refer when they say, תּוֹלֶה אֶרֶץ עַל בְּלִימָה (literally, *the world hangs on nothing),* which is expounded to mean: The continued existence of the world is based upon the merit of those who close (בּוֹלֵם) their mouths in the face of an argument. Although they are naturally stirred to anger, they overcome their anger and remain in control.

However, the paradigm of proper conduct with respect to anger is Hillel the Elder, who, as the Gemara (*Shabbos* 30b-31a) relates, could not be roused to take offense or become angry at all, even under extreme provocation (see Gemara there). Such a person is truly free of *kaas.*

HALACHAH OF THE DAY

פרשת ויחי

THURSDAY

PARASHAS VAYECHI

Yesterday, we began discussing some of the activities that are forbidden as part of the prohibition against *shearing*. We mentioned that cutting even a single hair off a human body or off an animal's hide is forbidden. In addition, there are other activities, which we will enumerate later, that are forbidden because they will inevitably lead to the pulling out of some hair.

We will now continue discussing in detail some of the other activities that are forbidden as part of *shearing*.

It is Biblically prohibited to trim nails with a scissors or nail clippers. Biting or tearing off nails is Rabbinically prohibited. There is, however, one exception to the Rabbinical prohibition against biting or tearing off nails. If a nail (or a piece of a nail) has become detached more than halfway *and* it is painful, one is permitted to bite or tear it off. In all other cases, however, removing nails is prohibited on Shabbos, even in an unusual fashion.

Removing loose or dead skin also falls under the prohibition against *shearing*. Once the skin is partially detached, it is no longer considered to be an intrinsic part of the body; rather, it is like hair or nails that grow from the body. Thus, it is forbidden to remove dead skin, warts, and the skin of blisters or boils on Shabbos.

Removing loose or dead skin with an instrument is Biblically prohibited, while doing it in an unusual manner, such as by peeling or biting, is prohibited Rabbinically. However, in the case of chapped or dried skin on the lips, biting the skin off is considered the normal manner of removing it, and thus falls under the Biblical prohibition.

Removing a scab from a wound does not fall under the prohibition of removing loose skin, provided that this can be done without inevitably drawing blood. Since the scab does not grow from the body, but is merely dried blood that adheres to the skin, removing it is not considered *shearing*.

The prohibition of *shearing* applies to removing hair from both live creatures and dead ones, even including hair from an animal's hide that has been flayed from its body. Since fur garments are made out of fur that is still attached to the hide, it is prohibited to pluck hair from any fur garment, such as a fur coat, fur hat or fur-lined gloves.

פרשת ויחי

THURSDAY

PARASHAS VAYECHI

A CLOSER LOOK AT THE SIDDUR

Before we take out the *Sefer Torah* for the Torah reading during *Minchah* of Shabbos, we cite the verse from *Tehillim* (69:14): וַאֲנִי תְפִלָּתִי לְךָ ה׳ עֵת רָצוֹן, *As for me, may my prayer to You,* HASHEM, *come at a time of "ratzon"* (favor). We also find a verse in *Yeshayah* (49:8) that speaks of the value of such a time: *So says* HASHEM*: I will answer you in a time of "ratzon."* What is the nature of this time of *ratzon,* which is the opportune time for our *tefillos* to be accepted?

Radak (to *Yeshayah* loc. cit.) explains that every person has the opportunity to create his own time of *ratzon,* simply by fulfilling the will of Hashem. According to this approach, having one's prayers hearkened to is a result of hearkening to Hashem's dictates, as the Mishnah in *Avos* (2:4) states: *Perform His will as if it were yours, so that He will treat your will as if it were His. Orchos Tzaddikim,* however, relates this to the concept of praying with proper concentration, and waiting patiently for Hashem to grant one's requests. One who is quick to anger, says *Orchos Tzaddikim,* is unable to reach this level, for his anger does not allow him to focus his thoughts in prayer, and he will become upset if his prayers are not answered immediately.

The Sages teach us that we must constantly pray for help in controlling our anger. R' Akiva used to pray daily that he not succumb to anger — *May it be Your Will, Hashem, that I not become angry, and that I do not anger You.*

R' Chaim Volozhiner taught that one should pray before entering any situation where there is a danger that he might become angry.

At the end of *Shemoneh Esrei,* in the closing prayer of *Elohai Netzor,* we ask: וְנַפְשִׁי כֶּעָפָר לַכֹּל תִּהְיֶה, *and let my soul be as dust before everyone. Reishis Chochmah* understands this request, too, as a plea to be protected from anger. Dust is continually stepped on and degraded by all; yet, it never complains or demands some dignity. So too, we ask for the fortitude to always remain silent even in the face of indignity and humiliation, without falling into the grip of anger.

A TORAH THOUGHT FOR THE DAY

וַיֹּאמֶר אֲלֵהֶם יוֹסֵף אַל־תִּירָאוּ כִּי הֲתַחַת אֱלֹהִים אָנִי.
וְאַתֶּם חֲשַׁבְתֶּם עָלַי רָעָה אֱלֹהִים חֲשָׁבָהּ לְטֹבָה
לְמַעַן עֲשֹׂה כַּיּוֹם הַזֶּה לְהַחֲיֹת עַם־רָב

But Yosef told them, "Fear not, for am I instead of God? Although you intended me harm, God intended it for good in order to accomplish — it is as clear as this day — that a vast people be kept alive" (*Bereishis* 50:19,20).

Ohr *HaChaim* compares the actions of Yosef's brothers in selling him to the actions of someone who tries to murder another by giving him poison to drink, and the drink turns out to be harmless wine. Such a person is not liable even to be punished in Heaven, because no crime was committed. Here, too, it turned out that it was beneficial for Yosef to be in Egypt; thus, Yosef told his brothers, they had nothing to fear.

Rabbeinu Bachya notes that although we see that the brothers tried to appease Yosef and ask for forgiveness, the Torah never says that Yosef actually forgave them for what they had done to him. We see only that Yosef spoke to them with words of encouragement, as in the above verse: *"Although you intended me harm, God intended it for good, etc."* Yosef assured his brothers that he loved them and that he would not harm them, but he never said to them, "I forgive you for taking me and selling me to the Yishmaelim, and causing me to be brought to Egypt."

Rabbeinu Bachya explains that if someone sins against his fellow, the offense does not get erased unless the sinner receives verbal forgiveness from the aggrieved party. Therefore, the fact that Yosef never clearly forgave his brothers caused them to leave this world with their sin still not fully expiated. This is why, centuries later, Hashem allowed ten great Sages (the *Asarah Harugei Malchus*) to be taken by the Romans and killed, with the murderers claiming that the Sages were being executed in the place of Yosef's brothers.

We may ask: Why did Yosef not forgive his brothers fully and explicitly? *Shiras David* suggests that perhaps Yosef did not forgive them with a full heart because they had never sincerely asked to be forgiven. It is clear from the Torah that they approached Yosef only after Yaakov's death, when they were concerned that Yosef would take revenge upon them. Yosef calmed their fears, and reassured them that he had no such intentions, but they did not specifically come to him to apologize and seek forgiveness; thus, he did not verbally forgive them, with tragic results.

פרשת ויחי

FRIDAY

PARASHAS VAYECHI

MISHNAH OF THE DAY: SHABBOS 13:4

The following Mishnah teaches the minimum amounts to incur liability for the remaining forbidden labors that are involved in the preparation of wool: שִׁעוּר הַמְלַבֵּן וְהַמְנַפֵּץ — *The* minimum *measure* for liability *of one who whitens and one who disentangles,* וְהַצּוֹבֵעַ וְהַטּוֹוֶה — *and one who dyes and one who spins,* כִּמְלֹא רֹחַב הַסִּיט כָּפוּל — *is double the width of a sit.* [1] וְהָאוֹרֵג שְׁנֵי חוּטִין — *And one who weaves two threads,* [2] שִׁעוּרוֹ כִּמְלֹא הַסִּיט — *his* minimum *measure is a full sit.* [3]

NOTES

1. A *sit* is the space between the index finger and the middle finger when they are stretched apart as far as possible. The space between the thumb and the index finger when fully spread apart, is twice this amount, or a "double *sit.*" If one whitens, combs, dyes, or spins enough wool for a thread of this length, he is liable to a *chatas* (*Rav; Rashi;* cf. *Rambam Commentary,* cited in *Gems from the Gemara*).

2. I.e., he inserts two weft threads between the warp threads (*Tiferes Yisrael*).

3. I.e., he is liable for weaving these two weft threads through a length of a *sit* of the warp, regardless of the length [or width] of the bolt of cloth that is mounted upon the loom (*Rav; Rashi*).

GEMS FROM THE GEMARA

The Mishnah stated that the minimum measure of one who whitens etc., is double the width of a *sit.*

The Gemara (106a) elucidates the measure of "double the width of a *sit*" and relates that Rav Yosef demonstrated it as a double measure, two times the size of a single *sit* — i.e., he measured the space between his index finger and middle finger [a *sit*] two times (*Rashi*). On the other hand, Rav Chiya bar Ami demonstrated it differently, as a simple measure — i.e., he displayed the space between his thumb and index finger, which is equivalent to double the length of the space between the index finger and the middle finger (*Rashi;* cf. *Sfas Emes*).

[As we explained in the Mishnah, *Rav* and *Rashi* do not distinguish between the phrases "a full *sit,*" and "the width of a sit." Thus, according to their view, "double the width of a *sit*" is twice as large as a full *sit.*" *Rambam Commentary,* on the other hand, explains a *sit* to be the distance between the index finger and the middle finger when they are extended but not stretched apart (which is explained by *Maggid Mishneh* to *Hil. Shabbos* 9:7 to be half the measure of when they are stretched apart), and "the width of a *sit*" to mean the measure between the thumb and the middle finger when they are spread apart (which is how *Rashi* explained "double the width of a *sit*"). According to *Rambam,* therefore, "double the width of a *sit*" is *eight* times as large as a *sit.* This fits well with *Rambam's* statement in *Hil. Shabbos* 9:18 that the measure of a *sit* is two fingerbreadths (or half a *tefach*), and his statement in 9:12 ibid. that "double the width of a sit" is four *tefachim.*]

A MUSSAR THOUGHT FOR THE DAY

As we learned in *A Torah Thought for the Day,* Yosef never forgave the brothers specifically, and this made it possible for punishment for this sin to be visited upon their descendants.

Rav Yisrael Salanter states that the power to forgive is a very important, yet dangerous tool. It may be used to complete someone's willingness to do *teshuvah,* for often a person's wish for forgiveness will spur him to mend his ways. It is critical, however, that a person asking for forgiveness understand that this is not just a formality. Rather, his request must stem from a true feeling and expression of remorse. If the aggrieved party feels that the one asking forgiveness is not sorry or sincere, he need not forgive him.

Rav Yisrael used to teach his students to get into the habit of forgiving anyone who hurt them, even before they would be asked for forgiveness. This, he used to say, is a method of taming one's own inclination to bear grudges and become angry. If a person becomes accustomed to quickly forgive anyone who wrongs him, he will more easily be able to control his wrath and ill feelings toward others. In truth, holding a grudge against a person whom one has already forgiven is actually forbidden. This, he explains, is similar to someone who loaned money to another, and then forgave the debt. Legally, the loan is now null and void. If the lender makes any attempt to collect the money, he is deemed a thief, because a loan that was forgiven cannot be collected. Although there are times where one may have a legitimate right to be upset with another person, this is so only as long as he has not forgiven that person. But once he forgives him, it is forbidden to still hold a grudge, as this would be comparable to collecting a debt after it was forgiven.

Rav Yerucham Levovitz says that it is human nature for a person being asked to forgive a misdeed to avoid answering the question directly, and just change the subject to other matters. This, he explains, is because the person feels that as long as he does not forgive the miscreant, he has some measure of control over him; once he forgives him, he cannot demand anything. Those who want to perfect their character, however, will look for ways to initiate the forgiveness. The Gemara tells us that Rav would pace back and forth in front of a person who had insulted him, to allow the man the opportunity to ask for forgiveness. There are also many stories of great sages who were heard saying under their breath, "I forgive you," to people who had just wronged or insulted them. These are ways in which a person can refine his *middos,* and become a true servant of Hashem.

HALACHAH OF THE DAY

It is considered *shearing* to pluck feathers from either a live bird or a dead one. It is permitted, however, according to most *poskim,* to pluck small feathers from a *cooked* bird, e.g. a *cooked* chicken. The distinction between the two cases is that the cooking process itself loosens the feathers, so that removing them is no longer a true act of *shearing.* Moreover, once the bird is cooked, its skin is now edible, and is no longer viewed as the hide of an animal. It should be noted, however, that although plucking such feathers is not forbidden as *shearing,* one must be careful not to violate the *melachah* of *boreir,* sorting, when plucking them. It is preferable to put the skin with the feathers into one's mouth and spit out the feathers. If this is not possible, one may pluck out the feathers from the skin as he is eating, but should not do so before the meal.

In addition to the acts listed above, we will now discuss several other acts that are forbidden because they will inevitably remove hair from the body.

It is forbidden to brush one's hair or beard on Shabbos with a brush or comb that has hard, stiff bristles. This prohibition applies equally to men and women. Since all people have some loose or knotted hair, brushing with a hard-bristled brush will inevitably pull out some hair. One may, however, straighten his hair with his fingers. The use of a brush on Shabbos is permitted only if it has very soft bristles (which give way when they meet with resistance), if one does not brush forcefully or excessively, and if the brush is specifically set aside for use on Shabbos.

[Using the same brush on Shabbos that one uses during the week is forbidden Rabbinically since it is considered עוּבְדָא דְּחוֹל, *weekday activity.*]

Since combing hair is forbidden, it follows that it is forbidden to remove nits from one's hair by combing it. It is permissible, however, to remove nits by hand, while being careful not to pull out any hair.

It is forbidden on Shabbos to remove chewing gum that got stuck in one's hair, as some hair will inevitably be pulled out in the process.

A CLOSER LOOK AT THE SIDDUR

In the sixth blessing of the *Shemoneh Esrei,* we ask Hashem for forgiveness:

> סְלַח לָנוּ אָבִינוּ כִּי חָטָאנוּ, מְחַל לָנוּ מַלְכֵּנוּ כִּי פָשָׁעְנוּ, כִּי מוֹחֵל וְסוֹלֵחַ אָתָּה, בָּרוּךְ אַתָּה ה׳ חַנּוּן הַמַּרְבֶּה לִסְלוֹחַ.
>
> *Forgive us, our Father, for we have erred, pardon us, our King for we have willfully sinned. For You are the good and forgiving God — Blessed are You,* HASHEM, *the gracious One Who pardons abundantly.*

The blessing mentions two types of forgiveness, *selichah* and *mechilah.* What exactly is the difference between them? It is also noteworthy that while the body of the blessing mentions both *selichah* and *mechilah,* its closing speaks only of *selichah.*

Eitz Yosef explains that when Hashem grants *selichah,* the sin is totally wiped away. On the other hand, *mechilah* means that there is only partial forgiveness [so that there will be no punishment]; but *selichah* is still needed to complete the forgiveness.

Malbim (in his *Ayeles HaShachar,* printed at the beginning of his commentary on *Sefer Vayikra*) states that *mechilah* is similar to forgiving a loan. One who forgives a loan does not say that the loan never took place; he merely says that he waives his legal right to collect it. Similarly, *mechilah* does not erase the fact that the sin occurred. Only *selichah* can do this; and the power of true *selichah,* explains *Malbim,* is reserved only for Hashem, as the verse states (*Tehillim* 130:4): כִּי־עִמְּךָ הַסְּלִיחָה, *for with You is selichah.* Only Hashem can regard a sin as if it never occurred, and He will mercifully grant *selichah* when a person asks for it with sincere feelings of *teshuvah.* A human being, as much as he is willing to forgive, cannot absolutely eradicate the memory of the wrong from his heart, as if it had never occurred. [Possibly, we can

explain that according to *Malbim* it is for this reason that we conclude the blessing by speaking only of *selichah,* which is an aspect of forgiveness unique to Hashem.]

Another approach to explaining the difference between *selichah* and *mechilah* is offered by *Gra.* In his view, *selichah* and *mechilah* are both necessary for *every* sin. *Selichah* is forgiveness for the actual sin itself; that is, for not having done what was commanded, or for doing something prohibited. *Mechilah* is necessary for another wrong — the fact that one who sins against Hashem has slighted the honor of the King of kings. This, explains *Gra,* is why we ask for *selichah* from אָבִינוּ, *our Father,* while we ask for *mechilah* from מַלְכֵּנוּ, *our King.* [Many other approaches to the difference between *selichah* and *mechilah* are suggested by the commentators; we will discuss additional interpretations as our studies continue.]

QUESTION OF THE DAY:

What did Yosef mean when he said, "For am I instead of Hashem"?

For the answer, see page 221.

A TORAH THOUGHT FOR THE DAY

וַיָּמָת יוֹסֵף בֶּן־מֵאָה וָעֶשֶׂר שָׁנִים
וַיַּחַנְטוּ אֹתוֹ וַיִּישֶׂם בָּאָרוֹן בְּמִצְרָיִם

And Yosef died at the age of one hundred and ten years; and they embalmed him, and he was placed in a coffin, in Egypt (*Bereishis* 50:26).

The Torah chooses to speak of the death and embalming of Yosef in the final verse of *Parashas Vayechi* and *Chumash Bereishis.* Generally, we find in the Mishnah and the Gemara that an effort is made to close a tractate on an upbeat note. Here, however, the subject seems very somber — the death of a great *tzaddik,* and his being placed in a coffin in Egypt. Why did the Torah choose to conclude *Sefer Bereishis* in this manner?

A closer look at the verse, however, reveals that there was more to the events described therein than meets the eye. The Gemara in *Sotah* (13a) notes that the verse does not state that Yosef was *buried* in Egypt, for in fact he was not buried. Rather, his coffin was placed in the Nile River, where it remained for over two centuries, until Moshe prayed for it to rise up so that he could fulfill the promise made to Yosef that the Jews would take his remains along when they left Egypt. [The Midrash cites differing accounts of *why* the coffin was placed in the Nile. One view is that the brothers placed the coffin there so that it would not be worshiped by the Egyptians. A second view is that Pharaoh placed the coffin there so that the waters of the Nile would be blessed. And a third view states that the Egyptian sorcerers knew that the Jews would not leave without Yosef's coffin, and they sunk it deep into the Nile so that the Jews would despair of ever retrieving it.]

In truth, the taking of Yosef's bones did far more for the Jews than simply fulfilling his request. The verse in *Tehillim* (114:3), which we recite as part of *Hallel,* states: *The sea saw and fled.* The Midrash comments: What did the sea see that caused it to flee? It saw the coffin of Yosef, who fled from sinning with the wife of Potiphar; the merit of the one who fled from sin caused the sea to flee.

Thus, the fact that Yosef was *not* buried in Egypt, but rather only *placed in a coffin in Egypt,* was actually a great blessing for the Jews, as the key they would later need to cross the *Yam Suf* would remain available.

Other commentators explain that the *parashah* ends by emphasizing that Yosef's coffin remained in Egypt to symbolize that his merits would remain with them through the difficult period that was to follow, until the eventual Exodus from Egypt.

פרשת ויחי

SHABBOS

PARASHAS VAYECHI

MISHNAH OF THE DAY: SHABBOS 13:5

The following Mishnah considers the forbidden labor of *trapping*:

רַבִּי יְהוּדָה אוֹמֵר — ***R' Yehudah says:*** הַצָּד צִפּוֹר לְמִגְדָּל — ***One who traps a bird*** by driving it ***into a closet,***[1] וּצְבִי לְבַיִת — ***or a deer*** by driving it ***into a house,***[2] חַיָּיב — ***is liable*** to a *chatas.* וַחֲכָמִים אוֹמְרִים — ***But the Sages say:*** צִפּוֹר לְמִגְדָּל — We grant that ***a bird*** is considered trapped only when it is driven ***into a closet,***[3] וּצְבִי לְגִינָּה וּלְחָצֵר וּלְבֵיבָרִין — ***but*** in the case of ***a deer,*** it is already considered trapped once it is brought to confinement ***into a garden, into a courtyard, or into enclosures.***[4] רַבָּן שִׁמְעוֹן בֶּן גַּמְלִיאֵל אוֹמֵר — ***Rabban Shimon ben Gamliel*** says: לֹא כָּל הַבֵּיבָרִין שָׁוִין — ***Not all enclosures are the same.*** זֶה הַכְּלָל — ***This is the general rule:*** מְחוּסַּר צֵידָה — If the animal is driven into an enclosure where it still ***lacks trapping,***[5] פָּטוּר — ***he is exempt*** from a ***chatas;*** שֶׁאֵינוֹ מְחוּסַּר צֵידָה חַיָּיב — but if the enclosure is small enough that ***it does not lack*** further ***trapping, he is liable.***[6]

NOTES

1. As explained at the end of this Mishnah, the halachic definition of *trapped* is that the animal's freedom of movement has been reduced to such an extent that it is accessible with little or no further effort by a person who wishes to seize it. Obviously, the precise confines within which this level of confinement is reached will differ from species to species. Following this general rule, a bird in a closet is considered trapped. However, a bird in a house — where it has room to maneuver — is not considered trapped (*Rav; Rashi*).

2. A deer is considered trapped when it is driven into a house and the door is closed. However, if it has only been driven into a garden or into a courtyard, according to R' Yehudah it is not considered trapped (*Rav; Rashi*).

3. I.e., on this point there is no disagreement between the Sages and R' Yehudah.

4. The Sages regard a deer as trapped even when it has been driven into a garden or a courtyard, and the door has been locked. Thus, they dispute R' Yehudah about the degree to which an animal must be confined to be considered trapped (see *Rashi* to *Beitzah* 24a).

5. I.e., if the enclosure is so large that the deer cannot be caught with a single lunge (*Rav* from Gemara 106b).

6. I.e., if the enclosure is so small that the animal can be caught with one lunge (*Rav* from Gemara 106b).

QUESTION OF THE DAY:

What praise of Yosef is found in the final verse of the parashah?

For the answer, see page 221.

GEMS FROM THE GEMARA

פרשת ויחי

SHABBOS

PARASHAS VAYECHI

The Gemara (106b) cites a Baraisa that offers more details about the *melachah* of *trapping.* The Baraisa states that according to R' Meir, one who traps grasshoppers, hornets or mosquitoes on the Sabbath is liable to a *chatas.* On the other hand, the Sages maintain that one is liable to a *chatas* only for trapping any creature whose species is usually trapped; one is exempt for trapping any creature whose species is not usually trapped. *Rashi* clarifies that according to the Sages, the forbidden labor of trapping applies only to animals or fowl that are usually trapped by people for use as food. Therefore, one *is* liable for trapping grasshoppers, which are suitable for consumption, but not for hornets and mosquitoes, which have no use.

The Gemara then cites another Baraisa that discusses the trapping of grasshoppers on the Sabbath. It teaches that one who traps grasshoppers during the dew season is exempt. [*Rashi* explains that during the dew season, the eyes of the grasshoppers are blinded, and they are considered to be already trapped, for they cannot evade those who wish to gather them. Since they can be easily seized, one is not liable for taking them.

Sfas Emes notes that this case is different from that of a blind deer, where one would be liable to a *chatas* for trapping it, for the following reason: A deer will run away from potential danger, for it is mobile, even if it is blind. A blind grasshopper, on the other hand, is completely immobilized, and will not try to escape.]

The Baraisa continues, teaching that one who traps grasshoppers during the hot season is liable. Elazar ben Mehavai, however, does not agree with this final ruling in all cases. He maintains that if the grasshoppers are coming in swarms, one who seizes some of them is not liable for trapping in any case. *Rashi* explains that when the grasshoppers are swarming, it is very easy to gather them up; accordingly, this is similar to a case where they are already trapped, and one is not liable to a *chatas* for seizing some of them in such a situation.

A MUSSAR THOUGHT FOR THE DAY

The Torah tells us that Yosef died at the age of 110. The Gemara (*Sotah* 13b) notes that Yosef died before any of his brothers, although he was younger than all of them, with the exception of Binyamin. [The verse in *Shemos* (1:6) states: *Yosef died and all his brothers, and that entire*

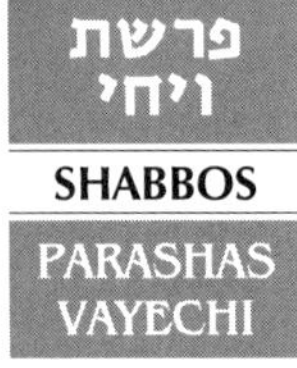

generation. This is understood to mean that Yosef died first (see *Rashi* to *Berachos* 55a).] Rav Yehudah stated, in the name of Rav: Why did Yosef die before his brothers? Because he carried himself with excessive authority.

This requires explanation. Surely Yosef did not put on airs of authority with respect to his brothers — all the accounts found in the Torah with respect to his relationship with them point to the contrary. And if he acted as a lord over the Egyptians, why should he be faulted for doing so? He was, after all, the viceroy of the land, and entitled to respect!

Maharal (*Chidushei Aggados*) explains that the shortening of Yosef's life that resulted from his being in a position of great authority was not a punishment; rather, it is an occupational hazard, so to speak, of being an authority figure. Anyone who finds himself in a position of rulership and authority, he explains, is by the very nature of his position not part of the *tzibbur,* the greater community; he is a *yachid,* a solitary figure. And it is well known, continues *Maharal,* that being part of a *tzibbur* affords protection; similarly, water in a river always remains fresh, while water that is drawn from the river and left in a pond will stagnate and turn foul. Thus, it is unusual for a person whose authority sets him apart from the community to merit living a long life.

Other commentators link Yosef's early death to the fact that his brothers referred to Yaakov in his presence as "*your servant, our father,*" and he did not react or prevent them from referring to him in this manner. This slight to his father's honor (despite the fact that it was not perceived by the brothers, who did not know who Yosef was at that point), resulted in Yosef losing one year of his life for each time he heard the phrase and did not react. Since the brothers used the phrase five times (see above, 43:28, 44:24, 44:27, 44:30 and 44:31), and the interpreter whom Yosef used to conceal the fact that he understood Hebrew (see above, 42:23) also repeated the phrase, Yosef heard it a total of ten times. For this reason, he died ten years shy of a full lifespan, at the age of 110.

HALACHAH OF THE DAY

Since *shearing* pertains only to detaching an item from the natural base from which it grew, removing hair from a wig is not included in the category of *shearing.* Thus, combing a wig is not forbidden as *shearing.* There are some authorities, however, who prohibit pulling hair out of a wig as part of the prohibition of *tearing,* and rule that one may not brush a wig on Shabbos except with a soft-bristled brush, without excessive force, and with a brush set aside only for Shabbos use. Others rule that brushing a wig is not prohibited as either *shearing* or *tearing;* thus, it is permissible to brush a wig in the usual fashion. It is preferable to abide by the more stringent opinion.

The above rule pertains mainly to wigs of human hair, in which the hair is generally attached more loosely to the base (cap) of the wig, and will inevitably be torn loose during regular brushing (thus violating the prohibition against *tearing* according to the aforementioned authorities). Wigs made of synthetic fiber, however, usually have the hairs more firmly attached to the base, so that they will not inevitably come out while brushing. It is therefore permitted to brush a synthetic wig on Shabbos in the regular fashion. One should test the wig on a weekday to see if brushing it forcefully removes any hair.

It is forbidden to pull a bandage (such as a Band-aid) off a hairy part of the body on Shabbos, as this will inevitably result in some hair being pulled out in the process. If a bandage must be removed because it is causing pain, or in order to apply some medication to the wound that it is covering, or because one must immerse in a *mikveh,* a non-Jew should be asked to remove it. If there is no non-Jew available, one may remove the bandage carefully.

There are a few other practical applications of this *melachah* that we will now discuss.

It is permitted to remove a splinter on Shabbos. If the splinter is deeply embedded in the skin so that it cannot be easily reached, one is permitted to cut the skin so as to expose the splinter and remove it. One should be careful, however, to avoid removing the splinter in a manner that will inevitably draw blood.

If a woman is scheduled to go the *mikveh* on a Friday night, and forgot to cut her fingernails before Shabbos, she may have a non-Jew tear or bite off the fingernails. If this is impossible, or there is no non-Jew willing to do this, she may have the non-Jew cut off the nails with an instrument. If there is no non-Jew available, she may not remove the nails, but should consult a competent halachic authority.

A CLOSER LOOK AT THE SIDDUR

After reciting *Vayechulu* in the Friday night *Shemoneh Esrei,* we continue with a short prayer that contains several requests. Although the section of the weekday *Shemoneh Esrei* that contains personal requests is omitted on the Sabbath, this is primarily because the

Sages wished to make the prayers of the Sabbath and festivals simpler and less burdensome than they would be if they included the regular prayer service plus additional passages for the Sabbath. Personal requests are not *inappropriate* on the Sabbath; they were just not included in the prayers. [For this reason, if one inadvertently began the fourth blessing of the weekday *Shemoneh Esrei* (*Atah Chonein*) during a Sabbath *Shemoneh Esrei*, he should finish it before reverting to the Sabbath version of the fourth blessing (see *Berachos* 21a and *Mishnah Berurah, Orach Chaim* 268:2).] Thus, even in the Sabbath prayers, the Sages instituted a short section of general requests. Furthermore, *Tanchuma* (to *Parashas Vayeira*) explains that the weekday requests were omitted so that a person should not recall his personal troubles (for instance, by thinking of an ill family member while saying the *berachah* of *Refa'einu*) and disturb his Sabbath tranquility. The Sages therefore couched the requests found in the Sabbath *Shemoneh Esrei* in more general terms, so they would be less likely to evoke disturbing thoughts.

This section of the prayer begins with the words: אֱלֹהֵינוּ וֵאלֹהֵי אֲבוֹתֵינוּ רְצֵה בִמְנוּחָתֵנוּ, *Our God and the God of our forefathers, may You be pleased with our rest. R' Chaim Friedlander* explains that there are two ways a person can rest on the Sabbath. He may simply be too tired from his weekday efforts to exert himself further, and he welcomes the Sabbath as a respite, resting to replenish his physical strength in advance of the coming week. Or, he may "rest" in a greater sense, removing all material thoughts and concerns from his mind, and concentrating instead on the spirituality of the Sabbath, and the closeness to Hashem that he can attain on the holy day. Hashem, of course, wishes for us to indulge in rest of the second kind (indeed, this is the meaning of the phrase found in the *Minchah Shemoneh Esrei* — מְנוּחָה שְׁלֵמָה שֶׁאַתָּה רוֹצֶה בָּהּ, *the complete rest which You desire*). Thus, we open this prayer with the hope that Hashem will be pleased with our rest. *Eitz Yosef* adds that although the Sabbath is celebrated with material indulgences such as fine clothing and good food, and we may sometimes tend to overemphasize this aspect of the Sabbath over its spiritual nature, we ask that Hashem not take this as an indication that we regard the Sabbath just as an excuse to indulge our physical selves.

Next week, we will discuss the requests found in this prayer.

ANSWERS TO QUESTIONS OF THE DAY

Sunday:

The verse states that הִנֵּה, *Behold,* Yaakov was ill, and the numerical value of הִנֵּה is 60. After Yosef arrived, it states that Yaakov sat on הַמִּטָּה, *the bed,* and the numerical value of הַמִּטָּה is 59 (*Gra*).

Monday:

Tosefes Berachah suggests that the tremendous love Yaakov had for Rachel caused him to recall her by name when speaking of her.

Tuesday:

In *Parashas Bamidbar* and in *Parashas Pinchas,* the census taken by Moshe begins with the words *Reuven, the firstborn of Israel* (*Numbers* 1:20,26:5).

Wednesday:

Pinchas, who slew Zimri to uphold Hashem's honor (see *Numbers* 25:6 ff.), was descended from Levi; also, the tribe of Levi was the only tribe that rallied to Moshe's side after the sin of the Golden Calf (see *Shemos* 32:26).

Thursday:

This alludes to the fact that one's nostrils typically flare when he is angry (*Rashi* to *Shemos* 15:8).

Friday:

Rashi explains that Yosef meant to tell his brothers: "The ten of you tried to harm me and did not succeed, for Hashem did not wish it to happen. Am I more powerful than Hashem, that I can harm ten of you against His will?"

Shabbos:

Although Yosef was known as Tzafnas Pane'ach while he ruled in Egypt, the verse tells us that he died as *Yosef;* he retained his Hebrew name despite its non-use. This inspired his descendants to keep *their* Jewish names — and this was ultimately one of the merits that brought about the Exodus from Egypt (see *Pardes Yosef*).